One Wild Life

*a journey to discover
people who change our world*

Clare Mulvany

The Collins Press

First published in 2009 by
The Collins Press
West Link Park
Doughcloyne
Wilton
Cork

British Library Cataloguing in Publication Data

Mulvany, Clare
One wild life : a journey to discover people who change our
world
1. Mulvany, Clare - Travel 2. Social reformers - Interviews
3. Social entrepreneurship
I. Title
303.4'84'0922

ISBN-13: 9781905172887

Design and typesetting by edit+
Typeset in Adobe Caslon Pro & Myriad Pro
Cover design by bite!
Printed in Spain by GraphyCems
Cover and inside of this book have been printed on FSC paper

CLARE MULVANY from Dublin is a graduate of Queen's University Belfast and of Oxford. Her working life has spanned a number of areas including teaching at Peking University, working for NGOs and social sector groups, and as a freelance researcher, writer, photographer and consultant on social change and development education. In recognition of her work Clare received a 2007 Social Entrepreneur award from Social Entrepreneurs Ireland.
www.claremulvaney.com

contents ☞

Part Three: Asia

Part Four: Australasia/Pacific

Part Five: United States

Resources

Acknowledgements

It is never just one . . .

Researching and writing One Wild Life has been an incredible journey, both while on my travels and on returning home. I may have stepped onto the plane alone, but all along there were friends who supported, colleagues who inspired, strangers who went out of their way to help, and family who put up with me. Without them all, this journey would never have happened. To each I owe a huge and unending thanks. Indeed there have been so many who have helped along the way, I fear I may forget quite a few names. Please forgive me if I do.

I'm grateful to the staff of The Collins Press for believing in this book.

I am very grateful to Social Entrepreneurs Ireland for their generous support, and would particularly like to thank Sean Coughlan, Lynda Stopford, Annalisa O'Carroll and Clare Murphy for their fantastic work in building the field of social entrepreneurship in Ireland.

For their remarkable hospitality and help – whether offering a couch or a contact – I would like to thank: Jackie Achello, Irene Oker Adokorach, Min Ameen, Harry Andrews, Rochelle Arms, Ned Augenblick, Amy Banzeart, Jeff Biggers, Jeroo Billimoria, Don Blanks, Norie Blanks, Sohelya Boluri, Maureen Bryan, Jean Callanan, Rebecca Cook, Tom Dawkins, Philip de Chazel, Chris de Souza, Bronwyn Feldwick-Davis, David Fick, Nick Flegg, Lara Galinsky, Manisha Gupta, Micheala Hackner, Ben Heath, Michaela Howse, Amy Jaffe-Barzach, Richard Johnston, Cathal Kearney, Robyn Keech, Sam Keech-Marx, Arron Kennedy, Catherine Lambert, Don MacLurcan, Tony Marx, Mark Mc Donagh, Conor Mc Hugh, Ceppie Merry, Carlos and Ruth Monteagudo, Josephine Nazziwa, Cameron Neil, George Ngesa, Joseph Ngigi, Linda Nowakowski, Titipol Phakdeewanich, Amy Prior, Dan Prior, Andie Razionzer, Jordan Riber, Brigette Riber, Kevin Rice, Priankya and Bhuwan Satyarthi, Severine Saxena, Sagun Saxena, Jared Tham, Sarah Wagner McCoy, Jennifer Wetter, and Wiseman.

I am indebted to a special group of strangers who found out about my work along the way, and who were remarkably helpful and encouraging. I am fortunate to be able to call them friends now: Anne Marie Bellevance, Chris McCrea, Nathan Cryder, Susan Megy, Greg Murray and Jean Russell.

The staff in Ashoka were always generous with their time. In particular I would like to thank: Sohini Bhattacharya, Bill Drayton, Jennifer Fry, Marita Oosthuizen and Beverley Schwartz.

While on my travels, my interviews were many and the conversations intense. Praise and thanks must go to this incredible group of changemakers, who were extremely generous with their time and continue to inspire: Rotimi Adebari, Victor d'Allant, Flick Asvat, Sujartha Balaji, Srey Bandole, Michael Bauwens,

Paul Basil, John Berger, Charles Best, Kelly Betts, Taddy Blecher, Frank Buckley, Caroline Casey, Solomon Cidile, Youk Chhang, Ian Clarke, Sasha Constable, Tara Cunningham, Nick Cuttriss, Andal Damodaran, Mary Davis, Tony Deifell, Trevor Dudley, Don Edkins, Derek Ellerman, Craig Esbeck, Kim Feinburg, Matt Flannery, Jim Fruchterman, Amy Gillespie, Peter Haas, Joan Hamilton, Mark Hanis, Salome Henry, Lisa Heydlauff, Barbara Jackson, Christian Jordan, Margarete Junker, KK, Johnny K, Delfine Kassam, Kim Keiser, Sr Stan Kennedy, Veronica Khosa, Eva Koncazal, Melissa Kwee, Dana Langlois, Mary Lawlor, Colin Lennox, Sue Lennox, Sébastien Marot, David McKiernan, Ruairí McKiernan, Anne Merriman, Jyoti Mhapsekar, Nick Moon, Gareth Morgan, Peter Mugyenyi, Sr Margo Mulvey, Mwalimu Musheshe, Joyce Mypanga, Eva Mysliwiec, Nicky Newman, Betty Nyagoha, Mardie Oakes, Marcie Odell, Ben Ogunyo, Colm O'Gorman, Stella Omunga, Fred Ouko, Sheela Patel, Davie Philip, Uma Prajapati, Douglas Razionzer, Louise Riber, John Riber, Tina Roche, Rathnaboli Roy, Deval Sanghavi, Patrick Schofield, Allan Schwarz, Sheela Sengupta, Bob Seward, Abhay Shah, Jack Sim, Nina Smith, Dear Sourm, Sarah Symons, Artur Taevere, Vipin Thekkekalathil, Nancy Thomas, Adam Tuller, Rajiv Vartak, Thangavel Velandi, John Weeks, Sri K. Vishwanthan and Kyle Zimmer.

I am fortunate to have a group of friends in Ireland who are simply magical. In particular I would like to thank the following for their unwavering support and cheerleading: Marion Berry, Méabh Boylan, Lissy Clarke, Louis Crowe, Jenny Dungan, Regina Fallon, Valerie Ringrose Fitzsimmons, Karen Furlong, Ita Harnett, Tom Lyons, Deirdre Mackey, Beverley Maxwell, David Moffitt, Tessa Normond, Tomás O'Connor, Joanna Rea, Philip Regan, Severine Reneaud and Susan Walsh.

Thanks also to the all dedicated staff in Suas, who still fly the flag so well. Special thanks to Emer Butler, Jordan Campbell and Bryan Patten, for their editorial and publishing suggestions and friendship, and to John Travers and David Bornstein for their valuable advice. Also thanks to Julie Ann Matkin and Alan Higgins for their photographic prowess.

A very special thanks must go to Colman Farrell for believing in me all along, pushing me to go the distance and supporting me, whatever the outcome.

And finally to my amazing family: my mum, Geraldine, and brothers, Brian and Paul. And to Adrianna, Aria, and surrogate sisters, Evie, Astrid, Irene and Vivienne. I am blessed.

'So tell me, what is it you plan to do
with your one wild and precious life.'

– Mary Oliver

Introduction

This journey started life as a fridge magnet. On it was written the following:

WHATEVER YOU CAN DO, OR DREAM YOU CAN, **BEGIN IT.** BOLDNESS HAS GENIUS, POWER AND MAGIC IN IT. [GOETHE]

The quote, living on my fridge door, was a reminder of a dream I had. It was a dream that would not go away, no matter how hard I tried to ignore it. Every time I looked at the fridge door out the dream would pop. 'Whatever you can do, or dream you can do . . .' For months and months it lingered and intensified. 'Begin it . . .'

It was the type of dream that told me there is something better than this; that the world doesn't have to be the way it is. It told me that there were parts of myself yet to discover. It told me that there are ideas that could shape me, places I could learn from, people who could teach me. It seemed to know that life could be richer, better, fuller, not just for me, but for everyone.

But it was an annoying dream. Because I was too busy. Because I didn't have the money. Because I was frightened of pushing myself. Because I didn't want to do it alone. Because I was scared of how it would change me. But the dream insisted.

'Begin it.'
Every time I opened the fridge door, there it was: three-inches square and staring me in the face.

'Begin it.'

It was telling me to wake up to possibilities. I wanted to ignore it but it was calling me to venture, to explore, to learn, to ask questions, to tell stories . . .

'Begin it.'

'But I am nervous . . .'
'But I don't have all the skills . . .'
'But I don't think I can do it . . .'
'But why me . . .'

'Begin it.'

So I began.

Two and a half years on, that was the best advice I ever got from a fridge magnet. Never before did I realise that a three-inch square could be so powerful. Never did I realise that the people I would encounter along the way would change the way I think and feel so dramatically.

The Dream and the Journey

So what was the dream? What was I being told to begin?

The shorthand version is 'to tell inspiring stories'. But in order to tell the stories, I had to find them, plus I was interested in a particular type of story. Over the past few years, through my work with a youth organisation in Dublin, and through some previous travels, I had been coming across stories of individuals working for social change around the world that filled me with inspiration and intrigue. They were tales of daring, compassionate 'social entrepreneurs': people who could see a problem with the world and were working to solve it in innovative ways. They were stories of people like: Betty Nyagoha, a courageous head teacher in Gatoto Primary School in the slums of Nairobi; or Taddy Blecher, a South African who set up CIDA University in Johannesburg for people from the townships; or Kailash Satyarthi, who is working to free children from child labour in India; or Matt Flannery in San Francisco who set up Kiva, a microcredit lending website; or, closer to home, Caroline Casey, who is the founder of Kanchi, and who is working to promote the full integration of people with disabilities into society.

They are people who are challenging the status quo. They dare to be different. They rarely take no for an answer. They work for children, women, the environment, small farmers, the disabled, human rights, the marginalised, the oppressed, the downtrodden and the forgotten. They are activists, campaigners, inventors, business people, teachers, film-makers, advocates. They come from all walks of life: some formally educated, some not; some from the professions, some not. Some are known locally, some nationally, some internationally. In my eyes they are visionaries, dreamers, doers, leaders, role models, pragmatists and optimists. I knew they were people I could learn from.

In reading more about these individuals through blogs and books, I became more interested, not only in what they are doing and what social impact they are trying to achieve, but also how and why they do what they do. What motivates them? What challenges them? What inspires them? What skills did they have to learn? Where do they find their courage? Did they have mentors? What advice would they give to others setting out on their own journey?

And then the idea for the journey emerged. What if I could meet these people and ask them these questions directly? Even better, what if I could also capture and share their stories and advice with others? And so it was that the dream was planted: the journey and this book. My travels became a quest to find these individuals and ask some questions. I wanted learn from their visions of social change and how they make a difference. I wanted to hear the story of their solutions and understand more fully about the choices and chances in their lives which enabled them to do what they do. I was curious too about their dark side: their challenges, their failures, their struggles and their obstacles.

In the end my journey took me across five continents in eleven months. I started off with interviews in Ireland and then headed down to East Africa, landing firstly in Nairobi. Then it was on to Cape Town via Uganda, Tanzania and Mozambique. From there it was to Asia, spending three months in India, Singapore, Thailand, Cambodia and Vietnam. Then to Australia, New Zealand, Tonga and Samoa. The last leg of the journey took me to the United States – West Coast first, with San Francisco – then to the East Coast trio of Washington, New York and Boston.

Finally, with a host of experiences and lessons to last a lifetime, I closed the circle and returned to Ireland having met some of the most interesting people who populate our beautiful planet.

The travel was as intense as it was rewarding, but it was not always easy with an oversized rucksack and with laptop and camera at the ready. There were lots of trains, buses, planes, boats, bikes, pick-ups, rickshaws, taxis and even canoes. I walked a lot, sometimes much more than I ever intended to. I got lost – a lot – constantly testing my already dubious sense of direction. But no matter how many times I got lost, I would – usually with the help of a stranger – always find my way again.

I travelled over rough terrain and smooth terrain, sometimes over roads that bore the label of road but really did not deserve it. There were times when I was lonely, times when I was not.

I was confronted with poverty and a scale of problems that I never thought existed.

I was in slums and five-star hotels, sometimes on the same day.

There was heat that made me want to drop, humidity that made me think I was evaporating and tiredness that made me want never to get up. Sometimes I liked the food. Sometimes the food didn't like me.

I laughed. I cried. I cheered. I danced. I swam. I sang. I listened. I shared. I smiled. A lot.

I stayed in hotels and hostels, in people's homes, in bus stations, train stations, tents and airports. I spent a lot of time waiting in queues. I spent a lot of time in Internet cafes, and, if I was really lucky, I even had a fast connection.

There were moments of intense happiness and moments intense pain.

I encountered some very smelly armpits and, at 5 ft tall and reaching average armpit level, it did not always make for the most pleasant of adventures.

But along the way, as I travelled over those bumpy roads, meeting changemaker after changemaker, visiting project after project, in the five-star hotel and in the slums, in Ireland or in India, my understanding of myself and the world was altered. I did things I never knew I could. I went to places I never knew existed. I met people who I never realised would change me.

Travel does this to you. It enriches as it shakes. Perceptions start to shift and alter. You start to shift and alter. You take a step and the world unfolds with colour and learning. You take a step and the world takes the next ten. The world? Well, it's the people you meet along the way who point you in

the right direction. Or a book you read which clarifies a point. Or a film you see which sparks a train of new thought. Or that kid you play football with. Or that mother you make eye contact with. Or that beggar you pass on the street. Or the visionary who believes, and continues to believe, that the world can and should be a better place.

Along the way I was certainly inspired, and life may just never be the same again.

The 'Social Entrepreneurs'

Different labels are often applied to the people I interviewed: 'social entrepreneur', 'changemaker', 'change agent'. Sometimes they run businesses, sometimes social enterprises (a business aiming for financial and social profit), and sometime NGOs or non-profit organisations. However, whatever the label, it was the individual's character and contribution I was particularly interested in.

Of all the labels, though, 'social entrepreneur' seems to stick best. It combines the innovation of a business entrepreneur with the heart of a humanitarian. It makes for one hell of a combination.

My criteria for choosing people were not particularly scientific but I was generally looking for someone:

- with an innovative vision for social change and the drive to execute it
- who has high integrity and strong ethical fibre
- who could be working in the 'for-profit' or 'non-profit' worlds, but always with a view to creating social wealth or impact
- and, practically, who would be willing to meet with me!

Collectively, I was looking for people from a cross section of life and disciplines (art, media, medicine, business, entertainment, education etc.), from a variety of age ranges and from both developed and developing countries.

In setting about refining my list of people to meet, I contacted several organisations that support social entrepreneurs around the world, namely: Social Entrepreneurs Ireland, Ashoka, The Skoll Foundation, and the Schwab Foundation for Social Entrepreneurs. That at least was a good starting point, and I am very grateful for their support and encouragement. Word of mouth, online networks, blogging, and going with the flow did the rest.

This book

Within these pages you will find interviews with people I met on my journey who, I believe, are offering something unique to the world. They are positive, engaged and, most importantly, trying to put their ideas into action. They are people I have learned from and I believe their stories need to be told. As much as possible I focus on the solutions and not the problems. We hear about the problems every time we switch on the news. So, in writing this book I wanted to offer something different, focusing instead on the journey others have taken to get where they are and the advice they would share with others starting out on their own journey.

I also share some snippets from my own travels. I'll be upfront: in writing this book, I found it difficult to know where to place 'myself' in it, and the manuscript went through many renderings. 'Who am I compared with all the people I have met? Aren't their stories more interesting than my own?' But along the journey, as I continued to publish a travel blog and wrote letters home, I found people responding in the most open and beautiful ways when I, too, was open and honest about my experiences, questions, observations and challenges. Some would email me about their own questions or their search to make a difference. Others, often strangers, would leave supportive comments on my blog. That, in turn, inspired me. So, in writing this book, I decided to share some stories from my travels, snippets from my journal, extracts from my blog and selections from my letters home. They capture some of the questions I set out with, the questions that were generated, and the questions that remain. There are also a few funny anecdotes and some tales of the inevitable travel hiccups. Where words fail, I hope the pictures help to fill in some of the gaps.

A note about how this book was written

Sometimes my conversations with the people I met went on for many hours so, in order for it all to make sense in the context of this book, I had to condense and restructure them, extracting the bits which I think will be the most interesting or useful. In writing the profiles I had to juggle the words a little, sometimes reordering the sentence. In many cases I have changed the overall order in which things were said, but in all cases have maintained the context in which it was spoken.

In selecting which interviews to include in the book (out the 100+ to choose from) I have tried to select a wide variety of people, backgrounds, nationalities and disciplines and from a range of the countries I travelled through. I have listed the names of other people I interviewed in the acknowledgements section. Their stories deserve equal praise and merit, but space did not permit it here. I hope my final selection is a good reflection of the diversity of people, solutions and approaches that are out there.

All dollar amounts are US$ unless otherwise stated.

At the back of the book back you will find a list of resources about social entrepreneurship and travel which I have found useful or interesting. I hope that they too may be of help to you as your journey along your own One Wild Life ...

Clare Mulvany
Dublin, April 2009

Part One: Ireland

It was important for me to start on my doorstep.

Before my departure I was living in a fairly rough part of Dublin city. At the end of the road, about 200 m from my doorway, was one of the major heroin-dealing points in the city. I just had to look out of my window to know that things could be better, much better.

When we think about development, the stereotype, at least in Ireland, is of some distant place. Most Irish people probably think of Africa. Images of famine and drought are predominant in the media and the problems seem distant and unconnected to life in Ireland. But there were

two realities I wanted to explore while on my travels. Firstly, that life in the so-called developed world is intrinsically linked to life in the developing world. And secondly, that we do not have to fly off to a distant place to make a difference, we just have to open our door. The people I met in Ireland are doing just that.

The interviews in Ireland gave me a taste of the variety of people I was to meet ahead and the stories of their fearlessness and feats. Their commitment lent further momentum to my decision to head off on my

Caroline Casey

Kanchi

www.kanchi.org

www.theabilityawards.com

Dublin, Ireland

Themes: Human Rights, Business, Media

The world owes us nothing, we have to go out and get it.

Caroline Casey, tall and graceful, oozes passion and intensity. Meeting up with her, it is difficult not to be taken by her energy. She speaks with conviction and has a rare innovative spirit that brings entrepreneurial ideas to life.

Caroline is the founder of Kanchi (formerly the Aisling Foundation) and the O_2 Ability Awards. Through high-profile media she works to enhance the relationship between society and disability.

As a flagship programme the O_2 Ability Awards are changing the way corporate Ireland integrates disability into workplaces. The Awards are televised annually and have become a showcase of best practice among Irish businesses in areas such as leadership, environmental accessibility, and the recruitment and selection of employees with disabilities.

Legally blind, Caroline can only see about 3 ft in front of her. But she certainly does not let the label of disability define her. It did not stop her becoming a mahout or elephant handler, for instance, when she trekked across India on the back of an elephant, Kanchi, in 2000, a journey which sparked her current work.

For her efforts, Caroline has been recognised as one of the World Economic Forum's Young Global Leaders. She was also the first Ashoka/Social Entrepreneurs Ireland Fellow in Ireland and has an honorary degree from the National College of Ireland.

The Ability Awards are about telling a story of a life that could be different. It is not just about Africa or India but also Ireland. **If we ever want to change the world we have to understand the value of the person, whoever they are, wherever they are.**

My only real conscious decision was, 'I will do the elephant trip'. Everything else was a natural thing – it is amazing how many things happen without having to make decisions. I initially set up the Aisling Foundation (now Kanchi) as a vehicle to raise money for the elephant trek and I have learned that once you make a good decision, lots of things conspire to help you.

When I decided to do the elephant journey I was scared. I didn't really like myself an awful lot and I'd forgotten where I was going. At the time I was working with Accenture [a management and technology consultancy company] as a consultant, but somehow I knew instinctively I had much more to give. When I came up with the idea for the elephant trip, it wasn't because I wanted to show the world that I was able, I just wanted to believe that I was. I wanted to regain some sense of my own ability, and it was only when I was planning the trip that I realised I could use it as a way to talk about the problems of having a disability in a corporate environment.

The more I looked into it, the more I realised nobody was talking about disability in the workplace. When I was looking for sponsorship to do the journey nobody wanted to touch 'disability' as a subject. It was too risky. 'Who is this girl?', they were saying. 'Will she fall off the elephant?' 'Is she mad?' Disability was clearly not something organisations felt comfortable about. So by this stage in my preparations it wasn't just raising the sponsorship that was bothering me, it was the question 'why won't the corporations talk about disability?' The elephant trip started to look small in comparison to this huge question.

Right before the trip I had a very rare opportunity: I was invited onto the *Late Late Show* to talk about my plans. Three days after the show I got a call from one of Ireland's most successful business people who said 'I want to give you €100,000'. I nearly dropped the phone! At that stage I literally had €67 in the bank but I needed to reach my fund-raising target of €250,000. When the cheque arrived, written on the bottom of it was 'if there is anything I can do to help . . .' So I decided to take him up on his offer. I knew what I wanted: I wanted to meet his friends who ran companies – some of the most successful business people in the country – and ask them why disability is a taboo in corporate Ireland. He gave me that wonderful opportunity the day before I went to India. I sat with sixteen of Ireland's top business people, all men, and told them, 'I want people to see ability, not disability. I want people to see that we all have capacity and capability. I'm visually impaired, I'm legally blind but I didn't accept it until I started doing this, but I know I can do this trip'. And because I was working in a top consultancy firm, I knew all these men were wondering, 'How can she work there when she is blind?' I told them it was because **I'd never labelled myself as being disabled.** Then one of them replied, 'Wow, I would never have thought about it like that'. His words stuck with me. You see, they had never come across a disabled person who was positive and saying 'this is what I want, I know I can do this'. I just engaged them. I left the room, raised the money – way above what I intended – and, as I was leaving, three or four of them told me they would help me when I got back to Ireland.

When I came home from the elephant trip I thought, 'Right, where do I pick up?' After the journey I did go through a bit of a low – the media had crowned me as an extraordinary human being, which I'm just not. But I said to myself, 'Let me remember the CEOs who sat around that table. What lessons can I learn?' I remembered what they had said – they had told me I was easy to talk to and that I listened, so I condensed these lessons, which I still carry with me today:

If I want something done,
I go to the top.
If I want them to hear,
I give them a solution.
If I want them to believe,
I energise them with passion.

Around this time I came up with the idea of doing Ability Conferences, aimed at CEOs. The goal was to completely throw the idea of disability on its head. I designed a large-scale multimedia event with music and even included a performance from a comedian. I spoke publicly for the first time about my disability. We got video clips of people working with disabilities. Even though it was a business conference, people were blown away – they had never seen anything like it. I just thought, 'Wow, it works!' It got the companies talking about disability in a new way. So we did that for two or three years but I soon realised that conferences alone were not enough: **companies needed solutions.**

Then the idea for the Ability Awards emerged. The idea was to have an awards programme for the business sector, based on praise. We wanted to

have a high-profile awards programme, which would be televised and be in all the main newspapers. 'Here are some companies who are fabulous and I will make them feel even more so. It will be an ego boost for them.' Business by its nature is competitive, so if Allied Irish Bank sees that Bank of Ireland are getting an award, they'll say 'well, we want to get one also'. Kids like to be praised, and businesses are not much different!

…

On my seventeenth birthday my whole life changed. Mum and Dad gave me driving lessons for a present. I was seeing an eye specialist that day who told me I'd never be able to drive because my eyesight would never be good enough. It was only then I acknowledged I had a disability – I have about 3 ft of sight.
I went to university in UCD and studied Archaeology and Classics. I wanted to be an archaeologist. After my degree I was told my eyesight was not good enough to be an archaeologist, so instead I went travelling around the world, trying to prove that I could. When I came home I said, 'What will I do now?' I was a waitress for a while and then thought I would do some horticulture – it meant being outdoors and was the nearest thing to archaeology. Again I found out that my sight wasn't good enough. So I decided to do a Diploma in Business Studies in the Michael Smurfit Graduate School of Business. I followed it with a master's in Business which got me into Accenture. Being with Accenture was brilliant. I learned that business

25

etiquette is so important and it showed me just how tough and competitive it is in that world: high expectations, the importance of money, the importance of bottom line and presentation. It was work hard, play hard. I was working with some fantastic people and I learned that in order to be taken seriously you have to be the best.

My biggest personal journey has been accepting that I'm fallible, that I'm disabled, that I'm not perfect, and that my eyes are never going to get better. People say, 'Do you think you have achieved this because of your eyes?' I don't think they have anything to do with it, actually. I think other things are involved, including family life. I think an insecurity has driven me from a very young age. I look at most entrepreneurs and I think there is a reason to prove something and for me it began with needing to prove to myself that I am an OK person. I also think of it as having a hole in my chest. The hole feels like it could be a wound, which could grow to be quite sore; a gap which so desperately needs to be filled. I just know I'm here to do something, so I think part of my work has been about proving I can close this gap.

Entrepreneurship can be quite lonely, especially when you are beginning. Because you are so driven, you are engulfed by it. And how do you deal with the alone part? You don't. You surround yourself with people who are exactly the same. **I have learned to surround myself with people who are high-energy, motivated and a bit mad – I love the madness.** I love people who don't look at the world in a box. I love people who do things completely differently.

I have also learned that the biggest barriers to anything that we do are mental. **Most of the work of social entrepreneurs is about changing mindsets. Because the minute we change mindsets, the resources will come.** Whereas business people are about selling us something, social entrepreneurs want to change minds. That is the clear difference.

In seven or eight years' time I hope that there will be no Ability Awards in Ireland because we will be beyond the need for them, but until then, there's lots to do. I want to bring the Awards internationally.

There are 400 million people in developing countries with a disability, and nobody knows about them. From a developing-country perspective, we hear about HIV/AIDS, we hear about poverty, we hear about gender, but we don't hear about disability. Where is it? Disability is hidden under poverty. If you have a disability and you are poor, you are the poorest of poor. If you have a disability and you want to get an education, you can't. If you are disabled and you're a woman and you are poor, you are in big trouble. So yes, there is still a huge amount of work to do.

Advice

Be curious. Being curious is so important. Why is it that people's eyes sparkle when they are in the right place at the right time? Be curious about how things are done, what makes people tick, or why people do what they do.

Have the questions. If you don't have questions I'm scared for you. If you don't have dreams or ambitions, you have to find one, because dreams keep us alive. Have sort of a silly game plan – even if it is just a silly game plan – but believe in it.

Also remember, **you are entirely, utterly responsible for yourself** and the quicker you realise that the better off you'll be. We can blame everyone for our circumstances, for where we live, our eyes, or whatever, but the reality is that if you want a better life it is up to you to make it. **The world owes us nothing, we have to go out and get it.**

Also remember that **life and business are about people**. Every time you talk to someone you have an impact on them. Being a good business person is about people. Getting an idea off the ground is about people. You are going to need them.

Believe you have the capacity. Believe. Because we all have hidden potential. It is one thing that we all have in common, but what is the point of having the potential if it stays hidden?

If you have an idea, picture it in your head. Close your eyes. See the picture. Don't assume you have to do the same one as everybody else. You are unique and different: look at what makes you unique and different.

If I sat with you seven years ago, I was a completely and utterly different person. I'm still Caroline, the same girl, but I am also different. I have grown. Know that you will change.

And **you need to know when to compromise**. Compromise is important, but never compromise on your vision or quality, and never your integrity.

Know there is no full stop. There isn't a 'eureka' moment. There isn't a moment of perfection. It just doesn't exist. The minute you know that, then you know that when you fail you will get back up again. Life is just like that.

And don't listen to negativity, because the amount of people who only want to be negative with you is unbelievable. Surround yourself with people who go for it. Then **go for it**.

Know there is no full stop. There isn't a 'eureka' moment. There isn't a moment of perfection. It just doesn't exist. The minute you know that, then you know that when you fail you will get back up again. Life is just like that.

Tara Cunningham
Release Speech Therapy
www.release.ie

Tullamore and Dublin, Ireland
Themes: Education, Health, Business

I knew there was a problem, I knew there was a solution and I knew I could do it. The other choice was to sit back and complain that nobody was doing anything.

Tara Cunningham is the founder of Release Speech Therapy, an organisation that provides holistic care and education for children with language difficulties. Her model is to bring children and their carers into the classes together, equipping both to develop language skills.

Despite not having a background in language therapy, Tara saw a critical need for language services. Knowing she had enough managerial, business and marketing experience to start an organisation, she trusted enough to find the right people along the way to fill in the gaps. One of those is Jennifer Wetter, a speech therapist, who has been working alongside Tara to develop the organisation. Tara and Jen work as fuel and engine, and it was hard to know really which was which.

Tara's optimism is infectious. She has a giddy, almost childlike charm, which is intensified when she is speaking about the positive impact Release has had on children who attend the classes. She has certainly come a long way from her early career ambitions – to be a US senator on Capitol Hill.

I am from a little town in the States called Tom's River, New Jersey. Being half-Irish, half-Italian, I suppose there is a bit of a rebel mixture in me! My father was a staunch Democrat. To rebel I became a Republican. I'm not one now but I was very involved in my late teens and was even the youngest delegate at the Young Republican Convention. I even spoke in front of Bob Dole and 12,000 other people. They all had great hopes for me. I even converted my parents to Republicanism – I was very, very into it!

I studied history and political science at university. So it was politics, politics, politics. I didn't drink. I didn't do drugs. I didn't go to parties where there were drugs. I was going to become a politician and my slate was going to be clean. I had ambitions: I wanted to be a Senator.

While at university I got an internship in DC with the National Federation of Republican Women. There are four girls who get accepted each year and, that year, the other three were daughters of congressmen. I was a child of the early 1980s and I loved Reagan! The idea in America is that you don't have to be from 'somewhere', that you can make it on your own: I just loved that. My father didn't even have a high school diploma when he arrived over to the States from Ireland in the 1950s. From the Republican perspective, it's not the government's role to provide a service, you should do it for yourself, which is why I liked the Republicans: they were all about, 'You can do it yourself'.

Right before graduated I got a job offer as a legislative assistant for a Congressman on Capitol Hill. But something very odd happened. Before I started I went down to DC to meet the people I'd be working with. But I just got this huge block. A voice within me was saying 'Don't do this. Don't do this.' To this day I don't know why, but all of a sudden I shut the door on the job and all of my political ambition, instantly. Instead, the very same week I went to a headhunter and got a job as an administrative assistant in an architectural firm. Everybody was saying, 'What the heck is going on with this girl?' I was twenty-one.

It turned out to be the best thing I ever did. The new job was full of architects and interior designers. Everyone in the firm had travelled. Half of them were gay, and being a staunch

conservative Republican I had thought gay people had twelve heads! They were into things that were not part of my old world. They thought I was hilarious and that I'd a stick up my arse so far! I spent a year and a half with them and it was fantastic. **My family thought I'd lost the plot.** I'd gone from being this big conservative Republican going somewhere, to basically a secretary working with a bunch of gay people. They had no idea what was going on.

The head of the firm, Rusty Meadows, took me under his wing from the beginning. He showed me the business side of things. I was able to go to meetings, which gave me a grounding in business, and that has been so valuable. I also got training in marketing. So suddenly I had switched from history and politics to business and marketing. I realised that business is very similar to politics but on a more practical level. You take the ideology out. You have problems, you have the solutions and you have to figure out the best way to get from point A to point B. But business is not about serving a personality, and I loved that.

After a year and a half Rusty took me aside, and said, 'You've done all you can here. You need to leave and I think you should go to Europe'. All of my friends in the firm had travelled. I was the only one who hadn't – I didn't even have a passport! So I quit my job and told my family I was leaving. I got my passport, went to Ireland with a cousin and travelled around Europe for a while, falling in love with it. I wound up temping in Dublin, working for two different technology companies. With both jobs I was only supposed to be there for two days but ended up being there for two months. I didn't want to go back to America. My mother couldn't understand it and begged, 'Please come back for a year, but if you don't like it you can go back to Ireland'.

Almost a year to the day I came back to Ireland and joined Baltimore Technologies, running their international emarketing. My politics were gone at this stage. Instead, I was volunteering with Clongowes Youth Club, the second oldest inner-city youth club in Ireland, and loving it. I was with Baltimore Technologies for nine months and afterwards headed up Ogilvy Interactive, also in marketing. But I hated the work. I was getting more and more involved with the inner-city kids and was getting more out of my voluntary work in one evening than I was with weeks of paid work. I didn't care if a leading brand went up 0.5 per cent in market share – it didn't mean anything to me. **I realised that I didn't want to die thinking I hadn't made a real difference.** So I was having a serious mind-shift. I didn't know what I was going to do, but I knew it wasn't going to be on the path I was on. I began thinking that if I started working for a charity, at least I could use my knowledge for greater good. I looked around and managed to get a job as a fund-raiser with Down Syndrome Ireland.

In that role I had to travel around the country, meeting parents to discuss a large fund-raising event we were going to host. We were raising money for a centre of excellence for children with Down syndrome. But wherever I went, no matter which county I was in, all that the parents said they wanted was speech and language therapy for their children, and that they needed it immediately. They couldn't wait the ten years until the centre was built. If their child couldn't speak, they wouldn't be allowed to stay in mainstream school, and if their child was put into a special school they wouldn't acquire the skills they need to integrate into mainstream life. Every day the phone calls kept coming in, 'Does anyone have a speech therapist? Does anyone have a speech therapist?' I just thought it was bizarre. I'd been **thrown into the deep end and had absolutely no idea how bad the situation was.** Literally I was only with Down Syndrome Ireland six weeks before I realised 'it can't go on like this'. **I knew there was a problem, I knew there was a solution and I knew I could do it. The other choice was to sit back and complain that nobody was doing anything.**

The idea for Release came one day when I was driving down the country with my boyfriend Mark (now husband). I was almost in tears. I'd just had a solid week of negative, negative, negative from all of these parents and I was saying '**geez, Mark, why doesn't somebody do something?**' He replied, '**Why don't you?**'
'**What the hell am I supposed to do?**'
'**You're Tara J. Liston – go figure it out!**'
'You're Tara J Liston, go figure it out.' Those words really stuck. So I sat there

31

and thought 'OK, what if I brought therapists over from the US and taught the parents some basic speech therapy techniques, then they could help their children.' I started doing research and found out that the government recognised that there were 372 vacancies for speech therapists in Ireland. Each therapist is responsible for 100 kids, so if there are 372 vacancies there were over 37,000 people not getting weekly speech and language therapy. I knew something had to be done, quickly. I also knew that parents were an integral part of the solution. Nobody knows their child better than their parent so if the parent can learn some skills to develop their child, then that child is going to do better. The parents needed to feel empowered to do something about it.

So basically I saw a need. I got a feasibility grant from the Dublin City Enterprise Board and I went to America to meet with the top people of ASHA – the American Speech Hearing Association. They validated the programme on the spot. They were all commenting, 'It is so simple, why didn't we come up with the idea?'. One person said, 'Because she hasn't learnt theory'. **All I did was listen to what parents wanted**. If they had listened to what parents wanted, they would have come up with the idea as well. It really was so simple: invite the parents in for a group session. It is not a miraculous process.

When I started doing this everybody asked me, 'Well, what is in it for you?' The best thing that could happen to me is if the Minister for Health rang me up tomorrow and said, 'We are stealing the programme from you, we are going to run it throughout the country'. I would be doing backflips down the hallway. **We want to do ourselves out of our job.** A lot of social entrepreneurs are not getting money for the work they do. It is very hard because we are told 'success equals money'. I'm not getting paid much but I have never worked harder and I have never tried harder for success. The business may stay afloat but as social entrepreneurs it doesn't mean that you are washing your own back with cash! You become secondary to the cause.

I think the real litmus test of how a society is working is how you work with the lowest people on the totem pole, your most vulnerable people. In Ireland, we should be ashamed; we have a disgraceful record in our ability to provide services and support to people with disabilities. Sometimes I get so mad, but that in turn motivates me to do this.

I could never have done it without Mark or without Jen, the speech and language therapist whom I first hired from the States – not in a million years. They are incredible people. The people you have around you are so important. Now I feel it is too late for me to pull out of this – we have come so far. But really I would just love for the government to say 'we are taking it off you'. Then I could become a housewife, or work in an accessory shop, or in ten years' time I could even be a soccer mom!

Ruairí McKiernan

Community Creations and SpunOut

www.spunout.ie

Galway, Ireland

Themes: Technology, Media, Youth

Following several years of travel around the world, Ruairí McKiernan returned to Ireland to set up an organisation called Community Creations which operates the award-winning website, www.spunout.ie. Based in Galway, the site is regarded as a pioneering channel to get young people involved in issues that concern them most. Topics range from dealing with exam pressure to sexual health, from money matters to relationships, and the articles have been read by thousands of visitors to the site.

Ruairí's own story is one of persistence. From running the website on a very bare shoestring (even hiding out in Internet cafes to tap into free Wi-Fi), he and a dedicated team of staff and supporters have grown the organisation into one of the leading youth sites in Ireland. And he is still barely into his thirties.

We are living in unique and challenging times. We therefore need unique recipes for social change.

Looking back on how my journey has come about so far, I suppose I was always involved in some kind entrepreneurial activity or other. Between the ages of eight and eleven I had a few different ventures, including a bird-table manufacturing operation, door-to-door holly sales at Christmas, and later on I sold marbles to my schoolmates. I think I can justify these as being ecologically, spiritually and recreationally oriented social enterprises! Between the ages of thirteen and fifteen, when there was no Internet, I got into computing and set up a mail-order software business operating out of my bedroom. It got fairly successful and at one stage I had to start mitching school to process my orders. It wasn't really about the money though – more a bit of a challenge and it was probably more stimulating than school. School to me seemed more like a conveyor belt churning out ready-made minds, rather than a place for fostering creativity and discovery.

I did fairly well at school but not good enough to get into top courses in Ireland. That didn't bother me too much and after a summer backpacking around Europe, I ended up going to Scotland where I did a degree in Business Management. For the first couple of years I acted the eejit and was partying a bit too much. In my third year I landed an internship at a major multinational computer company. Here I found the corporate environment and pressures, combined with my night-time student lifestyle, to be a strain. This resulted in major health problems and, at the age twenty, I ended up hospitalised with a ruptured stomach ulcer.

In hindsight I think a lot of this was to do with not having a clear vision of who I was or what I wanted to do and I just ended up getting pulled in all sorts of directions. I think this is something many young people are up against, which is why they need support, guidance and opportunities.

This whole experience gave me room for reflection so I knuckled down and got a distinction at university, and headed straight for California the minute I finished. This began three years of travelling and adventure that led me all around the world. I ended up doing all sorts of jobs ranging from security guard and gardener, to web designer and researcher. However, it was my volunteering, campaigning and involvement in health, social and environmental projects that really buzzed me up. One experience that stands out was, after finding city life a bit hectic at times, I ended up living, working and studying at an Ayurvedic healing centre. This gave me a completely different, more interconnected, way of looking at health, well-being and society, which has stayed with me and influenced my work. I travelled for the next few years. I would work a bit, get some money, and then travel a bit more. At one point I ended up in Canada, but there weren't many jobs going that I was interested in, or at least qualified for, so instead I spent time in libraries and got involved in social justice and activist initiatives such as Critical Mass bike riding [gathering as a large group of cyclists to reclaim the streets from motor traffic], the anti-war movement and the Free West Papua Campaign. I also helped out on organic farms for a while. I was on what I call a 'self-education' process, learning and becoming more involved generally in social justice issues.

A while later I found myself at a protest gathering in Melbourne, at a rally against the World Economic Forum. The idea of a thousand unelected business leaders coming together to 'set the global agenda' didn't wash with me, and still doesn't. So, not having any other outlet to engage with – like many citizens, particularly young people – I found myself protesting out of frustration. I got involved in a non-violent direct action protest, which was about being confrontational but doing it in a non-violent way – in the spirit of Gandhi, so to speak. The first day of the protest was successful in that it actually prevented the forum from going ahead. On the second day the World Economic Forum threatened to pull out unless there was immediate action taken. At 7 a.m. that morning 300 riot police attacked myself and about 50 others, who were sitting in a huddle on the ground with our backs to them. We got beaten with batons and I ended up with a broken nose and back in hospital. There has since been legal action and the police have paid compensation to some of us. Obviously confronting the law isn't something to take lightly but it's vital to remember the law should exist to serve people before corporations, and history is full of celebrated examples of confronting power.

In Australia the incident spurred huge social debate and awareness. We were all over the media. The activists were being vilified as hippies, anarchists and hooligans, whereas the vast majority were concerned, active and peaceful citizens that were simply disempowered. I was a business management graduate who didn't have accessible ways to participate, other than a vote every four years or so. At the time I was working in the financial services sector (ironic, I know) in Sydney's business district and had taken three days off work to attend the protest in Melbourne, something my colleagues only found out about when they saw me on the evening news.

After Australia, I became more active in my community. I organised various gigs for asylum seekers and marginalised groups and was generally more involved in community-related causes and issues. One of my major interests was forging links between peoples and issues. **I believe that you can't look at problems in isolation. Issues need bridges and people to see the problems in an interconnected way.** Following a stint doing youth media work in Canada, I was asked by former colleagues at the North Western Health Board to do research into young people's behaviour, based back in Donegal, where my grandparents lived. My grandparents were getting older and, as the Celtic Tiger roared on around us, I saw this as a great opportunity to spend time living with them and learning more about old Ireland, before it disappeared from around us.

I did the research and by end of the study I had a report mapping out how the Internet could be used to empower young people in Ireland. However, the health service was undergoing reform and there was no money available for the project – I became unemployed. Then aged twenty-four, I considered leaving Ireland again but instead decided to channel some of my frustration at not having avenues for participation and engagement into setting up an organisation that could provide meaningful channels for other young people. I set up Community Creations, an organisation that had the very broad vision of promoting positive social change. Together with another young community worker, Keith Corcoran, we spent the summer organising public events on a range of issues in Donegal town, working with the rural community

on health, social and environmental issues. We worked from home in what we joked was our 'cottage industry'. I had a cottage in Leitrim, Keith had a cottage in Donegal. Our Internet connections were so slow that it would take ten minutes to send an email, not ideal for harnessing the power of the web! We initially undertook loads of small projects – from helping to launch a public health report to designing websites. We earned some money here and there. It was during this time that SpunOut emerged, so we set about developing the site, and Anna Lally, our editor and backbone of the site, joined the team.

Over the next year and a half we did loads of stuff but spread ourselves way too thinly. We were notching up little successes but there came a point where we knew it was unsustainable. Keith decided to go to India and Anna was actually living in England, working online – it was all a bit crazy. I decided to move to Galway and to some extent had to start from scratch. The website was still running but we had no real systems or structures behind the organisation. In the meantime we were winning awards for the site! **I was working at home without a proper Internet connection and was hiding out in coffee shops with free Wi-Fi.**

It took over six months to find and set up another office. Anna was managing the website which was really critical. From the site it looked like all was well but the back engine was in danger of going to the wire. We still had no money. **It is the usual social** entrepreneur story: **I nearly quit a million times.** I worked fourteen hours a day. In fact, I pretty much feel like I've lost my entire late twenties and can't really remember large chunks of the last four or five years, something that has affected friends, family and my health. There was a point where I was starting to get resentful of all the difficulties we faced but now I wouldn't change the experience for the world. It was a seriously intense baptism of fire. Ultimately it has made me a stronger person and in the end we turned the organisation around to the point that it's now winning awards and thriving with eight full-time staff, several part-timers and freelancers, over 300 volunteers and is reaching over 250,000 young people per year. I feel proud that SpunOut is providing resources and opportunities for young people and creating a platform for them to engage in creating the positive personal and social changes that are so badly needed in today's world.

When I first started out I had a relentless drive for change and **I suppose the energy, ideas and enthusiasm of being in my mid twenties – without an office or an income – was the best advantage I could have possibly had.** I couldn't have foreseen the zillion barriers I've since come up against. I think therein lies the power of resourcing young people – they have less baggage and will kick down walls with gusto.

Whether people took me seriously or not, I'd say those that knew me or worked with me did, but certainly the mainstream 'establishment' didn't. I still get looked up and down when I attend meetings and spend the first ten minutes having to prove I'm not off the wall. Then again, who's to say I'm not? I've noticed there is definitely a tendency to dismiss younger people, to make assumptions and to prefer the old-school system of importing 'experts' and people with PhDs, rather than utilising the skills and ideas of the community. **My experience is that it is often the people on the ground, without the academics or jargon, who hold the energy, keys and solutions to success.**

I'm still several years younger than many of my colleagues in similar positions and the reality is that this brings many upsides as well as downsides. The fact that I'm still just about rooted into youth culture (only just, mind you!) gives me some degree of credibility when talking about youth health and social issues. Also, sympathetic people with experience often give up their time and expertise to provide a mentoring role, which is something I find very valuable. I have learned so much about patience and commitment. And focus. Obviously, I wanted to do lots of noble change-the-world-type projects. I've since realised that focusing my energies into tapping the power of hundreds of thousands of young people is a much better use of my time and skills and will hopefully bring about the change I know is possible.

Sr Stanislaus Kennedy

www.srstan.ie

Focus Ireland: www.focus.ie

Immigrant Council of Ireland: www.immigrantcouncil.ie

The Sanctuary: www.sanctuary.ie

Young Social Innovators: www.youngsocialinnovators.ie

Dublin, Ireland
Themes: Education, Youth, Human Rights

A nun by vocation, a social entrepreneur with passion, there is a long list of organisations associated with Sr Stan. From helping the homeless with the establishment of Focus Ireland, to promoting young social innovators, she is a well-known name and respected among a cross section of Irish society. At the heart of her work is the voice of the marginalised, working to bridge social and economic divides while drawing out the best of multicultural Ireland.

My story is a simple one. I was drawn into community action and social services, and then saw a need to establish new services and systems.

In 1958 I joined the Sisters of Charity because I wanted to work with the poor. As a child I became aware of inequalities in society. Back then I had no notion of becoming a nun, but I was always conscious of inequalities. I knew there were people who could afford books, and people who couldn't. There were some who could pay fees, and some who couldn't. And, even from an early age, I knew there was something not right about it. I can remember my mother telling my sisters, 'Always be good to the poor ones'. My sisters went on to become teachers and nurses, but I thought that even those professions would not bring me to work directly with the poor. So instead I entered the Sisters of Charity, believing that it would give me that opportunity – oddly, I didn't really enter to become a nun. I suppose when I stayed with them, I became more aware of the spiritual dimension of life and it became important to me. So I entered for one reason, but I stayed for another.

I initially worked in London with the Irish, in social services, and a few years later, in 1964, returned to Kilkenny where a new social services

When important work is begun, nothing can stop it.

programme for the marginalised was being designed by the church. It was a liberal and radical move, and was a real breath of fresh air in the Ireland of the 1960s. Up to that point there were no social services or social workers. The work was very challenging, interesting and inspiring and I stayed there until 1983. In the meantime I also trained as a social worker and returned to university as a research fellow. My research was on homelessness and through it I realised that there were basically no services for homeless people. Following the research I spent a year living with eight homeless women, to understand their lives better and the situation better. By the end of the year all the women were out of their homelessness. So building on that experience, at the end of that year I set up Focus Point as a response to homelessness, providing immediate care: a 24-hour phone service; services on the streets; youth reach; a drop-in coffee shop; a drop-in information and advice service. That was the beginning of what is now a very big organisation, Focus Ireland, employing many people in Dublin and throughout the region. I'm still involved with Focus but after about ten years of running it, I decided to pull back.

Stepping back was a deliberate choice – I knew it would grow more if I did, but it was not an easy thing to do. Looking back now, though, other initiatives emerged which, had I stayed full-time with Focus, wouldn't have developed.

In 2000 I set up The Sanctuary, which is a place of renewal and inspiration for people who work in care. I realised what it was like to work very hard in services and also saw that there were not many places for people to be renewed, revived and inspired. The Sanctuary is on a quarter of an acre in Dublin, with a lovely building and garden – the very environment itself aims to be inspirational. We also offer night courses to help people find their inner selves, harmony in their lives, and a balance in this world which is so unbalanced. The centre has evolved in its own way. Meditation has really developed and we also run a course on Mindfulness – developing the art of being still. We also run a programme for schools. In all there is an emphasis on finding stillness to be able to go back into the world again.

Then I set up a company called Social Innovations Ireland, which was established to respond to new needs in Ireland. Two needs were identified very quickly: immigration and youth. Out of that came the Immigrant Council of Ireland – which offers advice and information on immigration issues and tries to influence policy – and Young Social Innovators (YSI). We saw a need to find structures whereby young people could commit themselves to society. The idea of YSI emerged as a way for young people to develop projects for the community while also developing their consciousness.

The key thing to remember for

any entrepreneurship is to take risks. There were never any resources, we had to seek them out and believe that they would come. To this day this is true. But I continued because it comes from a belief that this is important work, that it is needed, and that it is possible. **I think that when important work is begun, nothing can stop it.** It is a very simple approach, but it is very real. A lot of people would say 'there is no money for this', but I would always believe that the money would come and I would start. And the money did come.

I think I have an ability to identify and see needs, plus I think I have an ability to see a solution to a need. I also have some organisational ability. Fortunately I have been able to get extraordinary people to work with me – people who are much more skilled than I am and who can do much more than I ever could. The right people always seem to come – they are attracted to a vision.

The spiritual dimension to life also keeps me going. I believe that there is more to life than the concrete things of everyday – there is the whole person: mind, body and spirit. Keeping the spirit nurtured is very important to me. I believe that my spiritual development keeps the rest of me alive. Sometimes it is a struggle, though, and it has not always been so easy to balance my life. There were times when it was really hard and challenging and I was on an edge, but I always had something that pulled me back. **Often when you are driven to the edge, it helps you to understand others at their edge.** If everything were so well balanced, we would not see the needs of others. I think it is that link with the edge within myself that links me to the people on the edge. Working to my own limits, seeing my own fragility and my own brokenness has helped me to see the brokenness of the world.

I feel a sense of urgency in my work – there is a lot to be done. I'd love to be young again, to start again, and to be able to work in the developing world. I would love to be able to do a lot more – I have always been looking for the next thing, wanting to do more, wanting to be more for people. But there was been a change in my life: now it is not necessarily me doing the thing, but instead making myself available to others as a guide and mentor. It is a turn my life have taken, which sometimes is a struggle also, because one part of me is very much a doer and the other part of me is very much a mentor – so I've had to learn to balance these things also.

Don't be afraid of your intuitions or your limits. Allow yourself to be influenced by the needs of people who are fragile, who are broken. Allow yourself to listen and to hear them. Allow yourself to hear it in your heart, not just your head. Allow them to change you. And remember: you have an absolute right to speak out against injustice and inequality. You might evoke criticism, but try to find opportunities to get involved and to be open to the world that we live in. Allow yourself to be touched, to be moved. That is what the great people in the world allowed: Gandhi, Mandela, Martin Luther King. The cause took them over.

Joan Hamilton

Slí Eile

www.slieilehousing.com

Cork, Ireland

Themes: Health, Human Rights

'There must be another way,' thought Joan Hamilton after successive years of seeing her daughter's mental health progressively decline, despite successive years of psychiatric treatment. Prompted by frustration with the lack of services for people with mental illness in Ireland, Joan, together with family members and several other concerned parents, pooled experiences and came up with the idea for Slí Eile ('another way').

The organisation now provides residential housing for people who have been released from care, aiming to support their transition back into mainstream society. But setting up it up has been far from easy. There have been broken windows and even abusive threats hurled at Joan for her efforts to break down some of the taboos associated with mental illness. Yet still she continues with a graceful and determined charm. Like so many parents, she wants the best for her children, but seeing that 'the best' was not available, she found the motivation and courage to try to create it.

I have learned that the only way to get change is to just do it.

Slí Eile was established to help people with mental illness recover in an accepting and supportive environment. It was set up by a group of concerned parents, including myself, who each had a son or daughter caught up in the 'revolving door' of the psychiatric system. When our children had a breakdown, they would be admitted to hospital, and appearing to respond to drug treatment, they would be discharged. But the problem was they would be discharged back into their original environment, without having addressed the root cause of the problem – so inevitably they would be back through the revolving door. Gradually, the length of time between admissions became shorter and the stays became longer. It was soul-destroying to watch my daughter and others in hospital. They would just sit there, waiting for their medication. They started to believe that they were incapable of anything else. So we started looking for a way to break the cycle.

I learned about therapeutic communities from a friend of mine, and was very attracted to this model of support. It is about helping people take back responsibility for themselves and their behaviour, and helping them to think more positively about what they can do with their lives. When individuals are released from hospital they have a choice to come to the Slí Eile home. Firstly they visit the house to see if they like the place, then they have

the option to apply for tenancy. We then enter into a formal tenant's agreement with them, whereby they undertake to pay rent, pay board, manage the money and run the house – as a normal tenant would do. The role of staff is to support and to facilitate. We have a big round table, which we can sit around to sort out problems and plan the day's activities – the shopping and cooking for instance. It is just humbling to see a person gain confidence through it, and the model really is very simple. It is based on supporting people to lead normal lives and reintegrating them back into the community.

There are no time limits for someone to stay in the house. Six months to two years is standard – anything longer and there is something not working. The expectancy from day one is that this is transitional. If it is not working for an individual we have to question whether it is what the person wants. We hope that our tenants will be able to make the transition back to leading normal lives and we link them into personal and professional training to help them do so.

Initially there was a lot of reaction to the idea – even protests from local people. We had received money for a house from the county council, but when neighbours heard that it would be for people with mental illness, they reacted – badly. The county council had put an advert in a local newspaper announcing that the money had been granted for the house. That night I had a phone call warning me that nobody with mental illness would be living in the estate. Over the next few weeks the neighbours started picketing in the housing estate with placards: 'Will not accept'; 'Get the message'; 'No support, no project'. They threw stones; they broke a window.

One weekend, as I tried to move into the house with a prospective tenant, the keyholes were all blocked up. We got the locks fixed, but it happened again and again. My family were starting to be seriously concerned about me at this stage. The third time it happened, I got out a credit union loan and installed a CCTV camera for security reasons – and that was the end of that! It was all rather sad really.

In the end we had to move to a different house. It was such a shame – the community would just not accept it. The tenants would have been victimised and we decided we had to move. **It is a case of 'win the battles that you can'.**

The house we have now is on a main road. We notified the new neighbours, who thankfully did not object. But I still feel that we shouldn't have to ask permission to move in. Imagine if you went around informing your neighbours that five black people would be moving in next door – it would be ridiculous! What is the difference? We don't need permission: people with mental illness have every right to live wherever they want to. And the really sad thing about all this is that in the time it took to find a new house and relocate, there were two suicides. I don't think they would

have happened had the original house been up and running. It was just a terrible shame.

...

I was born in Jersey, on the Channel Islands. I'm what they call a 'war baby' – that would be the Second World War! Jersey was under German occupation, so somehow I innately understand protest and justice. But having said that, it was a lovely place to grow up – there was great freedom. I was born into a large family with four sisters and two brothers, but my parents separated when I was about eight. I went to an Irish Catholic secondary school, but I hated it – I was treated terribly there – and left when I was fifteen. I was married by seventeen and had four kids by the age of twenty-two. Talk about innocent!

After a few years of marriage we decided to move to Ireland. We borrowed something like £1,400 and came to Cork. I didn't think Jersey was a place for four children; there was a floating population with a lot of drinking and drugs. Jerry, my husband, had a trade – carpentry – and he wanted to set up a business on his own.

We ended up here in Charleville, in the house we are still in now. It is an old thatched cottage with a rose garden, which we bought for £710 pounds. I thought the house was fantastic. I remember the seller asked for £1,400 and I said 'gosh, that is all we have got'. Jerry bargained him down. We had very little in the beginning, we were all sleeping on the floor – on mattresses, mind you – but we just accepted it. So we had four kids, and then another one after a few years. I think people thought we were exotic – I was the first woman in the area to wear trousers and Jerry had long hair! Everything, we thought, was rosy.

It was all fine until Geraldine, my daughter, was about fourteen. She started getting very withdrawn and introverted. Her teachers became concerned about her, feeling that she didn't fit in. She started saying very strange things and thought that we had come to Ireland to hide her away. We didn't know what was going on. A friend of ours was a GP, and after a few months said he would try her on medication. She became worse. He stopped her medication but about a week later was her first suicide attempt. She went missing one day – Jerry found her at the railway line. That was the beginning of it. Over the next few years she was in and out of hospital, getting worse. She developed tremors and shakes and had difficulty walking. I remember her asking me 'Why are you torturing me?' It was all so terrible.

Around this time I started my own business. It was mad, I know, but I just wanted to do something, and I knew I couldn't just sit and watch her. So maybe it was my escapism. I set about building the business – we made garlic bread and butters, growing it to seven people and stocking the likes of Dunnes and Superquinn. I got some training with FÁS on how to run a food business. Then I just kept going. When I was out working Geraldine started helping around the house a little. Soon she went from doing nothing to

working full-time in the business – so I knew she was capable and I could see what she could do.

I ran the business for seven years. It was invaluable experience and I know that I wouldn't be able to do what I do now without it. I learned about management. **I also learned that you have to work *with* the system.** I can see now that if we don't learn to work with the health board, Slí Eile will never grow and the model of therapeutic care will never take off.

In 1994 my food business was wound up. It left a huge gap in my life. Geraldine was back in hospital. I knew I needed to be doing something so I enrolled in a rural development course in UCC, which got me back into formal learning and was fantastic. But Geraldine was not so good – she was in a 'hospital', locked up in a room. I was able to visit her, but I would have to knock on a glass door to get in and the door would be locked behind me. It was horrible; there was no human dignity in it. Patients were rocking back and forth in the wards – it was just awful.

I decided to write to RTÉ in Cork and tell my story – I didn't believe that we were the only families suffering. A reporter asked to interview me, but rather than doing a direct interview with me (which I did not think the hospital would like) I brought her to meet my daughter. I think she was a bit freaked out when we went to the hospital and had to knock on that big door. The interview with Geraldine went ahead, and a copy was sent to the health board. The health board said that if it went out on air that they would sue RTÉ – they believed I was abusing my daughter's rights. But the interview was aired and I put out a call for other families to contact me. Five others got in touch, and that was really the start of Slí Eile. I began to hear what other people were going through and knew something more had to be done about it . . . however, things had to be put on hold for a while because I was diagnosed with cancer.

This was back in 1997, and while I recovered from chemo and surgery, nothing much happened. After a while, when I was getting back on an even keel, I contacted the families again. I was still a bit cautious about myself – that was another lesson: **you are no good if you are dead, you have got to look after yourself.** So once I felt ready, we decided to hold a conference in Cork, to bring all stakeholders together. I wrote to *The Irish Times* and had a letter published, and the then Minister for Health, Micheál Martin, agreed to attend the conference. RTÉ Radio contacted me again, asking me why I was doing it. I went live on air and spoke about my daughter. After that, the phone never stopped ringing. I was hearing horror story after horror story about what families were going through. In the end 700 people turned up at the conference.

The phone still kept ringing. There was just this huge outpouring and because of the interest, we organised a second conference. At the first one we asked 'Is there another way?' At the second one we said 'There are other ways.' From that, the idea for the Slí Eile model emerged, and now here we are.

I have learned that only way to get change is to just do it. You can keep talking and talking and talking . . . but I wanted to do. I knew there was another way to treatment. It has taken years to get here. I used to have a feeling of inferiority because I had dropped out of school, but I don't have that now. I have learned so much and I would not be as strong now if I hadn't been through it. I have learned that you have to take small steps to get to the dream.

If you can see what you want, you can do it. Unless you have a very clear picture, you will not achieve it. But if you can picture it, you can do it. And if you can't picture it, how can you expect others to? I suppose I've a very clear picture of the normality of living in any of the Slí Eile houses. If people aren't integrated, how can we learn to normalise mental illness?

There have been many times I've wanted to walk away from this – I thought it was going to kill me. But I can't *not* do this. I think about my daughter, and about all the other people who need support. I had to ask myself a while ago, 'If anything happened to Geraldine, would I continue with this work? And I would. I have seen the need. I have built connections with other stories. I don't know what we can expect for Geraldine, but it can work for others.

So I see another way. And because I can see it, I know it can be done.

Tina Roche

Business in the Community Ireland: www.bitc.ie
The Community Foundation for Ireland:
www.communityfoundation.ie

Dublin, Ireland
Themes: Business, Philanthropy

Tina Roche loves lots of things: art, advocacy, business, children, family, humanity. She has let those passions guide and direct her decisions in life. They have led her to be the treasurer of Amnesty International Ireland, a mother of one, a foster mum of three, lead fund-raiser for the Millennium Wing of the National Art Gallery of Ireland, and currently CEO of Business in the Community Ireland (BITCI) and The Community Foundation for Ireland.

With the Community Foundation for Ireland, her aim over the next ten years is to channel €100 million to community-based organisations in the country which are promoting issues such as social inclusion and civic leadership, while her work with BITCI sees her promoting corporate social responsibility (CSR), or good business practices. To Tina, good business CSR policies go beyond community involvement: they are about how businesses conduct themselves as a whole and how they contribute to the holistic growth of society. 'Imagine if you work for a business which is inspiring,' she says, 'imagine if, instead of just producing a drug, it was about curing AIDS – that it was a business which is about the health of a nation, not just about making money for shareholders.'

You will need an open mind and an open heart, and you can learn the skills along the way.

I've always been a community activist, even when I was working full-time in commercial work, it didn't matter. I've always been involved in one way or another and I think I always will be. It is just part of who I am. It may be how I grew up, it may be how I see the world, but for whatever reason, that is just the way it is. **It is not even a choice for me any more – it is part of what I've become. If I see an injustice I respond by wanting to do something about it.**

I was raised in Dublin. I'm the eldest of seven children. My father came from a dairy farm in Kilmainham. So while we were born into a working-class area, we also had this farming background and a country lifestyle in the middle of the city. I learned to milk a cow when I was five, which I suppose was unusual for a city girl!

My parents were young when they got married and were constantly involved with the community – they were very kindly and neighbourly people. My father was always taking care of the local community, whether on the school board, or looking after people when they were ill. I also spent a lot of time with my grandmother, who had a major effect on my life – she too was a wonderful person. So I was raised in a very open and warm way. My father was one of the people who started James' Street Credit Union, and we all volunteered there at some point or another. So I suppose the idea of social justice and community involvement was embedded into my upbringing.

Primary school was not a good experience for me and I hated it: our teachers were very unkind and would bully us. Some teachers were violent and I often saw them hit other children. I can remember on my second day at school, when I was just four years old, seeing a teacher lock another small child into a cupboard because the child had wet her pants. Even at that age I can remember thinking, 'This is so wrong', and that feeling of disgust has never changed – I've never understood how they could slap us and I've never understood that someone could have that level of power over another.

Out of the forty in my class, fourteen went on to do the Inter Cert. I was one of the really lucky ones whose parents insisted that we continue school. Out of the forty, five went on to do the Leaving Cert. The rest ended up working in factories. **My father knew that education was a real way out** and so we were all taught to read and write very early. He would sit us at the table and go through the paper with us – we were expected to be able to read the headlines.

After school, I started an accountancy course at night, and worked in accounts during the day. I worked in accounts with a number of publishing companies and landed a job in the *Sunday Tribune* as an assistant accountant, where I worked for ten years. Later I became the distribution manager, then financial controller, then company secretary and, after that, was on the board . . . so I worked my way up gradually.

All the time I remained active as a volunteer in the community. I got involved in the Irish Travellers' Movement and with the Simon Community. While with Simon I trained as a counsellor and worked on the first AIDS helpline. I also got involved with Amnesty International, where I became the treasurer and got very involved the area of human rights in business.

While at the *Tribune*, I decided to get a formal qualification and chose to do an MBA, with the support of the *Tribune*. It was a huge amount of work, and looking back now, I ask 'did it really help? Does it give me credibility?' Now I don't really think so and I don't think the qualification matters that much. However, in saying that, it did give me a chance to dip my toe into a lot of behavioural sciences, and it gave me the confidence that I could learn new things. Now, when I want to learn something new, **I'm not scared and I say to myself 'I can read a book about that!'** That is really how I ended up in a management role – I would always put myself forward, believing I could learn to do it, and have an opinion about what should be done.

Being the eldest of seven also really helped – it makes you naturally bossy and opinionated! **Opinions were really sought in our house.** We talked about politics and what was happening in the community and the wider world. I would always be around adults and would be exposed to their conversations. Being the eldest also meant that I was given responsibility at a young age. And because we were allowed to play out on the streets, we learned important people skills. We would go and discover new things. And because we were allowed to do that from a young age, we learned, little by little, that we could take on the world.

I have one son myself and three foster children. How we came to have the three foster children is an interesting little story. I was setting up Business in the Community and Adam, my son, was doing his Leaving Cert that year, so it was a busy time. Adam and I were driving somewhere one day when he saw an advert in *The Big Issue* magazine which read, 'Looking for foster parents for three children'. At that stage I had a mortgage, was a single parent, and was working full-time. Adam turned to me and said, 'We should do something about that, Mum.' 'Adam,' I replied, 'do you seriously think that they are going to give three children to me?' 'Well maybe we should just give the number a ring.' So we rang and left our name and number. After many interviews and lots of training, we eventually were accepted, and the three children joined our family. To take three kids into our lives in one go was a big adjustment. It was tough initially but it was also brilliant. My parents treat them like their own grandchildren. We go on a large family holiday every year, so from the very first year all we needed was a slightly bigger house so all twenty-eight of us could pack in! **The kids have transformed my life in a wonderful way.**

After leaving the *Tribune*, I wanted to work for Amnesty, where I had been volunteering. But just as I was about to go full-time, I saw an advert for the National Art Gallery – they wanted to build the Millennium Wing at the time, and the job was for Head of Development. My passion is Art. I go to every museum and art gallery that I can, and I have been going to the National Gallery since I was a child – my father used to take us there on Sunday afternoons to get us out of my mother's hair! When I read the ad I knew immediately I wanted the job. I had never fund-raised – they were trying to raise €5 million – but I went to them and said 'if I can do anything to help, I will'. The actual amount did not faze me and I just thought 'I will have a go at that'. In the end we raised €20 million and I worked there until the first sod for the wing was turned. It was then time to move on – my job was done.

So again, I still wanted to work for Amnesty. But around this time I saw another ad for a foundation for investing in communities, looking for a CEO. It sparked my interest and I went into meet the people behind it. It was an extraordinary opportunity and there was huge scope to do something. I spoke with them about their own ideas and presented my thoughts on what could be done, which is how I got the job. I ended up splitting the foundation into two – Business in the Community and the Community Foundation for Ireland, and we have grown from there.

Advice

Go for what you are passionate about, even if you can't do it full-time now, do it at night. Keep the passion alive and always have it in your mind 'I'm going to work at that'. **It took me nearly thirty years to get to where I am now, but on the way I was learning all the time and have always been involved in the community.** Being involved is so important. It is not important what you do but the engagement makes your life worthwhile. You could just sit in front of the telly and go to the pub, and that is a life, but you could also have a life that is engaged with people from all over the world, from all walks of life, and you can make a difference to their lives. Just think of it – that you can actually have an effect. So you just have to choose the life you want to live.

You will need an open mind and an open heart, and you can learn the skills along the way. It is an attitude . . . and just be open to it and try to see how you can make a difference with whatever you can bring to the table. When your heart and mind are open, you can do anything.

You see, I always thought that I was going to work with Amnesty . . . and you never know, maybe one day I will!

Davie Philip

Cultivate

www.cultivate.ie

Dublin, Ireland

Themes: Environment, Business, Education

It is not only technological solutions to environmental change that we need, it is a switch in the way we think about these things – we need to think about the bigger picture and move from being global consumers to being global citizens.

'Build your own solar panel', 'Art of Living', 'Low-cost design and construction'. These are just three of the courses on offer under the Cultivate roof, a sustainable living centre co-founded by Davie Philip. A self-confessed 'sustainability zealot', his environmental work centres around educating people about low-carbon lifestyles and building local, sustainable communities.

Previously a professional skateboarder, it has been quite a journey since his skateboarding competition days, bringing him from his native Scotland to Ireland via India. Now he is laying some roots, in an eco-friendly way, as a founding member of 'The Village', a sustainable living community in Cloughjordan, County Tipperary.

Before all of this, I was a professional skateboarder and a businessman. I started riding a skateboard when I was thirteen, in the craze of 1977. Everyone had a skateboard but as people stopped, I kept going – until it was a completely underground thing, which reminds me a little of sustainability right now. Because it was a tight community, I got to know everyone. I ended up travelling around the world because of my skateboard: competitions, demonstrations, tours, etc., having a great time.

During it all I also set up two businesses with my business partner: a clothing company making streetwear – baggy trousers and hoodie sweatshirts – all made from natural materials, so we had a little bit of an environmental edge. This was in the mid to late 1980s when most of the clothes you got were neon-coloured! I also co-owned a skateboard/surfboard/snowboard shop. Both of those companies got quite big, very big in fact, and in 1989 we (myself and my business partner) won the UK Young Entrepreneur of the Year Award. I was suddenly on *The Clothes Show*, a popular UK fashion TV programme at the time, but I was no fashion designer. All I'd really done was draw ideas on the back of an envelope and bring them to the factory for a sample to be made. Then I would wear them for a week and make changes based on feedback, and somehow they were popular. So I was no clothes fashion guru but suddenly we had all this focus on us, and I just started to feel that the whole fashion business thing was a load of nonsense.

Then, with the skateboarding, I didn't want to be competing any more and when you are not competing, you are not in the magazines, so you are not sponsored – then all of a sudden you are not a professional skateboarder. I knew I didn't want to be a businessman either – I just felt it was all about money and there was something missing for me. **So, at twenty-eight, I stopped. I decided I was going to leave everything** – not just the businesses – but everything. I sold all I had, packed my bags and got a one-way ticket to India.

I suppose I just felt I wanted to know more about myself. I was not being fulfilled by being this successful business person – **there was some sort of searching,** and something I wanted to know more about. So for a year and a half I ended up in Asia, wandering around from ashram to ashram, and yoga practice to meditation. It was the best year of my life and I think all young people should be given some money and, instead of going from school to university to work, be encouraged to wander around, get some life experience, and try to work out what they are actually interested in.

I ended up moving to Ireland from Asia, filled with a wonderful sense of connection. I realised I needed to study new things so I went to study anthropology in NUI Maynooth. On the course we were introduced to sustainability and world systems. I started to have a very similar feeling of connection to the one I had sensed in India: a feeling that everything is connected into a web of life, that we are not separate. So sustainability for me is almost a spiritual thing, for lack of a better way of saying it. **Nature is not something that is out there – we are nature, we are part of it, and what we do is also part of the problem, and the solution.**

A number of the anthropology students set up a sustainability society in the college, and we started getting people together around Ireland who were interested in the issues. Using the facilities of the college and some finance from people in the society, we started to educate ourselves and others on how we can live more sustainable lives and see the bigger picture. I started to see that climate change and peak oil are just symptoms of much bigger problems and that the whole system we are living on is unsustainable. On a finite planet you can't have constant growth, so I believe we need to start changing that system. I left college saying 'I'm just going to work in this field, it is where I want to be.' I'd spent all my twenties putting my energy into skateboarding and my businesses, and after Asia I was looking for something else to put my energies into – and sustainability was it.

Having a bit of an entrepreneurial background also helped. I found it relatively easy to scale up some of our ideas, like running the Convergence Festival on Sustainability, and developing Cultivate. I was also involved in the company that set up the eco village, which a group of us are developing in a town called Cloughjordan in County Tipperary. The eco village is so important to me as it will enable me to 'walk the talk' – we are not just talking about sustainability in a classroom any longer, we are talking about immersing learners in a sustainable community.

With Cloughjordan, we are really trying to show a renaissance of village and rural living. Because there has been so much urbanisation, we are going to need more people living in rural areas and working on rural, local projects in the future. We need to make rural living attractive and build our local economies and communities again. Interestingly the people who are moving to Cloughjordan are doing so for many reasons – they are not all sustainability zealots like me. Most of them have young families and want a safe and healthy environment for their kids to grow up in, or they are people reaching retirement who want to have a healthy community around them, rather than be shuffled off to a nursing home, and there are also a lot of people who have a business or an idea for a business in the area of sustainability.

It is not only technological solutions to environmental change that we need, it is a switch in the way we think about these things – we need to think about the bigger picture and move from being global consumers to being global citizens, engaged in the issues in a

very creative way. We need to move from saying, 'Someone should do something about that', to saying, 'We should do something about that', and have a bit of entrepreneurial spirit about it.

There is so much scope in all of this and there are so many opportunities to get involved. **All business in the future is going to have to be sustainable – if you are not investing into sustainability, you are so last century.** There are massive entrepreneurial opportunities in food, energy and building design for instance. And there is scope in developing local businesses, supply, and in the provision of community services.

Building communities is one of the most important things. For a lot of people right now, their sense of community is through *EastEnders* – they know the characters in soaps better than their own neighbours. It is better for consumption if we all live in individual worlds, but when we start to gather as communities and do things together, we can pool our resources – we can put up local wind turbines, or put in community gardens, and local energy systems. By working together as communities we can achieve so much more'.

Having the confidence to jump in and do something rather than waiting until you have been trained or you have the funding to do it is so important. I grew up through punk rock with a philosophy of life that said 'you can do that, you don't have to be an expert'. There was a sense that you don't have to be a professional musician to start a band, you can just do it. It was a DIY culture, and really I think that is part of why I have been able to do this – I will just jump in and give it a try. I'm not afraid to potentially fail, but seeing what needs to be done I just try to do it. And, with time, you start to build your confidence, your networks and your relationships to be able to do it more confidently.

Plus I love a bit of chaos! We sometimes call our productions 'Seat of our Pants Productions', because for some reason they all go smoothly but they have the potential to go horribly wrong, where no one turns up and everything fails! So it is chaos management and I think we need to be able to pilot through the chaos that we are living in and not be afraid of change – I hate when there is too much order. Change is the only constant. Chaos will always be there, so we need to learn how to surf it. I love that metaphor. In Cultivate, we are trying to train people to pilot the chaos.

I know that I have become a bit of a bore at dinner parties. 'Oh Davie, don't talk about sustainability again!' I suppose I'm not the best at small talk because I'm on such a mission. But I feel so privileged to work where I work and to do what I do. I meet brilliant people from all sectors. I feel lucky to play a part and we need to think about how to encourage more people into this area.

So, my advice is: just do it. There are so many opportunities to get involved, socially and environmentally. **Find something, jump in and give it a try. And if it is the right thing, you will get the support for it.** There are so many opportunities to pick something up and start a business around it in the sector. Look at what is going on, jump in and do it. And you need to be flexible. At times you may have to put a suit on. At times you may have your hoodie on and go surfing, or whatever, but be flexible, it is a great trait to have. I think of it as 'shape-shifting', which gives you the ability to move between communities of people, where you can put a suit on and be with government ministers or in an office, or you can interact with young people or different communities. We need that flexibility now, and not to be so rigid about how we see the different sectors – let's merge these things.

Occasionally I still get on my skateboard. My past catches up with me sometimes!

Mary Lawlor

Front Line

www.frontlinedefenders.org

Dublin, Ireland

Theme: Human Rights

Arriving into Mary Lawlor's office, Director of Front Line, I found her preoccupied. A human rights defender from Tibet had just been detained by the Chinese authorities. She was talking on Skype to his wife and explaining her course of action. 'I'll contact the Irish Embassy and try to get some legal representation.' As the conversation continued it was hard not to marvel at what technology enables when coupled with the will to use it wisely.

Her conversation, I learned, is typical of much of the work of Front Line, an organisation which Mary established to support the work of human rights defenders who may be at risk because of their work, and advocate for their safety. It is demanding work, requiring 24-hour attention and a team of very dedicated supporters, but as Mary explained, once they see that their efforts can be effective it is impossible to stop. Mary's own life story is evidence of such, working for twenty-seven years with Amnesty International and going on to establish Front Line. A map on her wall was a reminder of her remit, while another Skype call from China was evidence of their reach.

I have learned that once you know that you can be effective there is no way you can stop.

It takes an exceptional form of courage to be a human rights defender. Many of them get up in the morning not knowing if they are going to be alive that night. Some are imprisoned, some are intimidated, some lose their jobs, some have lawsuits taken out against them that have no basis, some are tortured, some are even killed. We all have to have courage to get over natural things, like bereavement or heartbreak, but **to think of people who choose to put their lives in danger, not for themselves, but for other people – I find it really inspiring.**

Front Line is about trying to keep people alive. We want to ensure that human rights defenders don't get persecuted for their non-violent, legitimate work on behalf of other people. We are trying to create a space where they can carry out their work in safety.

I began my human rights work with Amnesty International in Ireland. I was there for nearly three decades. Firstly I was on the board and later I became the Director of the Irish Section. I got involved initially through Séan MacBride, one of the founding members of Amnesty and a Nobel Peace Prize Winner. He was an incredible, devoted man. My sister had been working with him. One evening, when he was coming

back from an international meeting I was sent to the airport to collect him – he was in his seventies at this stage. I remember asking him how his trip had gone and he started to describe what he'd been doing. When we arrived at his house he asked if I could help him to open his post – at this point it was nearly midnight. I agreed. Late into the night he opened and responded to every letter, from all over the world. I remember thinking to myself, 'God ... at his age, would he think of taking a rest!' After that I was inspired to get involved with Amnesty.

After twenty-seven years with Amnesty I decided it was time to leave. I'd been the Irish Director for twelve years. The organisation's membership had grown and we were strong, but I wanted to get out before I was carried out in a coffin! It was time for fresh blood, plus I could see a need, or a gap. In 1998 I'd attended a conference for human rights defenders at risk where I met all these people who just blew me away. To hear the testimony of the work they were doing and the dangers they faced was just amazing. They completely inspired me and I decided I wanted to work full-time for them.

At that time there was no organisation focusing all of its activities on human rights defenders at risk. There were some organisations that had programmes for defenders, but it is not the same. I really do believe that if you choose to work with people at risk, you have to change your mindset – it is a different way of working. We have a 24-hour mentality here. We run a 24-hour emergency phone line in five languages – you never know when these people are going to need emergency help and you need to be ready to respond. If you work with us, you need to be willing to go beyond nine to five. If there is a crisis at the weekend, you deal with it. But we are very lucky, the staff here are very dedicated. This is not a soft job in human rights and they understand the level of commitment required.

When I had the idea for Front Line I was fortunate to find a very supportive and generous donor who really believed in the idea and gave us funding to launch the organisation. **Like a lot of these things, there was a mixture of luck and timing getting the money.** The donor's first baby had been born the night before I went in to ask him for the money – so I could not have picked a better time!

For the first year of Front Line, there was just myself and one other person working full-time. **When you start off something, you are never really sure how it is going to go** – you have an idea and a plan, and you know what you want to do, but there is no guarantee that you will be successful – there are lots of international organisations and it is difficult to succeed on an international level. I wanted to take it slowly at first and build up contacts with human rights defenders and other international and intergovernmental organisations. We have grown support and our programmes gradually.

Everything you do in life you learn from. I did philosophy and psychology in college, then Montessori teaching and then the Institute of Personnel Management exams – so I've been able to touch on lots of different disciplines. **I feel incredibly lucky to be able to do what I do today – I never really planned on it.** A man came to me one day for career advice and I was amazed at how he was plotting his future because I never did any of that – I have just been exceptionally lucky. It doesn't mean I didn't have challenges along the way. Raising a family while trying to do this work has been difficult because I was split in two, always trying to make sure that the children (I have three) were getting enough attention. I always felt guilty, thinking that I wasn't giving enough.

One of the hardest times was when my father was dying. It was a brutal four-and-a-half-month death, in 2004. I was spending most nights with him and working days. At the time we were in the middle of trying to get the EU to prioritise human rights defenders at risk through the Irish Presidency of the EU. This was an absolute priority for us because the adoption of the guidelines would bring about systemic change in the way Ireland and the EU worked to protect human rights defenders. The Department of Foreign Affairs called me in to tell me that at a meeting with the relevant EU partners they had got absolutely no support for the draft guidelines. I remember thinking things couldn't get any worse – I was in a state of pain and grief for my father and was physically and emotionally exhausted. But inspired by my father's tenacity and courage I somehow found enough will to discuss a plan B. We embarked on a different political approach, which was successful. So **I learned a valuable lesson: to hang in there when all seems bleak and hopeless.** To this day when I am down about something, I try to reverse it by doing something positive.

I think attitude is very important. The attitude you bring to the way you live your life is crucial. It saddens me when I see people who don't believe that they can do something. They look at the problems rather than the solutions, they don't have the confidence or they say that they may not have the qualifications. **But having an attitude of believing you can do something is the best qualification** – an attitude of positive engagement coupled with tolerance and respect for people. At least, I know it works for me!

When you work in human rights you learn that little things, bit by bit, can improve a situation. And I think that can apply to our own lives too – **we should not expect things to happen or change immediately but if you do the plugging, it will happen.** I used to be very, very shy. I hated speaking in public and I could hardly string two words together in front of an audience. I remember my first public talk for Amnesty. It was to a group of middle-aged women, far from

a hostile audience, who were literally willing me to the end of it. I was so nervous I could hardly speak. However, just by doing it, and practising, I have improved. I still get nervous before speaking at big meetings but I generally know I will get through. It is bit like an exam. When you do something new, you are pushing yourself a little bit more and testing yourself. But that way you open yourself up to possibilities. You may have a noble failure, but you have tried and you learn from it. The more you do things, the more you can develop your confidence.

I believe that human rights defenders are the heroes of our time. And when our work helps to get someone out of prison, or saves someone from torture, then I know it has been worth it. But if I thought that we weren't being effective, there would be no reason for us to exist. Which also contributes to our mindset – **as an organisation we are only here as long as we are being effective.**

I have learned that once you know that you can be effective there is no way you can stop. On a daily basis we are interacting with people who are at risk for their human rights work and who need help. Once you see that there is something you can do, that these are the people who are building civil and just societies on the ground, then it would just be impossible not to. I think this work is embedded in me now.

Snapshot: Education

It is estimated that over 75 million children around the world do not attend primary school. Of these, over 53 per cent are girls. The statistics in some geographical regions are worse than others. Over 15 per cent of children in developing countries, for instance, do not complete a course of primary education and in some countries in sub-Saharan Africa, it is as high as 40 per cent. As a result, global illiteracy figures are staggering. It is estimated that one in five adults is still not literate, amounting to 774 million adults

and young people worldwide who cannot read or write. Of these, two-thirds are women. Currently in developing countries around 16 per cent of young people between 15–24 are illiterate.

There are many barriers to obtaining a quality education. High school fees, discrimination, unsafe environments, lack of educational facilities and insufficient funding are just some. Other factors, such as negative cultural practices, threats from natural disasters and civil conflicts, can also prevent school attendance or completion.

However, with the international community focusing on the Millennium Development Goals (a set of eight international development targets, of which achieving universal primary education is one), international enrolment figures have shown some progress toward the 2015 targets. Net enrolments for primary education in developing countries have risen from 79 per cent in 1990 to 86 per cent in 2004. The abolition of school fees in many sub-Saharan counties saw a rapid rise in school attendance. In 2003 in Kenya, enrolment grew from 5.9 million to 7.2 million. Uganda, Tanzania and Malawi all had similar experiences following school-fee abolition. However, while pupil numbers increased, adequate resources were not matched. In some schools where fees were abolished, for example, there is as high as a 100:1 pupil–teacher ratio.

Snapshot: Education

Colman Farrell

Suas

www.suas.ie

Dublin, Ireland
Theme: Education

Following a medical degree, a multimedia degree, a stint in software development, a job as a translator in Rwanda during the refugee crisis, another job as an organisational development consultant, and several years working with a community school in Nairobi, Colman Farrell's career path may not be exactly typical. But his choices and passion along the way have led him to be the CEO of Suas Educational Development, a Dublin-based organisation working to tackle educational disadvantage both in Ireland and overseas.

Coming to Suas in its early days, Colman has since led a movement of dynamic young people who actively promote social change, leadership and quality education, helping people fulfil their own potential, and in turn, play meaningful roles in shaping our world.

Try things out. Give things a go. Go places. Go in the same direction as others, but only it if is your choice.

I've been fortunate with Suas to have an opportunity to bring together things that I think are important. But, **like any venture, you don't do it on our own**. You get there with other people, and I've had incredible support along the way.

It is difficult to put a finger on my motivations. My father passed away when I was four years old, and people have asked whether it had any effect on me. But as I never grew up with a father, it is hard to know if it would have been different or not. My mum was fantastic and I had a very positive home environment, but circumstances just made me feel a little different. I never felt awkward, just slightly removed, and so I never felt I had to do things as part of a crowd.

All along I had great teachers and went to a wonderful secondary school, Belvedere College, a Jesuit school with a strong social orientation. For a relatively privileged school in Ireland, we were more exposed to social justice issues than many of our peers. The Jesuit ethos was 'debate the issues' rather than telling you what to think, and our teachers spoke openly with us about controversial issues. There were high academic standards, and we were encouraged in sports, but the social side was also integral and because it wasn't rammed down our throats, it was hard not to be involved – it was just part of

what you did. As part of the school's St Vincent de Paul society, we paid weekly visits to old people who lived in the flats and houses of North Inner City Dublin, many of whom lived on their own in very basic environments. So in retrospect I think all those things had an influence on me.

I always wanted to do medicine. I don't know where it came from. I have always liked science and understanding how things work. So when I got accepted into medicine I was delighted – there were lots of congratulation notes. But even in the first few years, I started to have doubts, wondering if it was the path I should be on. It was a six-year programme, with three years of memorising stuff, then three more years of memorising stuff. At one point, halfway through, I wanted to change. The advice at the time was to wait until the fourth year, the first clinical year, and see how it went. It was only later during my intern year that I began to be more critical of the whole hospital system and how it functioned. I saw senior doctors who were generally very nice people but who were also disillusioned, bitter and cynical. I think their frustration came from working within a very dysfunctional system. There was an extremely competitive career structure, which meant that unless you got a tenured consultancy position, you were always on one- to two-year contracts, doing exams, working long hours, under a lot of pressure, and had restricted freedom. And I thought 'that will be me, this is the path I am on'.

So my gut feeling was to leave. I could have worked for another year, but medicine wasn't where I was going to be in ten years' time, or even five years' time. I just knew it was not where my future lay.

A series of coincidences then led me to work in Rwanda. Louis, a friend of mine from school, was working as a doctor in Southern Uganda, with GOAL, an Irish NGO. I asked if I could join him, GOAL agreed, but I was then placed in Nairobi. I arrived just as the Rwandan war had turned and a million Hutu refugees were fleeing into Zaire. The agency's local field director urgently needed French speakers. And so after my seven years of medical education I ended up going to Rwanda as a translator using my French from school. I was there for about twelve weeks, organising trucks and teams to collect the bodies of people who had died of dehydration as they fled. We also set up mobile rehydration clinics. And so I witnessed all this horror first hand. My medical training was still useful as it helped me to disassociate sufficiently to be able to function in an emotionally very difficult situation.

At the time I didn't fully appreciate what a historic, pivotal event the Rwandan crisis was, either for me or for wider global affairs. I learnt that when you are directly involved, it is actually less traumatic than seeing such atrocities on television. When you are there, at least you are doing something, you are making, in a very, very small way, a contribution. I also realised that almost all of the people involved were just like you and me. This really hit me one afternoon when I was walking unaccompanied along the road several kilometres from our base, surrounded by thousands of refugees. **I realised that the only difference between me and all those people was my passport – I had a way out.**

After coming back to Ireland I got a job teaching anatomy in Trinity College, but my Rwandan experience had whetted my interest in overseas development. While the emergency work had a big adrenaline rush associated with it, I realised that intervening at that stage is just too late. It is like trying to put out a blazing inferno that is already out of control. Instead I realised my real interest is in earlier interventions: health, education, social services and taking a preventative approach. Things should never get to the point they had in Rwanda.

And so I reapplied to GOAL, along with my girlfriend at the time, Vanessa. We were placed in Nairobi, Kenya where we came across Gatoto School, a small start-up school in the slums of the city. We were very impressed with the lady leading it, Betty, and our gut sense was that it had a lot of potential. We were there for a year until GOAL experienced a financial shortfall and had to scale back their programmes. However, Vanessa, a few friends and I continued our links with Gatoto, getting involved with the development of its management structures.

Coming back to Ireland, I didn't know what to do. I'd seen a master's degree in multimedia advertised and, rather arbitrarily, applied for it and was accepted. This was at the start of the Internet boom and I was excited about its possibilities. Plus, as a broad, generalist course, it suited my approach.

After the course I again found myself saying 'what on earth am I going to do?' I was twenty-six, with a medical degree and now I had this multimedia master's, which was very interesting but didn't seem to specifically qualify me for anything. So, rather aimlessly, I applied for Milkround jobs and was offered one with Procter & Gamble. I was interviewed by an Irish lady who was actually interested in my experiences in Africa. Unlike other companies I had interviewed with, P&G took a broad view of people. That alone gave me a positive message.

So I joined P&G in Newcastle, England. I wasn't particularly expecting to enjoy the city but I found it great. Plus the company was very supportive. A few things really struck me there: how polite everyone was and how nice people were to you. I had an excellent manager, who saw it as his job to help you to learn, grow and do a good job. He saw his success as being based on your success. I had worked in health care and in overseas aid, and had been in systems and organisations where junior people were basically exploited by the people at the top. The whole system in P&G was much more humane. And I

was very conscious that this was within a company that was essentially there to make money.

However after a couple of years, I decided I didn't want to stay with P&G long term. It was not what I wanted my life to be. I was working with smart, capable people and in a very supportive environment, so it was hard to leave. But it was not what I was fundamentally about.

During all this time I had stayed involved with the school in Kenya. After P&G I spent six months in Kenya, again working on broad management support at Gatoto. When I came back to Ireland I managed to get a job in software development, working with General Electric. After a few months, I was leading a software development team. It was an 'in at the deep end' experience in a demanding 'deliver or else' company culture, and I was completely out of my depth. So, I bought some books on software development, and learned as much as I could from my colleagues. The team were technically competent, but the process of how they went from analysing needs to delivering products was very disjointed and confused. They just needed someone to help them bring it together. I learnt the importance of process and of open, effective communications within teams, and of what you can achieve if you are willing to learn. I worked there for a year, until the dot.com implosion, and then decided to return to Kenya.

I returned to Nairobi with two American friends, Ned and Jen, spending nine months with Gatoto. The school had expanded and was performing very well, but the internal systems were under pressure. We lived on a shoestring budget, and it was a very tough year. It was great working with the school, and with my friends, but being in a different country, without an agency, where we really didn't fit into any boxes was very isolating. It was good in one way because I realised I could get by with minimal support. However realising you can get through things on your own if you have to, you can also get into a space where you don't feel you need people, and so you don't open up to people. However, looking back, I do think that experience of working through challenge gave me the confidence to try it out with Suas.

Back in Ireland I got a job with Enterprise Ireland, a state organisation supporting Irish business. Again I was working with very nice people but there was a sense of being stuck in a large bureaucracy. I had hoped it would be more dynamic and then when a new CEO arrived, it was. I was appointed to a team to restructure and develop the organisation – essentially I was getting what I wished for. But I decided to leave.

At the same time, I had started mentoring a group of young people who were setting up Suas. I was very impressed with them, especially their openness to learning, which I hadn't previously seen in other organisations. And something just drew me to them. As Suas grew, so did the work, until I had to make a choice. Leaving Enterprise Ireland was probably perceived as an unusual decision. I had just been promoted to a great role then left to join a group of students who wanted to volunteer in Africa during the summer.

Getting involved with Suas was great fun. It was a combination of being extremely stressful and extremely mad. We were really just making it up as we went along. We were being wildly ambitious, stupidly ambitious, considering where we were coming from. It was high, positive energy and there was a big adrenaline rush. I have realised that the things that are important to me are who I work with and the reason I am working somewhere. Everything else is secondary. With Suas I met people who are passionate, committed and who were concerned about the purpose of what they are doing.

 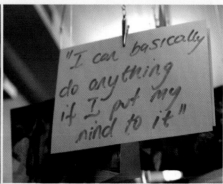

So that started a very intense journey, which has had its ups and downs. I think Suas is like an accelerated life journey. It is an emotionally intensive organisation, probably because it is fundamentally about people. It attracts younger people who have a combination of openness and trepidation, but who are willing to learn and share things and conversations, which older people tend to close down.

I'm really more of an observer than an engager, but my orientation has shifted more towards engagement. As a child I was relatively shy. I don't particularly like attention being drawn to myself. I am happy to be at the back. While sometimes that is strength it also holds me back from doing other things, so I have had to learn to change. I've also become more appreciative of the differences between people. I would like to believe that I am respectful of everyone, but equally I think I was intolerant of people who didn't approach things in the same way as me. Now I have come to see that people are just wired differently and that effective teamwork is actually making the best use of different skills and abilities. And I think I still have a way to go on that, but I think I have learned to appreciate differences more. And that has been liberating. I have worked with many people in Suas, each of whom I would consider much better at certain things than I am, and that is great!

I have also learned that the times of challenge are actually times of growth. I know that the best learning I've come through in Suas has been through the more difficult times. And, of course,

there have been moments when I've wanted to leave, but I have learned that in the times of change and challenge, sometimes you have to stick with the process. Many things I ended up doing came up because one thing finished, and another opportunity arose. But you learn to hold on tightly and let go lightly.

There is a quote I like about education: 'The purpose of education is to replace empty minds with open ones.' Whereas much of what traditional education does is fill empty minds with data, facts and figures. Instead we need to learn to develop and reframe our own relationship with the world, but that actually means letting go of a lot of stuff, which can be a very scary experience. It means letting go of your sense of self and allowing your identity to be fluid for a period of time. But I think that is also fundamental to real growth.

I'd encourage people to try things. If it does not work, try something else because you can learn from each one. **You have to zig before you zag.** You are unlikely to find your ultimate direction from day one. And if things don't work out completely, then you just know there is a different direction for you. I'd encourage people to take a step, and don't worry about it. I could not have conceived of where I am now even five years ago, let alone when I was leaving medicine. Try things out. Give things a go. Go places. Go in the same direction as others, but only it if is your choice. Learn from it all. And then zig after you have zagged. **The short version of that is this: when you look back, it looks like a straight line.**

Mary Davis
Special Olympics Ireland
www.specialolympics.ie

Dublin, Ireland
Themes: Sports, Business

Summer 2003. Dublin was awash with a flurry of yellow, blue, red and green
raincoats. Some 30,000 in total, each emblazoned with the Special Olympic
Summer Games logo and belonging to the volunteers, support staff and
athletes who had flocked to the city to be involved with the Games. It
was the first time the Games were hosted outside the US, and with 150
countries represented and 177 towns, cities and villages across Ireland
hosting delegates, the whole country was buzzing. U2 played at the opening
ceremony, Nelson Mandela turned up to support and never before had the

case for supporting people with disability in Ireland been given so much promotion and promise.

The woman leading the organising team was CEO of the Games, Mary Davis, who had the vision and determination to make them a success. Since then she has continued her work with Special Olympics both in Ireland and internationally.

Tireless in their efforts, Special Olympics Ireland's mission is to provide year-round sports training and competitions for people with learning disabilities. In doing so, they help individuals to develop strength and courage, experience community, share skills and gain confidence, whether as a volunteer or as an athlete.

The sheer ambition of Special Olympics could seem like a daunting challenge, but for Mary Davis and her team, 'Bring it on' was the attitude they chose to embrace. Their accomplishments are evidence of what can be achieved when we choose to see possibilities over obstacles and chances over challenge.

When I finished secondary school I wanted to study physical education. I'd been interested in sports from a young age – with brothers in the family there were lots of sporting fans! A cousin of mine studied Physical Education in Leeds, so I decided to apply there and was lucky enough to get a place. From Leeds I was then fortunate to win a scholarship for a year to attend the University of Alberta in Canada, to finish off my degree – and it was a fantastic experience. It was in Canada that I had my first exposure to the methodologies of working with people with physical difficulties, on a fourteen-week module in Adaptive Physical Education, which I got to participate in. Even though it was short it gave me some background in the area, which I was later able to apply to my work in Ireland.

When I returned to Ireland I initially did a few subbing jobs as a PE teacher but then saw a job advertised for St Michael's House which sounded really interesting – St Michael's House is a large organisation catering for about 2,000 people with learning disabilities on the northside of Dublin. I applied for the job and got it. However, when I actually began working I found it very different to the training I'd received in Leeds – **teaching people with disabilities was really a new experience for me and I had to adapt my skills, and try out new approaches.**

At the same time I started in St Michael's House, another PE teacher had started on the southside of the city. We got in touch with each other, and realised that we were each having similar teaching difficulties. There were very few teaching resources available to us at the time, so we would often get together to

Don't put any obstacles in your way because if you do, it will never get going in the first place. We would never have done the Games had we said 'How are we going to recruit 30,000 volunteers and where are we going to get €60 million?'

devise new methodologies – thankfully there is much more information now on how to teach people with a learning disability, but back then we were probably some of the first few people in Ireland working in the area, so it was very much trial-and-error for us.

Special Olympics came to Ireland in 1978 (the year we had both started working in St Michael's House). I'd vaguely heard about it in Canada, but didn't really know what it was or the benefits it could bring to Ireland. But hoping to be able to tap into it for resources and teaching guides, we thoroughly embraced it. When I say 'we', I mean myself and this other PE teacher, Julian – whom I ended up marrying in 1980. We both have remained very involved with Special Olympics ever since.

Our initial involvement was as volunteers, when we started working as coaches and helping out at events – Special Olympics was very small in Ireland at that stage. The first national Games were held in 1979 or 1980, but over the next few years we were gradually getting more support and learning from

expertise in the US about the wider issues of disability.

In 1985, when I was still working in St Michael's House, we decided to organise a European Special Olympics Games in Dublin. Nineteen countries participated from Europe and it was organised on a totally voluntary basis – Special Olympics had no paid staff and no offices, so we were begging and borrowing what we could. We were fortunate to get use of an office in UCD with a phone, **so when we were finished our day jobs we would go in there and do another day's work!** But we had a great team and the European Games were hugely successful. They became a model for the development of Special Olympics around other European countries, and gave us the confidence to further develop Special Olympics in Ireland.

In 1989 I decided to leave St Michael's House and became the first Director of Special Olympics Ireland. We'd been successful in retaining some of our sponsors from the European Games, and we were also given a small office. Because we now had a base, we were able to go from strength to strength: organising more fund-raising activities, obtaining government funding, and sustaining the activities that were already in place. I worked there for ten years until 1999.

Around 1995 we went to a Special Olympics World Games in Connecticut. By this stage Special Olympics in Ireland was developing at a fairly steady pace. It had good vision and a great leadership team behind it. **After the opening ceremony in Connecticut, we just sat around and said 'we could do this'**, and from that day on we started planning the Games, spending from 1995 to 1999 bidding for them in Ireland. It meant working with the government here, submitting the bid and working with Special Olympics International – we had to convince them all just how serious we were. The Games had never been outside the US so, naturally, they had lots of questions: How is it going to happen? Who is going to organise it? Did we have the capability? Did we have the facilities? Could we get the finance? **But sitting there that night we knew it was possible.**

There was a core group of about twelve who had been involved with Special Olympics in Ireland for years, and we had seen the Games develop to a very strong place. We knew if the Games were held in Ireland that we could do so much more for people with disabilities in this country, which really was our motivation – we felt that we could do it and we'd been to enough Games to see what was required to do them well.

In the end the bid document was

gigantic – it took us a couple of years to prepare it. The Special Olympics assessment team came over, assessed all the venues and met with the people who would be involved. I think the committee went back saying 'yes, with some adjustments, we think Ireland could do this'. Infrastructure needed to be developed, the traffic was a big issue; the fact that there was no 50-m swimming pool, and even the weather became an issue. But eventually we overcame all those things. We got the go-ahead for the 50-m pool. We brought together everyone who was involved with traffic management. And even if it did rain, we knew we had things like raingear! We were awarded the Games in March 1999. When it happened, we all looked at each other and said 'oh wow, so what are we going to do now?'

But we set about planning immediately. I vacated my role as Director of Special Olympics Ireland and moved over to become CEO of the 2003 World Games. I began working on the project and then gradually started to build a team.

At first the two biggest things we needed to do were to get the team and finances in place, so we put together a strategy for raising the money and got started. At the same time we were also figuring out what needed to be done four years out, three and a half years out, three years out of the Games. We planned in chunks of six months and built the staff team as we went along. Some people also joined the team as volunteers while they continued their day jobs. We ultimately built the team to 283 staff members and 32,003 volunteers. We had a board of directors, chaired by Denis O'Brien. The Board worked very well, supporting us and providing structure. We met with them once a month to check if we were meeting our milestones and reaching our fund-raising targets. We also had a patrons group which met twice a year – this was a wider group of professionals from business, religious groups and the entertainment world, chaired by the Taoiseach – who would help us overcome major obstacles, and their help was invaluable.

June 2003 arrived. The weather was great and we had the most incredible two weeks of our lives!

When we had the idea of bringing the Games to Ireland we knew it had the potential to make a difference, but **we had no idea the scale of difference it was going to make**. The impact they've had in raising awareness and generating a real depth of understanding about the capabilities of people with a learning disability is quite remarkable. There is now heightened awareness of disability in agencies, government groups and other sporting bodies. It would have taken Special Olympics Ireland forever to reach this level of awareness, and yet we were able to achieve all of it in four years with the Games, which was just fantastic.

So we had to build on that legacy. The Games finished in June but even before the closing ceremony we had a team in place to start creating opportunities in Ireland as a result of the success. **So instead of winding down, we actually started to rev back up**

again – there was never a feeling of 'oh, the Games are over' – we never had a second!

All the team grew hugely through the Games. Each time we did something – it may have been something new, it may have been something more challenging – we just took on the role and did it. It needed to be done and somebody had to do it. So personally I never had that fear, 'Will I be able to do it', I just had to say 'I believe in this'. So if something needed to be done, we threw ourselves into it and any obstacle that we came up against we would find someone who could solve it for us.

I talk a lot to students in universities and schools and there are a few things I always say to them. First of all: believe you can do it. If you really believe you want to do something, go out and do it. **Don't put any obstacles in your way because if you do, it will never get going in the first place. We would never have done the Games had we said 'how are we going to recruit 30,000 volunteers and where are we going to get €60 million'.** It would have seemed like such a mammoth task. But instead we said 'yes, we will meet every challenge and get over it'. So believe in yourself – you can do anything that you want to do. You are as capable as the person beside you. You may not think you are, but you are. So it is about seeing the possibility rather than the obstacles.

I remember a funny story, the first time we went to see the Deputy Chief of Staff of the Defence Forces back in 1999 to tell him our plans for the Games. The statistics alone of what we were talking about were mind-boggling: 10,000 athletes, 30,000 volunteers, 165 countries, 52 languages, 177 host towns, 70 venues . . . and on and on. This same man was at the opening ceremony and he turned to me saying 'Mary, after you left the room that first day we met, we looked at each other and said "that woman doesn't have a clue what she is letting herself in for".' He was probably right – **if we'd had a clue we would probably not have gone for it.** But we did go for it. So don't see the obstacles, just plough ahead and do it. You will get there eventually, you will get there. I have a great, great belief in that because I've seen it work time and time again.

And **age doesn't matter at all**. We had all sorts of age groups involved in the Games – the oldest volunteer was ninety-four and every single person, no matter what age, contributed in the most amazing ways to their success.

Business and finance skills are definitely something I had to learn. Running the games was like running a business – and was probably bigger than most businesses. I had a lot to learn. In terms of personal development it gave me more determination to succeed, and I would say I became a more determined person as I went along because I had to – I had to be determined and focused to meet the milestones we had set.

I suppose I would call myself a social entrepreneur now. When you look at a successful entrepreneur, they are usually quite creative in terms of their business and they are also quite focused and financially astute. They are people who go after something and

they have unshakeable confidence and determination. The difference between a traditional entrepreneur and a social entrepreneur is that one is working in an organisation that creates profit, and the other is working in an organisation that doesn't create a financial profit, but does create such huge social profit. And I think the whole idea of social profit – **what you have done in terms of making a difference in someone else's life – is so important. Actually, is there anything in the world that matches that?**

It all comes back to being centred around people. People are the most valuable asset that we have as a nation. You can get other things if you have the people. If you have the right people, for instance, the money will come because it is the people who will make it happen. But if you don't have the people with the drive, then you are not going to get far. Ireland may be more developed economically now, but let's not leave behind any person in our society. Let's develop them, let's ensure that we continue to look after each other in the way that we did years and years ago when we had to, when we all did neighbourly acts for each other.

Our future can be very exciting but it is up to ourselves to create it.

Colm O'Gorman

Amnesty International www.amnesty.ie
One in Four www.oneinfour.org

Dublin, Ireland
Themes: Human Rights, Law, Politics, Media

Colm O'Gorman, a prominent campaigner and advocate for the victims of child sexual abuse and sexual violence, believes in standing up for what is right. His stance led him to set up One in Four, an organisation which supports the victims of sexual abuse. Following a brief sojourn in Irish politics as a member of the 22nd Seanad Éireann for the Progressive Democrats, he is now the Executive Director of Amnesty International in Ireland.

Growing up in Ferns, County Wexford, at fourteen Colm was the victim of sexual abuse by local parish priest Fr Sean Fortune, an ordeal lasting several years. The acts, reported to the police, eventually led to the successful establishment of The Ferns Enquiry into clerical sexual abuse and the resignation of Ferns' archbishop, Brendan Comiskey. Colm has also been the centre of a number of high-profile documentaries speaking about how the Church handled the accusations.

Colm's strong reputation for standing up and speaking out against injustice is now taking shape in the international advocacy work of Amnesty, speaking out for the protection of human rights around the world, and particularly, giving voice to the thousands of people who are denied them.

It is one to thing to demand change, but you have to be part of the process of creating change.

I came into Amnesty after my role with One in Four and a brief sojourn in politics. It was fantastically timely for me. I personally needed to move on with a different kind of challenge. I have always been of the opinion that founders of organisations should be able to transition from their role, so that the organisation can grow from the original vision. So, after five years with One in Four, it was time for me to leave.

One in Four grew out of my own work as a psychotherapist in private practice in the UK. About 60–70 per cent of the clients I was working with there were disclosing experiences of childhood abuse, specifically child sexual abuse. Many of them were accessing therapy as they were finally at a point to begin to deal with these childhood experiences. I could see the need for an organisation that could help them to address some of the criminal justice and child protection issues that arose as they dealt with their own experiences as children, and also help them to transition into new ways of living. So I looked for one that could provide all of those things, to both men and women, and there wasn't one. So I decided to set one up, in a huge fit of naivety!

On some level, you don't know what it is you are setting out to do, but you know that it is necessary. I knew it was important that a space like One in Four exists.

Once we were established we quickly became involved in media work. Cases were presenting that demanded advocacy and the media was a hugely useful tool. Early on I found myself working with *Newsnight*, a UK current affairs programme, to make a documentary. A woman, Shy Keenan, had approached us explaining that she had been abused by her stepfather and a number of people in care homes and institutions she had been placed in. She had gone to the authorities to report the abuse but nobody would respond to allegations, despite the fact that she has a tape recording of her stepfather detailing some of the case. So we decided to investigate it ourselves. Together with Sarah McDonald, who at that time was a producer and director with *Newsnight*, we worked for nine months making the documentary. The programme eventually led to a criminal trial, which resulted in 140 years of collective sentences being handed down.

It was a huge case at the time, and was a great example of the power of the media to influence debate and raise public awareness of issues. **Change does not usually come from decision-makers acting on their own. Change comes from people dictating and demanding** change. Media becomes an important tool in trying to inform and challenge public debate and I have realised that it is one of the means through which I needed to do my work.

Following the first documentary, Sarah, whom I got to know well when making the film, asked if she could make another about my own case. I can still remember the first time she asked me to make it. My first reaction was 'you have got to be kidding me'. At that point I didn't want to bring my case up again but over a period of time she convinced me that it was a good idea to tell the story. 'Suing the Pope' went out in 2002. I'll never forget it. It was aired at 11.15 on a Tuesday night on BBC 2. I had no expectation of it really having an impact, especially here in Ireland but quite the opposite happened. The world went mad. There I was sitting in a little office in southeast London, with the Irish media going nuts and all these calls coming in.

The media started to talk about the fact that I worked for an organisation called One in Four. People started to contact us and it just started to build and build and build. Very quickly we were getting lots of information about allegations, complaints, concerns, and even threats. There were concerns around child protection in Ireland, predominantly involving clerics and the church. And we needed to do something with that. I decided we had to engage with the authorities back in Ireland, asking them how we could channel the information effectively.

We also decided to look at what supports existed for people here. The Department of Health at the time put in some money to help us respond to calls initially. And at the same time, there was pressure about whether or not the film could be shown in Ireland, and initially RTÉ were not clear about whether they would screen it. In the end RTÉ decided to air it on 2 April 2002. On 1 April, Brendan Comiskey resigned as bishop (he was the bishop who had covered up the allegations). That obviously sent the whole thing into overdrive. We held a press conference after the documentary went out, launching a website for Ireland. In the first 24 hours we had 6,000 hits, so we knew there was demand. By the end of 2005 there were 4 million hits a year on the site. As a result One in Four were asked to open up an office in Ireland.

In the middle of it all, I really was just responding to what was happening. Clearly I had choices. I knew I wanted to go public. I had made a choice when I was younger that, when the time came, I would not be anonymous about what had happened to me. When the time did come I had to be able to think on my feet, take advantage of opportunities when they arose and be able to make quick decisions. I knew that moving back to Ireland was the right choice.

I grew up in Wexford but had left at seventeen, hitching to Dublin. I had legged it, frankly. It was either leave Wexford or check out completely. **It was either the river or the road, and I choose the road. Really, it was that stark.**

I spent two years in Dublin trying to find my feet, with long periods of homelessness on the streets. I couldn't get help from social services because I was under eighteen. I got a bit of money here and there and some jobs. I got a job in a coffee shop that paid me ten pounds a shift. Ten pounds would get me a bed and breakfast for the night. So if I got a day's work, I got a place to stay. It was a difficult, challenging time. **I was running but I was not sure what I was running to**. I was just running and trying to find some place to find my feet.

Finally, I found a place to live in Dublin but soon after I got glandular fever and was unable to work, so I lost the house. From there I just kept moving. I think I lived in eighteen bedsits across Dublin in a period of about two years, one of them for two nights before the ceiling fell in. During this time I found the gay scene in Dublin, which was hugely important to me because it was a safe space. I had never in been able to address who I was, or my own sexuality because of all the abuse. Certainly any positive sense of who I might be in the world, or any positive understanding of my own sexuality was massively corrupted with the abuse. I was not even able to connect with it. I was operating in an immediate, reactive way to everything that was around me. Not in a considered, conscious way, and I certainly did not react from any sense of who I was or what I wanted to be in the world. I didn't live in my head, because it was too scary a place to go. So finding the gay scene was really important.

Then in 1986 I went to London. I was still finding my feet and I certainly was not dealing with anything in my past. **For about nine or ten years I just wandered, working in all sorts of jobs:** bars, agencies, hotels, security, trade shows. I have done so many different jobs it is ridiculous! After a lot of wandering I finally came to the decision to train as a physical therapist and drove a minicab for three years while I trained.

The decision to go into psycho-therapy came later. After deciding to bring my case to the Gardaí, I knew that one of the ways I could prove that I was fine was to go into therapy. But I still hadn't fully acknowledged what had happened in my past. So I headed off to therapy to prove that I was fine, and in six weeks found a therapist who told me I was. But of course I wasn't at all. I hadn't begun to even touch it.

Meanwhile, my father, who had been distant most of my life, and I had a number of incredibly honest, upfront conversations and became very close as a result. He died ten months after I went to the Gardaí and his death was another trigger which made me think 'you know, I am really not OK, but I need to do something with all of this. I know, I will become a psychotherapist'. It was kind of a classic number. Why does someone want to be a helper? Probably so that they are the ones doing the helping rather than the ones that need the help. I didn't want to be the one that needed the help.

Luckily I found a phenomenal course and the people who ran it completely nailed me. They just said 'no, you are not doing this. There are all these issues you need to deal with.' Because I wanted to be a therapist, so much, so that everything would be OK, I knew I had to deal with them. When I did, I discovered that it was really important, one of the most significant things I have ever done. My training lasted three years and I remember thinking, if I never become a therapist myself, then this is the most important thing I've ever done.

It was only after all of that, while working as a psychotherapist, that the idea for One in Four emerged.

...

I have learned over the years that it is one to thing to demand change, but you have to be part of the process for creating change. That is why the role in Amnesty is a good one for me. It is very much what I believe and it is very much what Amnesty is about. It is about holding people to account. But is not just about holding politicians to account, it is about holding ourselves to account. I am very passionate about this. The reason I got involved in parliamentary politics was because this is a republican democracy. We are literally the sum of our individual parts. We are, as a state, a collective of individuals. All the power of the state, the legislative, the judicial and the executive, as the Constitution states, is derived from us individually and collectively as citizens. So what happens in this country happens in our name and through our power. Government has no power. It has the power we vest in it, and in our name, so whatever this state does, it does in your name and my name. That then places a huge responsibility on us to be clear about the messages we send

and to be part of a positive expression about who we want to be, who we need to be and who we are.

We can talk about politics failing us, but we also have to recognise that we are failing ourselves. It is not politics failing us, it is us failing ourselves. Politics reflects our priorities. There is a reason why, parish-pump politics win elections in this country, it's because that is what we demand.

Advice

Take your time. Go easy on yourself. Don't push yourself in deciding who you are or who you have to be in the world. You will get there. Opportunities will be presented, the world will occasionally throw them your way. Be open to them and don't be afraid to take them on. And be happy.

If someone had said to me ten years ago 'you will be doing this', or listed all the things I have done, I would have laughed them, I wouldn't have believed it for a moment. And what that also tells me that in ten years' time, God knows where I'll be. I could be on the side of a mountain keeping chickens and saying that I have found my route to happiness, because it could well be. Or I could be doing anything else: who knows. **But there is one truth that I have learned: to be open to change, to be open to possibility and to never lose sight of the boundless possibilities within ourselves, and the boundless possibilities that exist for us in the world, without becoming trapped or paralysed by those possibilities.** You can do whatever you want.

R868	12		06:40	LONDON LHR
:1948	8		06:40	NAPLES
3152	6		06:40	PARIS CDG
4282	9		06:40	ROME FCO
254	9		06:45	FRANKFURT FR
192	4		06:45	LONDON LCY
514	4		06:45	POZNAN
62	8		06:50	BRUSSELS
42	8		06:50	FRANKFURT FR
02	7		06:50	LONDON LHR
22	9		06:50	NANTES

Diary Extract: The Departure,

It was a late night of packing, slimming my bag down to essentials until I could bear the weight.

Deep in my belly is fear and nervousness. I know I have travelled before, but this time it feels different, very different, never so unhinged, knocking on doors and seeing which ones will open. I think I am I on the cusp of something big, and I feel that this will change me – for the better I am hoping, but I know it will change me.

Passport: Check.
Visas: Check (I hope, I think . . . is it really right that I can get a visa for Mozambique on the border? I will just have to wait and see . . .)
Excitement levels: High.
Nerve levels: Moderate but rising.
Sanity levels: Questionable. What the hell am I doing, by the way? Am I mad?

EI152	3	07:20	LONDON	
EI450	5	07:20	MUNICH	
AF5003	10	07:25	MALAGA	
EI402	5	07:30	BARCEL
LH4985	2	07:30	VIENNA
AF5116	10	07:30	WARSAW
FR1974	7	07:40	KERRY
EI630	3	07:40	LONDON
EI650	5	07:40	SLIGO
BD120	2	07:55	BUDAPE
FR1986	7	08:00	CORK

written at Heathrow Airport

This morning an early lift to the airport. Dawn rising above the city. Dublin shrouded in an amber hue, all wrapped up in glow. Astrid (my cousin) came to see me off. I held it together until the last moment, until the tears came, the reality hit, and I was through the gates.

Beyond there is a world to be discovered. Now, sitting here, it is really hitting me. The dream is made reality. Pause went to Play. The shift from 'I plan to' to 'I am doing' has happened. Venturing though those gates is venturing on a path which I have chosen, which I have set, which is calling me to be something bigger than myself.

The excitement has pounced. Please fasten your seat belts, we are about to take off.

First stop, Nairobi, Kenya.

Part Two: Africa
Nairobi, Kenya

Picture this: a river that smells like stagnated slurry, once brown but now indigo blue, dyed from the washout of industrial waste. Channels of mud and raw sewage mixing with water. Plastic bags serving as toilets, flung into the air, tossed in the hope that they will just disappear. But they don't. A single step brings you through it: over mango pips, rubbish, wrappers, dust, festering flies, the rising mound of plastic bags. There is a young boy asleep in a wheelbarrow. Another plays with a pair of scissors. There is a main thoroughfare, lined with small kiosks, each decked with variants of rusted corrugated iron. A mobile phone rings with a techno ringtone, or maybe it is Wham: it is hard to tell.

The picture is hard to forget. Once you see it, once you smell it, the memory is there to stay. That is where my journey really began, in the Mukuru kwa Ruben slum on the outskirts of Nairobi. I was told that there are approximately 100,000 inhabitants in the slum. But it is hard to tell. Who counts anyway? There is a sense that this is a forgotten place, a place where the rest of the world stood on, forgetting to lend a hand to help it up again. But between the rubbish and the waste, the sewage and the smell, there is a sanctuary. It is called Gatoto Community Primary School, and it is run by a dynamic team of teachers including head teacher, Betty Nyagoha. It is a large open space, with classrooms, a library, a music hall, and latrines. There is garden planted, and more trees on the way.

I say my journey really started with that 'Begin it' quote. And it did. But in other ways it started here at Gatoto, back in 2004 when I first met Betty and visited the school as part of my previous work (I was managing a volunteer programme for an Irish organisation called Suas – see interview with Colman Farrell). Back then, Betty and the pupils at the school struck me with their hope and optimism. Despite the surrounding conditions, and despite all the things that they could legitimately complain about, they didn't complain. Instead they believe that things can be better, and they

work to make them so. Gatoto is an example of what raw belief can do.

There is an underpinning ethos in Gatoto. It is a belief in the ability and potential of every child, and it is not just lip service. The school enrols over 900 pupils, and exam grades are improving each year. They also perform exceptionally well in national music and athletics competitions.

On the day of my visit, over lunch I sat outside with the school's social worker, Rhoda Mutua. She started to tell me stories about each of the children as they passed by. One boy, in Grade 8, had disappeared for six months. After a tip-off, Rhoda found him living on the streets in Nairobi. Domestic issues had forced him to run away from home. After meeting with the boy's family Rhoda was as able to help alleviate some of the family issues and the boy returned to school.

At two o' clock the bell rang for the afternoon classes. The main yard was still buzzing with the play of younger children (the ones who only have morning classes). Rhoda told me that the kids stay around the school because there is nowhere else that is safe for them to play. Without Gatoto, she is not sure what these kids would do. Then she turned around and tended to a child who had fallen and cut his knee.

It seemed appropriate that on my first day overseas on this journey, I returned to Gatoto to say hello, for in many ways it sums up the essence of my entire journey: a belief that change is possible and a commitment to make it happen. I knew too that there are other Bettys and Gatotos out there. Maybe not schools, but perhaps businesses, or hospitals, or other organisations. And with that, I was off to find them.

Nick Moon

KickStart

www.kickstart.org

Nairobi, Kenya

Themes: Business, Technology

KickStart, based in Kenya, develop and promote new technologies in Africa. Founded by Nick Moon and Martin Fisher in 1991, the idea is to develop low-cost equipment, or 'appropriate technologies' that can 'kickstart' new businesses. Among the many innovations they have produced are: a building block press, an oil press (which can be used to extract cooking oil from seeds), and the most successful product to date, a manual water irrigation pump, otherwise known as 'The Money Maker'. In 2003, the MoneyMaker was named as one of *Newsweek*'s 'Ten Inventions That Will Change The World'. The figures which capture KickStart's impact are very impressive, and rising:

– Over 65,000 new businesses have started
– 800 new businesses start up each month
– Over $79 million per year (approximately €60 million)
  generated in profits and wages by the new businesses
– Revenues from these businesses represent 0.6 per cent of Kenya's
  GDP and 0.25 per cent of Tanzania's GDP.

Nick is a firm believer in market-based solutions to poverty and is convinced that simple technologies can lift people out of subsistence or hand-to-mouth living. The profits generated allow the families who use the pumps to plan for the future, look after their health, educate their children, and encourage many people back to rural areas from the urban slums. The fact that the technologies do not need fuel or electricity is yet another bonus in places where both are scarce and expensive.

But for Nick this is all just the beginning. 'What we have is not enough, you have to have the numbers, you can't just have nice little stories. If it is going to make a real, significant difference, on a large scale, it has got to be

I'm perfectly happy to take risks.

hundreds of thousands.' And that is indeed their plan. KickStart currently operates in Kenya, Tanzania and Mali and has an expansion plan in place to for the next few years. The day after I met him, Nick was heading down to South Africa to investigate options there.

I've learned so much through travel. So TRAVEL! We can only learn so much sitting at home and surfing the web. But nothing beats going into these places.

I grew up in India and later in Singapore. My parents were English and Irish. My dad worked for a shipping company. I was a nice middle-class boy and I went to school in England, where my grandmother was, but by the age of seventeen, I had left. I had developed some ideals to be the 'working man', the artisan, which I believed to be a truly valuable person in society. I worked on building sites – labourer, carpenter's mate, painter – for a couple of years. Then I did an overland trip to India, travelling on buses – it cost thirteen quid from Istanbul to Delhi. I'd an affinity for woodwork, so later I put myself through woodwork college and became a cabinet maker. I wasn't very good (not patient enough), so I switched to building carpentry – bigger things – and travelled around Europe in my early twenties with my toolbox and an earring. Afterwards I came back to London and started a business with a friend of mine.

We wanted to set up a socialist co-operative – to practise our craft but with some social or community benefit.

So we set up a workshop and did all kinds of odd jobs at first. But we had no idea how to run a business and we learned as we went along. At first it was just the two of us but we later expanded to three partners and four apprentices. We captured a niche market at the time, restoring Georgian buildings. It was Thatcher's yuppie Britain. There were a lot of young city types and a lot of money in the city to be made. But I didn't feel this was fulfilling the social side of our strategy. Not at all.

Then we had real trouble in the business – we were going under. One day I saw an ad for a French-speaking carpenter which paid £250 per week. This was a lot more than we were paying ourselves at that time and I thought it looked pretty good. I called the number and the voice at the other end said, 'I think the job is in Nigeria or somewhere'. I wasn't expecting anything that far away and initially said 'never mind', but then I called back the next day and found out the job was in Togo and that no one else had taken up the post. So I found myself on a plane heading to Togo to build a music recording studio with a bunch of guys. We were there for about seven months.

This was the early 1980s and was my

first experience on the ground in Africa. We were there long enough to get to know the city – Lomé. After seven months I decided Togo was a much more interesting place than I had first imagined. A few months later a Nigerian guy who had come to visit the site in Togo rang me. He wanted to build a recording studio in Nigeria and wanted my help. So I spent three months there – not a very pleasant experience (lots of business hassles) but I had 'the bug' and had decided that Africa was an interesting part of the world.

I went back home to bail out of the business. I sold my share of it to the others and joined VSO [Voluntary Services Overseas]. I've always liked to travel and thought I'd be in some tropical paradise for a few years. I also thought VSO would give me the chance to do something useful for a community. They hired me to go to Western Kenya, near the Ugandan border, to work as a carpentry and business skills teacher.

When I got there I found that the school had a Northern Irish headmaster who wanted to develop a vocational training programme. We had to build the classrooms and the workshops and plan the coursework. There were a lot of things I had to get used to: no electricity,

charcoal stoves, collecting water, using pit latrines, and a rural lifestyle. I was there for three years. It gave me insights into the values of rural people in Kenya, which I don't believe are that different from those of rural people all over sub-Saharan Africa. I finished with VSO in 1985 and still feel that the greatest beneficiary of those three years was myself. I had taught a few people how to make tables and chairs but then realised that there were no jobs for them to go to. I learned that even if you give someone a skill which you think might be useful, that because of the social and economic situations they are in, it doesn't mean it will be.

I went off scratching my head and was almost immediately offered a job by a large British charity called ActionAid. By this time I was married to a Kenyan woman, we had a child, so I was very pleased to stay on in Kenya. ActionAid offered me a job that took me to the slums of Nairobi, into a big shanty town. They were looking to build schools and needed someone to train community groups to build with low-cost construction materials, such as bricks and roofing tiles. So we built schools and clinics in the slum.

After about a year, ActionAid sent

me to northern Kenya to a town called Isiolo. This is where the tarmac ends – you head towards Ethiopia and you're in nomadic pastoralist country. So I travelled hundreds of miles in my big green Land Cruiser. I was very popular because I was the ActionAid guy, bringing 'the stuff'. Later I struggled because I felt like we weren't really accomplishing anything, however good our intentions were. I found we only made the communities more and more dependent on our services. But that wasn't so obvious then. **During all this I was feeling very puzzled.**

It was around this time when I met Martin Fisher, who had come to Kenya on a Fulbright scholarship from Stanford. He wanted to use his PhD in mechanical engineering design in some useful manner, not for the military or oil industry. He had come to see what kind of appropriate technologies there were and how they were being used in the context of rural development. We had a bunch of machines we'd built to make bricks, tiles, ploughs, etc. When Martin saw them he said 'these are terrible! They can be so much better designed – cheaper and stronger.' I replied 'well, you're the design engineer, join us.' So he did. Martin brought an enormously valuable skill.

We began working together to build up the technical support unit of ActionAid. Soon, however, we began to realise that NGOs were going into communities, training groups, assisting with loans but when they moved away these groups collapsed. Not only were we not creating new businesses, our

technology was ruining businesses that had already been established. So our idea was to approach the more entrepreneurial people in the communities who were interested in supporting the new technologies we were using. That way, when we left, they would be able to continue and grow businesses. So that's how we got started.

At the beginning, of course, we didn't have much money. Martin and I hired a few guys too. We worked voluntarily for quite a while. We took on some consultancy work to make ends meet. But then a friend of ours in Britain, who believed in our programme, applied to the British ODA (Overseas Development Administration – they call it DFID now) for funds to set up the business. It was a 50 per cent matching fund, so now we had to find a way to 'unlock' the ODA money.

In 1992, the political situation in Somalia exploded. Half a million refugees came into Kenya. The relief NGOs set up camps for 50,000–60,000 people. They set up waterholes, schools, clinics, etc. These new 'tented cities' had huge sanitation problems. There are a lot of taboos around sanitation with Somalis. They won't use common latrines. And for nomadic peoples, the fields became overwhelmed with excrement from people who were no longer roaming. We had to develop a new technology for dealing with this; and invented a system for making and installing really cheap, sanitary pit latrine cover slabs. We went to the camps and hired and trained teams to do all this, installing around 130 latrines a day at the peak.

We installed over 40,000 latrines in 5 camps on contract from UNHCR [the UN Refugee Agency] and different NGOs working in the area. We were allowed 6 per cent for overhead costs, so the money we got for this allowed us to match the ODA money.

So now we had the money we needed to start developing new technologies. We saw a need to develop agri-based small enterprises. We initially developed a manual oil press, which can be used to squeeze the oil out of oilseed crops like sunflower to produce nutritious oils. The by-product was a great animal feed. But it was all very small scale. **If we wanted to make a difference on a large scale, we'd have to improve the lives of 100,000 people, not 100.** We learned that we needed quality technology but the product also had to be 'sexy'; something desirable that people would really want.

We got into the area of irrigation and we saw the scale of the opportunity: people needed water pumps. So we've developed them in three different sizes ranging from $34–$94. **We're not in business to sell pumps as such – that's just the means to an end, to give people a tool to earn an income, so they can use the skills and the land that they already have.** Land is people's one asset. They have the skills to use that asset and a powerful motivation to use it.

People look at Africa and think 'those poor people, we must do something to help'. But they don't want handouts. Giving things away for nothing is unfair and unsustainable: unsustainable because it can't go on forever and unfair because you can't give it to everyone – how do you choose? It's also demeaning. People will say 'thank you' but they won't feel good about themselves. If you're able to tell someone 'here's something that might help you but it's up to you to decide if you want it and will use it', you provide an opportunity, so long as you make it easy and affordable and leave it to them to decide. People will make a conscious decision and then learn to use the technology to best benefit them.

Our guiding principle is to '**do the greatest good, to the largest number, in the shortest time, at the least cost**'. (I think that was John Stuart Mill – Brit philosopher from long ago.) We believe that you can take private sector practice and use it in the social sector. It is about profit but it is also about social values and environmental benefit. That's how these new 'responsible corporates' look at their work – supposedly anyway. The only difference between us and a 'for-profit' business is that we focus on the latter two first.

We have always said that people are not poor because they are sick but that they are sick because they are poor. There is a correlation; they are interlinked. We know this for certain because we find out what people have done with the additional income from our products. The first thing they do is put better and more food on the table – so then you have an immediate health and nutritional impact. The second thing they do is spend money on educating their children. And the third thing is to spend money on medical care. Once they've taken care of these things, they start making investments: buy that dairy cow, buy the solar panel. And they start diversifying their investment and making lifestyle choices.

I'll give you an example: one woman was in a desperate situation. She grew a few lines of beans and sold them to an exporter. She made $250 a year and was raising six children. Well, when she got one of our pumps, she began growing more beans. She now earns $1,500 a year, and with that extra money she's done exactly the things everyone else does. She's bought a cell phone and is sending her children to secondary school. She's buying shares in the Nairobi stock exchange and buying solar panels. I find it inspiring.

I've been self-employed all my life. I suppose I don't worry unduly about consequences – **I'm perfectly happy to take risks**; you can call it a quality or a defect. Fortunately I found a way to do something with my own skills.

I also think it's good that I was a woodworker. As a woodworker, you have to plan a product from its raw materials and see something through to the end. You understand operations. It's a skill I've had to apply here: translating strategy to actual operations on the ground. This is where development efforts so often fail. The policies and the background information is spot on: these are the causes and this is where we intervene. But then they still go and do the wrong thing. Builders understand implementation better than architects do!

I've also had to learn business admin- istration. While I did get technical qualifications and went to the university of life, I realised that our business was no longer a cosy operation and the challenges were different. So I went back later in life to do an MBA, which has really helped me. I don't think it would have been so useful to me when I was younger. As I worked my way through the course material though, I could pick up 100 case studies that I could now relate to. It all made a lot of sense to me after the experience I've had.

You have to believe things will work themselves out and that you will get there. **A little recklessness helps.** In my case, I've also had an inspirational business partner. I wouldn't have done this if I were on my own.

I'm pretty happy doing what I do now. I feel a sham when people say they admire what I do. They think that I've made enormous sacrifices but if that's true, it has never felt that way. I'm glad I am doing this and am pleased that I live here. My only regret is that of any middle-aged person – I wish I had done it all sooner and faster.

I certainly value enormously the three years I spent as a volunteer. Everything I do now is based on what I learned about the world through the eyes of rural Africans. I don't think I would have understood how to design or market and produce this if I hadn't learned that. I wish I had some more profundities but you know . . . don't take anything for granted, go see for yourself.

Diary Extract:
Travel to Eldoret, Kenya

The bus ride to Eldoret was supposed to take six hours. It took eleven. Not bad really, considering we got three flat tyres and the engine nearly went on fire. I was travelling on what was supposed to be one of Kenya's more 'de luxe' services and by the time we did arrive the dusk was just about dark and I wasn't too happy having to walk around the city with my bags looking for a place to stay.

Eldoret is not exactly on the tourist route. It sounds almost mythical, like Eldorado, land of golden opportunity, but it is not quite. Accommodation options are limited, and I decided on one that was listed as 'mid-range' in my guidebook. But 'mid-range' is the middle of undefined parameters and on this occasion they were very narrow. A big mama of a woman greeted me and showed me to a room. Bed, door, lock; three basic essentials. The darkness was well in at this stage, and I decided to pitch for the night, locking the door behind me. It was only then that I really noticed the grime, serious grime. I'm not looking for luxury, or spotless. I'm happy with basics. But basics in this room were on another plane to my definition. The bath was lined with accumulated slime. The sink a slurry of mould; the water a brown sludge. Not good. I looked around some more. Basics also seemed to constitute a complimentary bottle of vodka and a box of condoms. Hotel, hey? I was beginning to seriously doubt. But is got worse. I pulled back my sheets, only to reveal . . . a used condom.

I spent last night tucked up in my sleeping bag, in all my clothes, with a towel wrapped around my pillow, really not wanting to hear what was going on next door and this morning awoke early, up and out of the room as quickly as possible into Eldoret. Noise was blaring from every angle. Matatus (the local small buses) gathered and swarmed. It was market day, and it seemed like the town population swelled with every Tom, Dick and Jacinta wanting to sell their wares. Shoes, potatoes, radios, penknives, colour sarongs, fake Gucci bags – Eldoret has it all. It also appeared that it has a lot of banks. They seem to congregate on every street corner. The queues to some today ran the entire street. Comparing them, I was not sure if length was an indicator of popularity or inefficiency. Possibly both. But it wasn't the markets or the glitzy hotels that brought me to Eldoret, but Ben Ogunyo, who I met today.

Benjamin Ogunyo

Koinonia

Eldoret, Kenya

Themes: Youth, Education

'Koinonia' is a Greek work meaning 'together in partnership', a word which Ben Ogunyo thought best captured the essence of his work. Together with his long-term friend George Ngesa, he is changing the way children's homelessness is being tackled in the region. Rather than placing children in residential homes, Koinonia works with families to reintegrate the children back into their homes.

It can be a slow process, taking time to build trust among the children and families, but as Ben emphasised, it is working at the root of the problem. If children run away from home there is an obvious problem, and so it is in the home where the real solution to the problem lies.

Life on the streets is a rough ride. The children survive on slim pickings: scavenging, odd jobs, begging, crime. The life of drugs can suck them in. Glue sniffing is rampant among the street population, up to 2,000 children and teenagers in Eldoret town alone. Walking past the area in Eldoret where the kids congregate (on an urban dump), there were the empty bottles and some kids sniffing. Heroin is on its way too, smuggled in over the borders with Tanzania, often by the street kids themselves. But Koinonia is finding ways to break the cycle.

If a family agrees to take the child back into the home, Koinonia agrees to assist with school costs. Working with the family they discuss ways of generating income, linking them to microfinances institutions, for instance, or teaching them farm management skills. The method proves to be more cost effective than institutional housing for children.

In cases where the children cannot attend school, Koinonia links them up with vocational training: bike repairs, auto mechanics, tailoring, so that they can in turn set up their own small businesses. On the day I visited, George walked me around town and introduced me to some of the boys they were working with, and who are now successfully trained and off the streets. I met Martin, on the streets for several years, who now runs a bicycle repair shop, is married and has a young family of his own.

The journey we have in life is not very long, and with the little time that we have, we must spend it wisely.

I had some troubles growing up. My parents were not able to provide for even my basic needs like food and schooling. I was born in Kakamega, but my dad was working in Mombasa [approx. 750 km away], on the other side of the country. While he had a job, very little money came home to us. My mum worked very hard to get me through my primary education, but could not afford to send me to secondary school. I was the eldest of five children and some of my younger siblings did not even have the chance to finish primary school.

After primary school I was sent to live with my father in Mombasa, but because of his drinking, he was unable to look after me properly – it was very hard. I had to stay out of school for a whole year. I landed some casual construction jobs – working at the age of thirteen so that I could afford to live. I was staying with my dad in a tiny room where we were both just sleeping on the floor. It was pathetic. I never knew where we were going to get the next meal.

But things really changed one day. I was hitching a lift into town when a Canadian man, Ernest, stopped his car. He could see that I was very young. As we were driving he asked about my home situation. When I told him I was unable to go to secondary school, he offered to pay for my schooling in exchange for some household work – cleaning cars, washing clothes, etc. It

was the first time someone had really believed in me. **That moment did change my life. I had never thought I would be able to go back to school.**

So I went to school during the day and in the evenings and during the school holidays I would work in Ernest's house. I never had proper holidays but I knew I was lucky. How many people want such an opportunity, but never get it? I realised that when I grew up I also wanted to help others who did not have opportunities. It was a dream which has stayed alive within me.

When I finished school, Ernest told me about a children's home in Eldoret and suggested that I get involved. **Coming here I didn't know what I was letting myself in for.** It was a residential rehabilitation home for sick and street children. But I didn't know what to do. I was eighteen or nineteen. The children looked rowdy and unruly. I had never really been on the streets and I didn't know how to talk to them. But there were no separate houses for the staff, so we all had to stay in the same room, twenty-four hours a day. So I had to learn quickly.

It was a difficult time and I would ask myself 'why am I going through all this?' But I started to think about what I could do to help these kids. So I thought 'I have some knowledge, I can read and write. Why don't I share it'. The kids also really wanted to read and

write, so we began with small informal literacy classes, which grew and grew. **Within a year the street children were asking to do state national exams, just like the other kids in the mainstream schools.**

So we began a school in the dormitory – it was the only place we could go. By night it was a bedroom and by day a classroom. We would push the furniture around, sit on the beds, and the kids would write on their laps. There was only one exercise book being used for all the subjects.

I realised that we needed a few more resources, so step by step I got help and

support. In the end we had a fully-fledged school, with teachers and everything. Then we had to resister the school as a legal entity so that the students would be able to take the national exams. But the authorities said they couldn't register us 'because sick children don't have good brains'. They told us that we could not take the state exams because we would lower standards in the district. However, I convinced them to give us a go and let us at least try. And they agreed. Then I went back to the school and motivated the kids to study really hard. When the examiners came they brought in harsh supervisors to make

91

sure no one was cheating. In the end we were the second-best school in the whole district. The results were so good that the majority of kids qualified for the good schools, and some are now in university. **Remember, these were street kids, often drug addicts, who were told that they did not have brains.** Because the school performed so well, many rich parents wanted to send their children to our school. **We didn't have modern facilities, but we were disciplined and focused.**

But then it struck me that the school was losing some of its sense of purpose. I knew I was doing a good job there **but the school was not really solving the problem of why there were street kids in the first place.** The street kids were becoming attached to the institution of the school, to the extent that when they were leaving, they were social misfits. **I felt there was something missing: a link between the home and the institution,** which is how I came up with the idea of Koinonia, 'doing it together'.

I realised that we needed to talk to the families to discover the root of the problem. It is a slow process. Families usually have more than one child, but if one child is on the streets you will find that it is only a matter of time before the others are too. The same reason that made one leave would make the others leave also. So by working with the families we try to break that cycle.

Over time you start to build trust and confidence, and they will start to tell you more about their circumstances. **Trust is very important. When you build it you have to keep it.**

So I started with a very small number, and am growing it gradually. I would like to see the model extended beyond Kenya. If this is handled well, no child will be found on the streets. And if no child is on the streets, families will be intact and will be taking care of their children. It is about moving away from putting children in institutions to empowering families.

The journey we have in life is not very long, and with the little time that we have, we must spend it wisely. I find joy in what I do now. I realise that I have a talent in motivating others, but I also know I need to share that talent. In this world, there is so much evil around, we should not add to it. The next generation should be a generation focused on caring for one another and asking about what value they too can add. None of us want to be drug addicts, or social misfits, and because none of us want it, we should do our best to prevent it. So explore your talents to the maximum and use them well. You don't know why you have them, and finding them can sometimes be an issue, but look for good role models – people who think differently – and they can help you to discover who you are.

I am who I am today because someone helped me, and I tried to emulate him. I would have been on the streets if I did not have him as a role model. I have realised that it is not how rich you are but how many people you have helped to become who they are which is important.

Diary extracts:
First Impressions of Uganda

Arrival

A long bus ride later, I arrived in Kampala. Winding though plush, rich lands – fertile, green and hilly – through tea plantations, rice plantations, open fields, maize crops, tropical forest. Past baboons, past basketball courts, past sugar factories, past banana plants. Then through the border, where the guards welcomed me into the country with a handshake. Oddly and beautifully the 'flip' between Kenya and Uganda was noticeable. The Ugandan side seems more open, less cultivated, and less populated. And as darkness crept in, I caught a sunset which hued the sky with a golden glow. I am excited to be in Uganda, my first time here. I am excited by its scenery, its people, its possibilities.

Breeds of Transport

Transport in Kampala is as abundant as the sunshine. It seems to have a language all of its own, and clones overnight.

On first sight of the taxi park, I thought it was a labyrinth without a solution. Surveying it from above, it looked like one mass of discordant white, and fear was holding me back from jumping in. But once I did, I realised there was actually a sophisticated order, and help came to direct me, much help. A charming woman selling hard-boiled sweets silently accompanied me to the taxi rank and made sure I was on the right track. Others made similar offers. Had they not, another man, wearing white gloves and an official-looking jacket, would have pointed out the right way.

'Taxis', by the way, are shared buses, 'specials' are taxis. There are metered taxis too, of the yellow New York variant. 'Boda Bodas', my favourite breed of transport, are either pushbikes or scooters which carry pillion passengers (at your own risk). Then there are also buses of various shapes, sizes and states of disrepair. 'De luxe' can mean anything from a box of rust with wheels to a fancy passenger coach with seats which belong to first class in an airplane. And somehow, somehow, they all manage to get around – just about.

The other day on a Boda it was a 'take your life in your hands' moment, as we negotiated the early morning traffic – across roundabouts, along footpaths, over curbs, around the potholes, weaving though the taxis, and the specials, and the cycles, and the mass of pedestrians, and perhaps a chicken or two. I gripped on tight, hair on the back of my neck strictly upright. Who needs white water rafting when you have rush hour in Kampala!?

You also find some funny things written on the back of buses in Uganda. My favourite: 'Rich men also cry'.

Snapshot: HIV/AIDS

There are 3 million deaths from HIV/AIDS alone each year globally; 33 million people are living with HIV/AIDS, including 2 million children. In 2007 alone, it is estimated that 2.7 million people became infected with the virus and 2 million died from HIV-related causes. Additionally, up to 400 million people are directly affected by the pandemic.

Young people (under 25) account for over half of all new HIV infections globally.

Fewer than 50 per cent of all people in this age group are properly educated about the risks they face.

Sub-Saharan Africa is more heavily infected with HIV/AIDS than anywhere else in the world. An estimated 22.5 million were infected at the end of 2007 and nearly 12 million children under the age of eighteen have been orphaned as a result of the pandemic. Some estimate that this will be as high as 20 million by 2010.

The disease is having a devastating impact on all aspects of society. Life expectancy averages 47 in the region. Many households are losing their income earners. Health sectors are under strain to meet treatment demands. Teachers, health workers, labourers and farmers are dying. Others have to be trained to replace them and demand on services is high. Overall the disease is having a negative impact on the African economy, struggling in its ability to cope with the epidemic.

ARVs: Antiretrovirals

Antiretroviral drugs are medications for the treatment of infection, primarily HIV. While they are not a cure for HIV, they have the potential to improve dramatically the health and extend the life expectancy of people infected. However, the high cost of the drugs (particularly branded drugs) has put them out of reach for millions of people who are in need of treatment. Nowhere is this more evident than in sub-Sarahan Africa.

The introduction of generic, non-branded ARVs has helped to reduce the cost of treatment radically. However, despite the lower costs, millions are still unable to afford the drugs and remain untreated. In 2007 for instance, the estimated number of new HIV infections was 2.5 times higher than the increase in the number of people on ARVs.

Peter Mugyenyi

Joint Clinical Research Council

www.jcrc.co.ug

Kampala, Uganda
Theme: Health/Medicine

Founded in 1991 to serve as a national AIDS research centre, Uganda's Joint Clinical Research Centre (JCRC) pioneered the use of antiretroviral drugs (ARVs) in Uganda and now provides treatment in more than fifty clinics across the country. Much of the growth of the centre has been down to the stoic efforts of Peter Mugyenyi who joined the centre as its first director. It was Peter's 'mover and shaker' antics that enabled ARVs to become affordable to the masses, and which, he joked, 'almost sent [him] to prison'.

When I was in my early twenties, way back in the late 1970s, I had to flee Idi Amin's regime. I had done my undergraduate studies at Makerere University in Kampala and had graduated as a doctor. I'd even been admitted to Makerere for postgraduate studies, but conditions were so bad I couldn't continue. So I just had to leave. I first went to Lesotho and from there to the UK. I worked in the National Health Service and qualified in Child Health in Glasgow Royal College of Physicians and Surgeons and the Royal College of Physicians of Ireland. I loved my time in Dublin. I practised in the northeast of England and also in south Wales. So I moved around a lot! Along the way I made my way up the medical ladder, working as a Senior House Officer, then as Registrar, and when

I left to go to Saudi Arabia, I was a Consultant. I spent some time in Saudi Arabia, helping to expand their child health services, but I really wanted to practise in my own country. So I saved some money and returned to Uganda.

I came back to Kampala in 1989. To be honest I didn't know that I would find and I was really shocked when I did come home. It was a time of chaos. There was some odd sort of silence about and things were not going so well. The infrastructure was in ruins. Even on the road from the airport there were potholes the size of craters. The road had been bombed during the war and had not been repaired. Cars were just zigzagging everywhere.

I started working as a paediatrician at a Mulago hospital in Kampala and was also put in charge of paediatric postgraduate training at the university. But the situation was appalling. Kids were very sick and hospital facilities were terrible. I saw a job advertised for a newly created AIDS research centre, but frankly, I didn't want to apply. I was engrossed with my work at Mulago – there was so much to do – and I had already started some research work on AIDS. **But the sheer horror of what I saw on my wards motivated me to do more.** One day one of my colleagues said 'have a look at the kids we are treating, almost all of them have AIDS, something more has to be done'. My colleague was right. I knew AIDS was killing our nation and something had to be done. While I was a bit hesitant to take the research job in the centre, I thought that the role would offer me better opportunities to work on AIDS, so I came here at the newly created Joint Clinical Research Centre in 1992. It was then I really started my AIDS work and I have never stopped since.

My instructions were Mission Impossible. 'People are dying. You must find us a solution. You must find us a cure for AIDS. This is what you are here for.' From there it gets kind of complex. My salary was 16,000 shillings, which was the equivalent of $6 or $7 a month. We had just a small centre with two studies running. We started looking for partners, raising funds and building infrastructure. I found myself wearing many hats: I was the clinician, the chief researcher and also the centre's manager. There were not many other staff: another doctor, an administrator, a financial administrator, and a couple

of nurses. During the day I would treat patients and in the evenings I would send faxes all around the world, looking for international funding and partners. One of the projects we won was a WHO [World Health Organisation] project to examine attitudes to HIV vaccines, to see if our population would accept them if available and to examine what effect the vaccines would have. We also carried out other studies on TB in relation to AIDS, and conducted some trials on western and traditional medicines. **I also had a role in getting antiretrovirals (ARVs) distributed in Uganda. In fact, it almost sent me to prison.**

You see, **I never accepted that ARVs were impossible to use here.** At the time, three reasons were given against the use of the drugs in Uganda. One, that we lacked the infrastructure; two, that we lacked human resources; and three, that we lacked sufficient distribution mechanisms. But from 1992 we started importing and using ARVs as they came onto the market in the West.

Funding was scarce and the drugs were expensive. We would charge a little more to the people who could afford them and use the money to subsidise drugs for those who couldn't. That way we were able to expand. In fact the centre became known as a pioneer in ARV use in Africa. At one stage we were treating more people with ARVs than the rest of the African continent and, by the late 1990s, we had a lot of people on treatment. Unfortunately these were mainly the rich or those who had sponsors. It was then that the generic drugs started to be developed

Peter Mugyenyi (Joint Clinical Research Council)

I have learned that a lot of things that are said to be impossible are very possible if determination and goodwill is there.

and we became one of the first to start importing them, and it was that which almost sent me to prison.

I'll explain: It was 2000 and South Africa had been taken to court by a consortium of thirty-nine pharmaceutical companies because they were considering use of generic drugs in the country. The controversy was raging and while all the media attention was on South Africa, I imported the generic drugs here, and nobody realised. I knew people would think this was not a wise step to take. First of all there was the patents law; secondly, the National Drug Authority wouldn't allow them past customs; and thirdly, you must be crazy to import a drug that had landed a more powerful country in court! However, if I had looked for a licence to import the drugs, I would have been laughed at, and if I had asked the government, they would have read me the riot act. So I just ordered the drugs and didn't tell anyone.

The drugs arrived from India into Entebbe Airport, Uganda's main airport. I immediately told the authorities to declare them to the National Drug Authority and the government. Without a licence to import, I knew the Drug Authority was bound to take action. I was breaking the law and I knew they were obliged to arrest me. But while the arrest papers were being processed, the Minister in the President's office heard about it and I was called in to his office for a crisis meeting . . . it was exactly what I hoped would happen.

At the meeting I was asked why I had imported the drugs. 'Look,' I said, 'a huge number of patients are being referred to me with HIV. I'm a physician and my job is to save lives. I know there are drugs available to do the job, so I have brought them here. They are waiting at the airport. I have not tried to smuggle them in. The ball is in your court, you have to take the decision.' I told the President that I hadn't used public money to buy the drugs, that I had fund-raised for them, and that it was his choice whether to send them back to India. 'However,' I added, 'I have brought them to you because there is a national crisis. People are dying in this country in huge numbers, and these drugs can save them.' Phew!

The Ugandan government knew there was an AIDS crisis; they had to confront it. At the meeting, the Drug Authority was asked if there was a legal clause under which the drugs could be imported. 'Of course there is', they said, 'there is an emergency clause. We have a state of emergency in this country, and under it, the drugs can be used.' They took out a little book and showed me the wording. 'You can have your drugs', they said. But immediately I said 'no, I can't take these drugs. Things are not as simple as that. If you import these drugs, I do not want to be back here next week or next month. I want a guarantee that from now onwards I will not be threatened or harassed, and that any drug that comes in to this country for the right reason is not going to be banned . . . So take your little book out again.' A while later they said 'under the same clause, you can have the drugs'. BINGO!

It caused a revolution in access to life-saving drugs. Immediately the numbers of patients who could afford the drugs shot up. That action saved thousands and thousands of lives.

But the story does not end there. About four or five days later, I got some 'visitors', who were just 'passing in the neighbourhood' – of course, they were representatives from the pharmaceutical companies. It was hilarious because normally they would introduce themselves by flashing cards and shiny brochures, but on this occasion they didn't even introduce themselves as being from the pharmaceuticals.

'We understand that you have imported generics', they said. 'We are in the neighbourhood and thought we should just pass by.'

'Welcome', I said, 'what can I do for you?'

'We heard that you imported the generic drugs.'

'Yes.'

'Are you aware that South Africa is in court?'

'Yes, I am very much aware.'

'And you went ahead and imported them?'

'Yes.'

'Well, that was not a very wise thing to do. But we are not here to make any kinds of threats.'

'Well, that is great.' I explained the reason why I imported the generics. 'Our people are dying in huge numbers. These drugs are for them. We are trying to save some lives here.'

'How much did you pay for the drugs?'

I told them.

'Well, then', they said, 'there is no need to import the drugs from India, we will match their price.'

And I simply said 'thank you very much'.

It was smiles all around, but as soon as they were out, I was on the phone again to India. 'Guys, your cost has been matched.'

'Then', they said, 'we will halve our cost.'

'Well, that is wonderful news!'

So then the situation was never the same. The cost of generics kept coming down. The price was still high for most Ugandans, but at least middle-income people and some farmers could afford treatment and could survive.

From then on I continued the campaign. I ended up being one of the people who testified in the US Congress about the need for ARVs, and I was part of a delegation who met with special White House committees about requesting the US to approve funding for AIDS. Later on the US President announced the Global Fund for the treatment of HIV/AIDS, malaria and other diseases.

By this stage we knew that HIV/AIDS treatment was feasible in Uganda. We knew how to give it and how to train the people. Our main constraint had been funds. So when we got the grant, we quickly started expanding our practices. There are now over fifty clinics in all parts of the country, reaching people in their local areas. We have managed to put a laboratory in each region, so doctors don't need to send blood samples to us in Kampala any more. Now we are trying to reach sustainability. We don't believe that Uganda should be in the hands of donors, or that people can live forever on handouts. We strongly believe that we should build a self-sustaining health system, which relies on increasing our local capacity. We also know that 'free' is not best practice. Giving free drugs is OK for the moment because we have a catastrophic emergency – and in an emergency you have to do what you can – but our programme encourages those who can pay to pay, and those who can make only a small contribution to do so.

I don't want to make it seem that things just flowed smoothly and effortlessly: they didn't! **I have had so many frustrations. The biggest was watching people die in huge numbers: dying a death I knew I could prevent only if I had the resources.** That was mental torture. As a physician, I knew the treatment was there, but I couldn't get access it to it. The second biggest frustration was the incredible greed of the pharmaceutical companies. I appreciated that pharmaceutical companies needed to make some returns but **I believe that trade has to have some ethics whereby profits are not prioritised over lives.** I also had to go all over the world convincing people that AIDS treatment was possible in Africa. People said AIDS treatment in Africa was impossible, so we had to prove them wrong. We had to learn to do things ourselves, and to trust in ourselves, and above all, as physicians, to have compassion.

I have learned that a lot of things that are said to be impossible are very possible if determination and goodwill is there. There are a lot of people of goodwill all over the world. Building partnerships with others has helped us. I suppose my life has been about how to save lives, especially of the poor, and to make the life-saving drugs more accessible. I have learned how important it is to **have a cause in life.** You need to have one you believe in. I think it is important because it will discipline you to attain success in whatever area you choose. It doesn't matter whatever field you are in, see it through, and don't let difficulties distract. I have not yet succeeded – the problem is still very serious, especially as the cost of drugs still limits access – but I remain focused. I can say that a difference has been made, not by me alone, but by all of us who have worked on the problem consistently and persistently.

For us it became Mission Possible.

Trevor Dudley

The Kampala Kids League and The Kids League

www.kampalakidsleague.org

Kampala, Uganda

Themes: Sports, Education

Kampala Kids League (KKL), and The Kids League (TKL) were set up by Trevor Dudley to help to improve children's lives through sport. As a result thousands of children have taken part in sports across the country.

Trevor, a keen sports fan, quit his job as a quantity surveyor to run KKL full-time. He could see that sport in Uganda was in a dire state. Pitches were being handed over to make way for shopping centres or hotels and, in an effort to increase academic standards, new schools were being built without sports grounds. Realising the benefits of sport in his own education, Trevor saw a need to promote a balanced education. And so emerged the idea for the leagues, which despite continued funding challenges have grown with the commitment of players, their parents, community volunteers and the financial backing of some local corporate sponsors.

But for Trevor the leagues are about more than just sport. They create an opportunity to promote positive health messages and bring children from different social and cultural groups together who would otherwise not mix. Street children play alongside children from the wealthier neighbourhood, tribe plays with tribe and religion with religion. Irrespective of the label, the sports field is open to all.

Since beginning in 1993 over 14,000 children and 3,000 volunteers have taken part in a wide range of sporting tournaments, including football, basketball and cricket, in Kampala. The success of the organisation in the capital has given rise to further leagues nationwide, as far as the conflict area of Gulu in the north. Leagues have even taken place in Uganda's notorious refugee camps and such expansion nationwide has enabled a further 25,000 children to participate.

But the story gets better: Trevor, seeing huge talent coming through the leagues, realised a need to channel this talent to help players fulfil their sporting potential. So started the talented Kids League, in which the cream

of the soccer crop were given further training and coaching. Every year since 2002, KKL have been taking a team to the International Youth World Cup – and they have won it five times, and counting.

I learned so much on the sports field that I would never have learned in the classroom. I went to grammar school in Nottingham, UK, which promoted the benefits of a balanced education with both academics and sport. They worked us hard in the classroom but we also got to play lots of sport. I was captain of the school cricket team and I still play cricket to this day in Uganda. It was those schooldays that showed me the potential benefits of leadership and teamwork through sport.

After school I qualified as a quantity surveyor and also met and married my wife, Ann, and we had a son, Mark. In 1979, when I hit thirty, we were given an opportunity to work in Africa. Both parents and friends thought we were crazy to even consider accepting a job in Kenya. But one afternoon I went to visit my gran who surprisingly said, 'Go for it – in 1925 I turned down a job as a nurse overseas. Ever since then, I have regretted that decision.' That's why we are here today.

We lived in Nairobi for three years and really enjoyed ourselves. In 1982 there was an attempted coup, which disrupted the building projects I was working on and we had to leave Kenya. We moved to Jordan to work on the new international airport. While there, our son, who was five, joined an American-style Little League soccer programme and the organisers asked me to be a coach. I hadn't any experience but I went along anyway. I found out that I thoroughly enjoyed coaching. The experience again showed me how powerful sports can be – even for really young children. I could see the power of allowing kids of different nationalities to mix together through sport.

After three years in Jordan we went to Tanzania, where I worked for two years. Then the company I was with in Nairobi asked if I would reopen their office in Kampala. This was 1988. Uganda had just suffered twenty years of chaos under Idi Amin and Obote but things were now settling down.

The key for any social entrepreneur is once you've identified a problem to convert it to a challenge. Challenges can be overcome. To overcome you've got to have passion and enthusiasm to take it forward.

Kampala was a derelict city then but when I visited I was immediately struck by how warm and friendly everyone was, even after twenty years of the most horrendous war. So Uganda it was. There was a lot of work to do.

It was tough initially in Kampala. We had a hard time finding a school for our daughter Lauren (who had been born in Jordan). My wife got a job at a local school and we sent our daughter there. There were also lots of shortages – it could take two days to find bread, for example, and there were very few facilities. But it wasn't as dangerous as we were led to believe, and all these years later we're still here and still loving it.

I spent the first two years in Uganda with that company. Afterwards, I found a local business partner and we started our own company. We were always busy. Hospitals and schools needed renovating and then as economic confidence grew new commercial development took off. My wife, in the meantime, loved working in the school and obtained a teaching qualification. She now runs The Acorns School, an international pre-school here.

In 1997 things started to change in my life. I was volunteering, helping gap-year students from the UK at the time – working with seventeen-year-olds, who had come out to Uganda to volunteer on projects, mainly at schools. I used to visit schools to help find programme placements for them. On one visit I asked a headmaster about sports education. I learnt that since the President had pledged free primary education for all in his election manifesto the average class size had risen from 40 to over 100. There now was no time for sports with the overworked teachers under pressure to improve academic results.

Coupled with this, sports standards at a national level were declining because of mismanagement and corruption. Ugandans love sports and people were so disappointed with this trend. I could see the life being squeezed out of sports from both ends. Health in Uganda was also likely to suffer if sports were not a positive part of the education system. Everyone agreed something should happen, but I realised no one was going to do anything about it. So I started to develop some ideas based on my experience with the Little League programmes in Jordan. I sat down with a good friend of mine, Lesley Magnay, and we thrashed around a few ideas, working out how best to set it up.

There's always a bit of luck in these things. Around this time Stanbic Bank (one of the main banks in Uganda)

appointed a new managing director. It turned out that he was an old friend of mine who had sponsored a bank team from my Jordan days. We went out for dinner and I asked him if his bank would be willing to sponsor the new league. Because he knew exactly what I was talking about he said yes. That got us $1,000 and the impetus to open our own bank account and do the legal work to get us started as a voluntary association. And that was the beginning of the Kampala Kids League (KKL). We then got five or six people together and established the framework for what we wanted to do. We used the guidelines from Jordan as a template, adapting the model to Uganda. We visited schools to ask what they wanted. Most of the kids wanted soccer, and most schools said they would support the initiative. Some schools were suspicious that sports would 'interfere' with academics. We did surveys to find out when we should hold the sports and listened to what parents and the schools needed. Parents thought it was a wonderful idea.

The final piece we needed was

the sponsors and financial support to pull off the programme. We wanted certificates, free uniforms for kids, and all the equipment. It worked out to be around $50 per child, which was far too expensive for most of the parents. Having already persuaded Stanbic to provide start-up costs, we wanted to secure additional corporate donors. I realised that you have to become a beggar to get something like this off the ground. I had never done that before. I spent three months knocking on all kinds of doors and they were all very reluctant initially, some were quite rude. They thought we were crazy but my friend and I were eventually able to talk them into it. We had staked our own personal reputations to get the money, so we knew we had to succeed!

The press loved the League. Local soccer was in a disastrous situation and it was horribly corrupt. There was a lot of negative press about it. The media were desperate for something positive, and so there was an article about our kids' programme in the papers almost every week. The sponsors were absolutely delighted.

Season by season it grew. We got feedback from the kids and found that basketball and baseball were also popular, so we expanded the range of sports. Baseball turned out to be too expensive to run, but basketball was a big hit. And, in the last few years, we introduced cricket to KKL. We were so proud when the International Cricket Council [ICC] gave KKL the award for the best junior cricket programme in Africa in 2006.

Over 14,000 boys and girls from over 180 schools, orphanages and street children's organisations have taken part in 55 different seasons of sports in Kampala, supported by over 2,000 volunteers and 160 different sponsors. It has exceeded our expectations in so many ways.

Sport is such a powerful means of not only getting kids to run and kick a ball, but of bringing people together and breaking down barriers. **We just wanted to encourage them to play sport, but the social changes that have occurred are unbelievable.** The barriers that existed – class differences, religious beliefs, tribal or race barriers, etc. – are being broken down. Also 10–15 per cent of children in KKL are orphans or street children. So the teams are really diverse. **You might have an ambassador's child or a minister's child playing on the same team as a child who slept on the street the night before.** And in a matter of hours, they're all friends. The kids don't notice this type of thing, and you realise it's the parents you are educating in social change. This reinforced the power of sports for me – sport is a powerful tool in improving kids' lives.

The standard of play is not high in KKL as we follow a philosophy of allowing all kids to play regardless of skill, which means even children with disability get a chance to play. However, we observed that some kids were really talented and they lamented that they had nowhere else to go. There were no sports youth structures in Uganda at that time to encourage and support talent. So we gave some talented under-

13 kids additional training and support and found a very good coach. In 2002, we decided to see how good they were and we carefully prepared a team and took the kids to a tournament in Denmark. They won!

They then moved on to Sweden to play in the biggest youth tournament in the world – the Gothia Cup. This was mammoth. Over 200 teams competing in our category alone! We thought if we could finish in the top 16 we would make Ugandans proud. But we had underestimated the power of our team. Our captain and goalie, Benjamin Ochan, asked me as we stood in the middle of the magnificent Ullevi Stadium in Gothenburg, in front of 45,000 people for the opening ceremony, 'Mr Trevor, how do we get to play football in this stadium?' I had to tell him the sad news that only the final would be played there. Benjamin then said 'it's OK, Mr Trevor, we will win all our games and we will be back here next week'. He had planned it all and went off to tell his team. One week later we stood once again in Ullevi Stadium as, true to his word, KKL had won all their seven games and had stormed the final to play the might of FC Copenhagen. Seventy minutes later KKL were Gothia world youth champions after a nerve-wracking penalty shoot-out. **They came back as heroes!** Not only had they won, but they had won well, becoming known as 'the team that plays football with a smile on its face'. They became great ambassadors for Uganda.

On our return, the World Health Organisation [WHO] flew our team around the country to promote a measles immunisation campaign. It was unbelievable. Over 10,000 people were turning up to greet these little kids who had become such perfect role models and peer ambassadors promoting health and education awareness. The Ministry of Health followed us around and they ran out of vaccine as kids rushed to get the medicine that had helped create strong and healthy world champions. WHO told us it was one of the most successful campaigns they had ever run. All that gave me the spur to expand the programme nationally. I retired from my business to devote full-time to developing the programme. We set up a non-profit NGO called The Kids League (TKL) Uganda and a registered charity in the UK, Kids League Foundation (KLF).

My wife says she has never seen me happier than when I was developing KKL and TKL. **I have learned that passion and drive are important for success, and by tapping into my passion for sport I've been able to drive the organisation forward.** We have been expanding the programme into other districts in the country, including working in refugee camps where a lot of the children are not in school. In Gulu, for instance over 20 per cent of the kids in our programmes are ex-child soldiers, ex-abductees, have known conflict trauma or have witnessed some unimaginable atrocities. We have seen that by allowing these children to mix with others, to make friends with children their age, sport has had a tremendous impact on them and has helped peace-building within communities.

We have also been using sport as a way of getting the message across to both children and their parents that health and education are important. **Sport has changed parents' perception of education.** We want to continue using sport to encourage people to go to school. And a great thing about this model is that **it can be replicated, both nationally and internationally.** So maybe one day we will expand beyond Uganda but I first want to make sure that the programme here is sustainable. To make it a success we need to guarantee quality over quantity. The important thing is to keep growth slow – be conservative when expanding and keep quality high. At the moment we're happy to grow at a reasonable rate and grow from our experiences. We're making sure that our programmes take into account the feedback of the people that matter.

Listening to people has been one of the most important things for us. We have had to be tolerant and patient, making sure that as many people as possible are involved in the programme and have ownership over it. That way real solutions to problems will be discovered.

I would recommend that young people take a gap year and work overseas. When I first came overseas I learned so much in my first year. I learned a lot about the need for patience. Many people come from Europe and they want to change the world in a day. But you learn that it takes time.

The key for any social entrepreneur is once you've identified a problem to convert it to a challenge. Challenges can be overcome. To overcome you've got to have passion and enthusiasm to take it forward. So many things will try to pull you back. So you have to have patience and resilience. If you have the passion, it will come across in your face, in the way you talk, and in the way you enthuse others. That way you can inspire thousands and encourage good ideas to grow.

I'm positive about what I'm doing and I believe in what I'm doing. I unearthed a problem, I converted it to a challenge and by listening to people I think I've found a good solution. I'm just so pleased that this opportunity has come along, has given me something which has obviously been building up in me for over thirty years and which has given me more satisfaction that I could ever hope for in life.

Without doubt I have to thank my wife and children who have watched this crazy man give up a comfortable job to dive into the insecure roller-coaster ride that donor-driven non-profit programmes provide. Their support has always been unwavering even in times of need. When my wife and I left England we initially wanted to do two years on each continent, working our way around the world. But I suppose we got stuck in Africa. Maybe one of these days I'll pull up my roots and start heading around the world, but only once I feel I have achieved everything I want to do here.

Ian Clarke

International Hospital Kampala
(part of the International Medical Group, Uganda)

www.img.co.uk

Kampala, Uganda
Themes: Health/Medicine, Business

There is a gentle Northern Irish lilt to Dr Ian Clark's voice. It's a voice that belongs to the hills of Bangor or the wards of City Hospital in Belfast. But instead, choices and chances have led him to Uganda, where he has set up a private hospital, International Hospital Kampala (IHK), aiming to raise the standard of health care and diversify medical practice across the country. Despite twenty years in Uganda, the accent is still there: a reminder of his roots even among the red, dusty streets of Kampala.

IHK is now at the stage of attracting private sector sponsorship to support a charitable ward, 'Hope Ward', so that people who cannot afford the services can still have access to them. There are also plans for a medical university, to raise the bar in training and to expand clinical services regionally. It is also part of a larger medical group that includes: International Air Ambulance, the Ugandan Health Management Institute, International Hospital of Nursing and the International Medical Foundation.

I was a GP in Ireland, living in Bangor. When I was a medical student I always imagined I would do surgery, but by the time I qualified I was fed up studying and so decided to go into general practice. However, even though I had a good income, I soon got bored. So I started a business, running a bookshop, which got me into retailing. Afterwards I started craft shops and then furniture shops – as one does if you are a doctor! I had a farming background, and I suppose I was used to doing things with my hands. In retail it was certainly 'hands on'. Looking back now, I think I should have gone down the surgical route in medicine, because **I am the sort of person who needs to be able to see what I do.**

After some time, I don't know how many years, I was overtrading in the business (and running out of cash flow), so I had to cut back. I had about six shops, which I had to reduce down

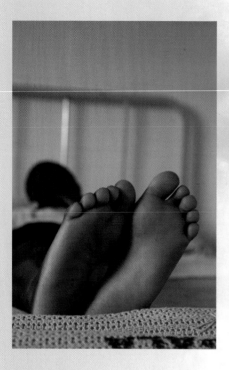

to one. That was the hardest bit of business experience I have ever had, but it was also really good for me. I realised that I could either trade myself out of business, which is very difficult, or I could close down. I had too much pride to close down, so I just worked twenty-five hours a day until I got the business turned around. I think it was in that context – of having to work very hard and having to turn a business around – when I said to myself 'so what is this all about? What am I doing this for?' At that time I was a strong Christian believer and I believed that we are all here to make a difference. I suppose I have always had a sense of destiny, that my life should have significance and I should make a difference.

By my early thirties I was married and had three kids. We had an overtly middle-class lifestyle – two cars, kids

in private schools and so on. But I was starting to question, 'is this what I really want? Is this what I want to do?' I think it is common for a lot of people in their early thirties to begin to question the direction of their lives. So both my wife, Robbie, and I began to think about making a major transition, exploring the possibility of doing something beyond that existence.

It initially resulted in a two-week trip to Uganda. A contact from our church was visiting Uganda, so I just decided to tag along on the trip and explore options here. Uganda would not have been our first choice but when I visited, my heart was really touched by the medical need that I witnessed. I had been dipping in and out of medicine in the eight or nine years before that and then suddenly I saw there was all this need. So I said 'this is it, if I want to be a doctor, this is the place to be one'.

Life in Uganda was hugely different from Bangor suburbia. Although we did not get here until 1988, the country still felt very much like 'post-war'. In fact, it was like nothing had happened since the war. There were skulls and an eerie silence and there was all this need.

We were supposed to be in Uganda for two years, but we kept extending our time here. But after about five to six years I developed cancer. It turned out to be testicular cancer, with secondaries around my body. I went back to Ireland for treatment, and when I saw the X-rays myself, I thought it was fatal. For a week I was totally sure that it was the end of my life – so it was a very interesting week! I remember saying to myself 'if I am going to die now, at least I have fulfilled something which I think is worthwhile and in line with my faith'. So it wasn't all bad, but I really thought it was the end of the line for me. After a week I got a CT scan, and the news was brighter. I went through treatment. It was very nasty but somehow I came through it. However, after that experience I was not sure I could ever go back and be a GP again in Northern Ireland. I felt I had all this valuable experience of working in a post-war situation, with the rural poor, with HIV/AIDS. Why would I waste all that?

After my illness Robbie said I began to get a bit more stubborn and more determined to return to Uganda. I decided to do a master's in public health in London, at the School of Hygiene and Tropical Medicine. So we sold up our house in Ireland and moved over to England. Then we came back to Uganda. At first I took a six-month job in Kampala, in what was called 'the surgery' – it was essentially an expatriate practice attached to the British embassy. But within six months I realised that this was not really for me; that although I was back in Uganda, it was not enough. It was around this time when I decided that my goal was to start a hospital in Kampala and to raise medical standards. However, instead of targeting the rural poor, where we had initially been working, I would target the emerging middle-income group in Uganda, and use the money raised to upgrade the overall medical services. It was a way to improve the overall level and delivery of services. So I thought **'if I raise the bar**

then it is going to have a ripple effect on medical services across the country'. So I had a **very definite vision** of what I was doing and I did not make any apologies for shifting from working with the rural poor to now working with urban middle income. There was a larger strategy at play.

When I was in Luwero (the first place I worked) our model aimed to bring hope. When I shifted to Kampala our core value was about making a difference to the health services in Uganda. Now those two things have started to merge for me because if you are making a difference you are bringing hope to people as well.

However, about six years on, my plans got interrupted again. The cancer had returned. So, in the middle of developing a small hospital, I had to return to Ireland and get more treatment. The treatment was again quite nasty but I came through. After I had the second bout of cancer I was fairly wild. Robbie said that while I was determined the first time, the second time I was absolutely determined to continue my work. It was an interesting time for me personally, including in my marriage. But interestingly, I don't think any of my difficulties shifted my belief in my destiny, my belief in humanity and a belief that I had a role to play in making life better for other people. **I have a very strong belief in people, and I think it is my belief in people that enables me to do what I do.**

We returned to Uganda. When I came back, I picked up the pieces of my practice and eventually got this small hospital going which gradually grew. We developed more clinics and a local medical insurance company, then this hospital, which has grown into quite a large organisation, with over 500 people.

And my work here is good fun. Of course, it can be quite stressful at times but I really believe that the hospital has had an impact on the systems here. **We have shown that you can be in a Third World country, but that the services do not have to be third rate.** My idea has been that if you develop the best you can with the resources you have, then you are sending out the message to other hospitals in the region that, at the very least, health centres should be clean. It is about setting an example. Many Ugandans have never had any medical training, and so they don't fully understand minimum standards. But when given training, they are really excellent and can deliver great services. That is one of the things I find so exciting about my work here – working with the people. We are developing young talent and skills. I am in this for the development of the people. That is what really gives me a kick. And I couldn't do it on my own. Unless I had people around me who believed in me and what we are doing, we would not be where we are today.

So, as part of that training, we have also started a nursing school and a Ugandan health management institute. We have also developed the charitable Hope Ward, so people who can't afford our services can still access them. There was one woman, for example, who had

been leaking urine for twenty-three years. She attended the Hope Ward and we were able to solve the problem. Being able to facilitate that is so good.

This work is difficult and takes time. I have learned that you don't give up and you don't expect to make huge strides at once. You just keep going through them incrementally, step by step. Then you look around after a few years and see the progress you have made. A lot of our success has been about being able to bring people along with us, people who believe in the vision of the hospital.

Life is a journey, and people find themselves at different stages of their lives at different ages. I think your life can be in seasons. It varies according to the person, and I don't think there is one formula for it. Some people are very focused and know what they want, whereas others don't discover it until later in life. My father died when I was nine, and I think that when I was younger I could have done with a bit more direction in my life. It took me a while, but I did find myself. **It may have been a bit of a circuitous route but I think it was worth it.** If someone feels they are just meandering and drifting in life, then I think they should keep reviewing what they are doing. But at some stage we've got to ask ourselves where we are going.

My own questioning led me to Uganda, and now I think I have found my home here.

Blog extract:
Further westwards the road continues

I have been on the road again, moving westwards. First to a town called Hoima, then to a smaller town called Kagadi, followed by a visit to the verdant Fort Portal near the Congolese border.

The bus journey to Kagadi resembled more of a roller-coaster ride than a bus ride. Red dust spewing from all sides, sending pedestrians in all directions. A live chicken on the seat in front of me. 'Shake your Bootie to the Name of Jesus' playing on the radio. Me, with my fingers crossed, hoping I make it.

From the window alone I have been learning. Watching how a whole family can squeeze onto a boda boda, or a whole community into a Toyota Corolla. Seeing how bunches of bananas are carried on bicycles. Seeing the transition from wattle and mud housing structures to local brick. Noticing that when tarmac comes, so too do little shops, more residents, more businesses.

Driving through tea plantations was a novelty. Their green seems to ripen the land. The order of the fields, each squared off into plots of equal size and looking as if they are hovering on the undulating hills, filled me with a sense of calm. Learning that the tea pickers get on average €0.13 per kilo of tea picked, however, did not.

But whatever the conditions, this place – its scenery, greenery and people – is nothing short of beautiful, and it is that which shouts 'return' to me.

Mwalimu Musheshe

Uganda Rural Development Training

www.urdt.net

Kagadi, Uganda

Theme: Education

Kagadi, a small town in Western Uganda, may be off the beaten track, but what is happening there in the form of Uganda Rural Development and Training (URDT), has more than a few things to show 'mainstream' development.

'Awakening the sleeping genius in each of us' heads the administration building, a motto filtering through all its programmes. Established in 1987 through the visionary leadership of Mwalimu Musheshe, URDT is based on a belief that individuals, when connected with their own goals and visions, are motivated to develop both themselves and their environment. They believe that only when the development process moves from 'reactive' to 'creative', and when people are viewed as 'active' rather than 'passive', will lasting change take place. URDT facilitates this planning at a village and individual level, and has built up a host of complementary projects to support the vision.

The programmes are designed to demonstrate the interrelationship between the various development disciplines, including: health, education, nutrition, sanitation, rural technologies, and income generation. Included are the following: a Land and Human Rights Centre, where the local community can gain access to legal information; a community radio station, broadcast to over 4 million people; an institute for Business, Vocational and Media Studies, with a demonstration farm, irrigation and solar technologies, bike and car maintenance, carpentry workshops, a mill, a large resource library, an Internet café, a 'green belt' around the campus, and a cultural museum; a girls' secondary school, specifically targeting marginalised and disadvantaged girls in the district. There are also plans in place to set up a rural university.

It took a while to track down Mwalimu, and figure out where Kagadi actually was. I couldn't locate it on any maps and nobody I spoke to in

Kampala knew where it was. But persistence paid off. After lots of emails and phone calls I did eventually get to speak to Mwalimu, who gave me directions: 'east to Hoima, south on the road to Fort Portal. Get off the bus when you see the big radio tower.' Sure enough, there was the tower, and I was very glad to have stepped off that bus.

We started URDT back in 1988 with a view that development can be very different from the stereotype of 'people are poor, let us help them'. Our motto instead reads 'Awakening the sleeping genius in each of us'. We believe that people have inherent wisdom and power within but they sometimes need help to discover and unleash it. That really is what we are doing here: we are endeavouring to create a centre of excellence by tapping into the experiences of the rural communities. We use their experiences to inform our plans, curriculum and community interventions.

When I was younger, I was always involved in school programmes and I **engaged in all kinds of sports. If there is anywhere you learn about how to deal with others, how to collaborate, how to build teams, it is on the sports field.** I used to have a lot of leadership roles among my peers, as a games captain or prefect. As a footballer, I learnt that it is about the team winning and not the individual. All of those things helped me to learn about people and the challenges of leadership.

I became a student leader at university, on the students' guild council and chairman of the student's hostel,

I believe the way we think determines the way we act. If you think you are powerless, you act powerless, if you think you are powerful you act powerful. It is all in the mind.

but some of my opinions got me in a lot of trouble. In 1980 a group of us were opposed to rigged elections and wanted to make the point that they were wrong. We believed that rigged elections were messing up democracy and that older politicians were teaching the younger generation that stealing was acceptable. 'If you teach someone to steal an election', I argued, 'where do you stop? Stealing is stealing. Rigging elections is not acceptable.' For that I was arrested and imprisoned for thirteen months in Mbuya military barracks, simply for challenging the elections and opportunistic politics. **It was an experience which really got me questioning how to change the whole system, and to see what I could do for society.**

After I was released I went back to university and trained as an agricultural engineer but by this the time I was really looking critically at other philosophies and was seriously thinking about what I could do. I started to work as a student volunteer in the villages of Kahunge, in the then Kabarole District, which is where a lot of the URDT model emerged from. I now tell people that I

went as a student volunteer to the village and never came back!

Before starting this I noticed that solving community problems in Africa was done mostly by external 'professionals'. They would arrive into communities and say 'there is a problem with this, let me fix it'. But it was a knee-jerk approach to development. Once a given crisis was over, they would relax and wait for another crisis. This is not sustainable development. I believe you can only talk about sustainable development when the community you are trying to develop are involved, and that they have a vision for their own development. So instead of a reactionary development model we help people to clarify their aspirations. We help them to crystallise their own visions for what they want to achieve for themselves and for their communities, and keep them in touch with those visions until they are realised. That tension between where they are now and where they want to be is the essence of the creative process.

We have developed a process for doing this, which involves shifting people from doing development as robots to doing development very consciously. We call it a 'visionary approach to development'. We try to help people to identify the reasons for their actions. We ask people 'what do you want to create for yourself, your family, for your community, for your country, and what will propel you to get what you really want?' We have found it to be a very powerful method for motivating people.

Historically, development is compartmentalised. People are agriculturalists, or health officers, or environmentalists – each working on separate projects. But this is not how families and communities are organised or operate, at least in Uganda. In a typical village here, a single household produces its own food and sells the excess in markets. So they are both agriculturalists and sales people. If a child in the home becomes sick, a family member will go to the bush and get some herbs to make medicine. So they also have local health expertise. In fact, they are experts in so many areas.

So the challenge for us was to develop individuals who have a holistic approach to development and to make connections between their areas of knowledge. That is what was lacking in our development process: the connections. We want communities to appreciate the interconnectedness of the issues and different disciplines of education, so that in their villages they will see the links between health and agriculture and education, and try to solve their own problems and create change in an interconnected way. I suppose we are trying to change the

way people see and think about issues. If you do not have a broader view of the important connections between issues, you will never see them, and the problems will remain unsolved.

So we use a process which first tries to change the way people think about their communities and future, and then help them to act. **I believe the way we think determines the way we act. If you think you are powerless, you act powerless; if you think you are powerful you act powerful. It is all in the mind.**

So that is why we try to make people more aware of the issues. But we also know that **awareness alone is not enough for change.** Smokers, for example, are aware that smoking causes cancer, but they still smoke. Drivers are aware that speed kills, but they still speed. So we try to create an environment where people move from just being aware of the problem to being able to take action. We call it 'consciousness raising', where consciousness is acute awareness plus action.

To achieve all this we have what we call 'Community Action Planning'. We work at a village level to help individuals develop a vision for their community. 'If the situation could change at all, what would it look like?' Whatever response they give, we then ask 'why?' Somebody may say that they want to build a good house, for example, but by asking them why, you learn that what they really want is a secure environment so they can be healthy. Through this process they learn that having a house alone will not guarantee their health, and that they may also have to develop their farm for food, for instance. By working in this way people start seeing the interconnectedness of issues.

The next step in the process is to connect the situation they are currently in – their current reality – to their desired state or vision. When you do this people start to see a discrepancy between what they have and what they want. Because of the discrepancy, they then also want to do something about it. That is where the structural planning actually begins: looking at what actions need to be taken. We don't do the planning for them, but **we facilitate the process of planning so they become change agents in their own lives.**

As we were developing this model, we also started noticing a high number of school dropouts in the region. Dropouts of today are the illiterate adults of tomorrow and if we do not intervene the cycle will simply perpetuate.

The idea of developing a rural university came in 1987. Back then the idea of a rural managed and focused university seemed like a crazy idea to many. At the time there was only one university outside the 'clutches' of the government and there was certainly no private education sector. But we could see a need for rural-based education, particularly for girls.

We had the idea of a rural university, which would develop local people to act as change agents in their communities. We also saw that girls are the first ones to drop out of school – especially if they are from very poor families. We wanted to do something about it before it got out of hand. We know that being

poor economically does not mean that you are poor in the brain. We wanted to identify bright girls who have an interest in education but who did not have sufficient opportunity because they are from marginalised families. So we developed a primary and secondary school for girls, which would act as a catchment model for the university. Alongside the school is a vocational institute teaching business, engineering, development programmes, and media studies.

Our system here is a little different to standard school. When the girls come we don't give them the same curriculum that has led to the big army of unemployed in Uganda. We educate both for the future and for now. We have dubbed the model 'two generational' because both girls and their parents are involved. The 'home-grown' curriculum focuses on issues that are relevant in the girls' homes – growing crops or looking after their health. At the end of each term the parents come to the school and the girls share some of their learning with them. This way it is helping to change the role of the girl child in the family. In a patriarchal society like this one, girls are at the lowest rung of the ladder. However, we are showing that girls are capable and should be respected. When the parents come here and see the girls speaking with authority they start to value their child more, and they begin to make plans with their children.

Essentially our model is about developing a critical mass of women as entrepreneurs, as leaders, as visionaries, as technologists, to enable communities

to get out of the malaise of poverty.

Developing the right values is a starting point for everyone. Values about life, peace, justice, relationships. Values are like your anchor in life, which will help you make all your other decisions. Secondly is the law of transcendence: to love oneself enough to allow yourself to love others. Many people do not love themselves sufficiently. I believe it is why we live in fear and suspicion and why we don't trust others. So to me, if people can transcend that fear and be open to different possibilities, they have the possibility to have meaningful lives.

Also I tell the girls here to 'get out of your jackets and start searching'. In most cases we have prejudices, for example,

that men should not do secretarial work. I think we should get out of those 'jackets' and expose ourselves to different skills and be open to building different knowledge bases, whether we are male or female. Exploring differences is so important. **It was really by accident that Columbus landed in America, but at least he set sail on the ship.** So people have to learn to set sail. It takes vision, commitment and courage. The values are the anchor or the rudder. Once you make fundamental choices at the value level, all other choices are based on that. These are a starting point.

So, set sail.

Travels through East Africa

The next phase of my travels brought me back to Nairobi, then down to Mombasa in Southern Kenya. From there it was on to Dar es Salaam in Tanzania, with a hop over to Zanzibar, and then into Mozambique, stopping in the towns of Beira, Chimoia, Vilanculos, and the capital, Maputo.

There were fewer interviews on this stretch. Partly intentionally (as I wanted to attend the Zanzibar film festival) and partly unintentionally. A bout of food poisoning in Mombasa meant I had to lie low for some time and the delay meant that some of the people I wanted to meet up with in Maputo were not in town when I was passing through. Despite having tried to pin down interview times it was somewhat frustrating to travel all that way and end up missing people by a couple of days. But that is the nature of travel. Sickness at some point along the line is likely and you can't plan it all. During this stretch I was learning to go with the flow and learn through observation, particularly in Mozambique, as these blog extracts recall . . .

The Darker Side of Innocence

It is a harsh reality when you start to question the motivation of children. Walking around the market in Vilanculos, a coastal town about ten hours by bus south of Beira, I met a group of kids and started chatting and joking. They loved my camera – particularly seeing their image on the digital screen. They started dancing and singing, and on the surface looked all sweet and innocent. However, it turned out that they were drunk, sharing beer between them. The oldest was no more than twelve. Then one pinched my wallet!

I did not lose much money, but my trust in there being a chance for childhood here has been robbed. Kids have to be streetwise to survive. Petty crime must seem like an easy option. All across the country I have seen small kids selling everything from pineapples to plastic bags on the streets. In all of central Mozambique, I did not see one school. I know that there are some, but they are few and far between. I hear that functional literacy is at about 10 per cent. Life expectancy averages around thirty. About one in three are HIV-positive.

This country is at the raw end of challenge. For these kids, what little future they have is uncertain. I will not condone what they did, but I have been trying to put myself in their shoes. Can I really be so self-righteous to say I would not do such a thing? No, I don't think so.

Had I not met people along the way on this journey who are working to change the system, working on the solutions, then I would be in a sorry state by this stage. The problems are vast, but there are people working on the solutions. I do still think that change is possible here, but it requires more people, with more commitment, who are willing to challenge the way things work. This particularly means local people who understand the system and will not tolerate the corruption that is rife in Mozambique. Do they exist? Well, let me continue to try to find out . . .

In Maputo, the confusion continued,

as another blog captured . . .

Maputo is a city built by revolutionaries and military men. Its socialist history is marked on its maps. Mao Tse Tung Avenue intersects with Kim Il Sung Avenue. Vladimir Lenin Avenue runs to Ho Chi Minh Avenida. There is a Robert Mugabe Roundabout. Mozambique's own Samora Machel takes pride of place, as the avenue running to the port. But there are ironies too. Between Karl Marx and Lenin Avenues, a huge church stands, carving out a bit of the Portuguese religious legacy. At weekends, Frederick Engels Avenue becomes a capitalist's catwalk, as BMWs and Mercedes swarm, dropping off high-fashion fourteen-year-olds to their dates at the gelateria. High-heeled ladies walk their poodles and carry bouquets of freshly cut flowers.

Across the city, in the bit on my map which has no names, kids continue to sell just plastic bags, or just sunglasses. There, the pavement looks like the site of an earthquake. The further away from the wealthy part of the city you get, the fewer manhole covers there are, and the fewer pavements.

There are times in the city when you think you have stepped into Portugal. Little pavement cafes, wide tree-lined streets, pastry shops and bakeries. There is prosperity and wealth. Sitting in the cafes, it would be easy to forget that you are in one of the poorest countries in the world. Maputo, in that sense, seemed very distant from the rest of the country.

Being in Mozambique has raised many questions for me about change, about social entrepreneurship and about the political climate which must be in place for that change to take place. It is clear to me that an enabling environment, politically, must exist and encourage the change (one only has to look across the border to Zimbabwe to see what can happen in a politically curtailed hotspot). In Mozambique, I heard story after story of the endemic corruption and bureaucratic warrens that must be navigated to make anything happen. Those who manage to do business here with honesty and integrity are stalwarts. The system does not make honesty easy. Back in Ireland, I for one take the democratic process for granted. I take the political lobby and freedom of speech almost as a given. I assume, as default, that the police are a generally benevolent force. I trust that when I dial the emergency services someone will at least answer the phone. Not so here. As default, the government is viewed as corrupt and the police as law breakers. I never had to dial the emergency services, thankfully. The fact that there are only 800 doctors in the whole country, and 600 of them around the Maputo

area (and this is a HUGE country, with some 801,590 sq km) – I'm very glad that I did not need to.

Leaving Mozambique, I am convinced that this a country with significant potential. However, I feel that the window to protect what is already there, particularly when it comes to protecting the environment, is already closing. Leaving the country, I do not know what all the solutions are, I do not know whether it is too late, but I do know that it is worth trying, and there are at least some people who are indeed trying.

. . .

My time in Mozambique brings back mixed memories. It is a tough environment. It takes tough people to tackle the tough issues. I'm not sure I am tough enough for it, but I am glad I travelled. In many ways, I'd like to travel back, spend more time, meet more local people, learn some Portuguese. I think it does take time, which is something I did not really give it enough of.

But it was soon onto South Africa, where the journey picked up pace again.

Taddy Blecher

CIDA City Campus
www.cida.co.za

Johannesburg, South Africa
Themes: Education, Business

A few years ago Taddy Blecher, a financial whizz-kid, had job offers from top international actuarial firms flying at him from all directions. He had chosen one in the US, his bags were packed and he was ready to go. But two weeks before leaving South Africa something pressed the pause button: he realised he had to stay and be a part of making the new South Africa. And that is exactly what he did, helping to set up and grow a new model of business education, creating a generation of people contributing to the economic and social growth of the nation, in the form of CIDA City Campus.

The first virtually free university in South Africa, CIDA now caters for thousands of talented young people from the townships and poorer black communities who ordinarily would not have an opportunity to gain third level qualifications.

CIDA's educational model has many innovative dimensions to it. While the main emphasis is on business skills, the model incorporates a personal development component, including the option of transcendental meditation, and a community service element. During the school holidays students are expected to return to their local communities, teaching or coaching others, and in doing so help to raise educational standards and expectations among their peers. Students are also required to take part in the management of the campus, helping to keep costs low and gaining valuable skills as the do so.

Taddy has enthusiasm in abundance. He also has a look of Harry Potter about him. There is a bit of magic about the place too.

Everywhere all around you there are innumerable opportunities to make a difference.

Consciousness is rising in the world, and the world is changing. Everybody you talk to is thinking differently, even some of the hardened investment bankers! We are getting more and more people phoning us up and saying 'you know, I have been working for years as an investment banker and I am burning out. I want more meaning in my life, I know that what I am doing is not what I am meant to be doing.' There are so many people starting to change towards this now and it is incredible when people find their place, because there is an **infinite amount of space in social entrepreneurship.**

When you **find your niche**, it is so addictive, so fulfilling, so meaningful. I often say to people that being a social entrepreneur and doing this kind of work is the most selfish thing you could ever want to do – you should almost have to pay for it. You just feel on such a high. But have no illusions, **being a social entrepreneur is unbelievably hard.** You have almost got to be mad. But provided that you are mad and provided that you can accept the hardship, it is just an adrenaline rush, it is just addictive. Being an entrepreneur you make some mistakes along the way. You are always trying new things. You are constantly thinking 'what more

could we do and how better could we do it'. Often people can't keep up with you because you are off doing the next thing. So you have got to **build a great team**, and just like any business, you have got to run it properly, with proper governance. But you must never lose the magic because that is the engine, that is the glue.

I believe that **it is absolutely possible to change the world.** When I was young and at school, we would study history, but it always seemed like history was something that happened 'to' you. Growing up in South Africa, as a young white South African, I would see the police beating people up and I would always feel so helpless. But then I made an internal mindset shift: that history isn't something that happens to us: it is something we create. I realised that every single human being is creating history everyday and that we have the potential to create a new history. I see it happening. We just need to **think in a more enlightened way** about how we do everything.

I have found is that it is a **journey of a long-distance runner.** If you want to be a great social entrepreneur you can't go through ups and downs. You have just got to take things as they come. You have always got to have a **crystal-clear**

123

vision of where you are going, and what change you want to see in the world. **Any meaningful change takes time**, there is no question about it. But you learn all the time and you grow all the time.

I grew up in a privileged white family. My family were social activists, but I was always the capitalist in the family. While they were fighting with the police, I would be the one running my own businesses and worried about making money. But things changed for me in 1994. We had the new democratic South Africa. Nelson Mandela came into power. For career reasons I had decided to emigrate. I had packed away everything, leaving only two suitcases out. I had organised a job in the US and I was off. **But literally just before emigrating I had a seminal experience: I realised that I didn't want to leave.** 'I don't want to do this, I don't want to go. I want to live a life of greater meaning. I want to see if we can make a more meaningful South Africa.' There and then I just decided that I wanted to stay in the country and help the poor and help them learn how to make money and become successful. I realised that I could never have done anything politically, but I that I could do something through education or teaching or human development – that was my real interest.

The deepest thing in my heart is that every human being has genius in them, their own unique gifts and if you write off any human being you have somehow broken the puzzle of life. So that was **the real calling** for me – to help others develop their true potential through education. Beautiful education will create a beautiful world. Whole education helps individuals grow and evolve. I had come across some years before a system of education called Consciousness-Based Education, which I love, which brings the practice of Transcendental Meditation into education, so that personal development becomes the basis of social and economic development. Socrates said the foundation of education is to 'Know Thyself'; Galileo said you cannot teach a man anything, you can only help him to find it within himself. This is the missing link in education today. That's the goal, to turn an educational institution into a lighthouse, where each and every student is a light within, and all the lights together brighten society and reduce all unwanted and unnecessary suffering around.

I am also a very values-driven person. I think that if people can grow up in communities which have values, which are like a family and where people take care of each other, they end up getting a lot more from life. I think that if people can grow up in that sort of way we will have more stable and productive societies.

CIDA has emerged as a model where people who have been privileged, who have been well educated, can give a bit of their time to teach and help others. Our focus is on social economic transformation and **our philosophy is that you don't end poverty by giving people money, you end poverty teaching them how to help themselves.**

You don't end poverty by making people dependent and weak, you end poverty by creating wealth. Crime is caused by poverty. You can put more policemen on the streets, but it is superficial. So you have to ask, **how do you deal with the root cause of things?**

The root cause of problems in life is people having no skills, no education, no human dignity and not being fully awake inside. Without the skills and education, they are not able to create what they would otherwise create. Our

students (17–21 years old) have come from nothing. Most of their parents are uneducated and unemployed. Many have been growing up without parents because of AIDS. They have been through absolute hell, and they don't believe in themselves any more. They have essentially given up on life. But you will never build a constructive society if millions and millions have given up on life. We are trying to change that in South Africa.

We want the CIDA students

125

to become role models for the next generation, showing that there is a way out of poverty. That was really our concept: to take that band in society and provide them with a high-quality education. Professionals in the top accountancy and law firms come in to teach at CIDA. It does not take a lot of their time, but it has a ripple effect. They teach 1,000 people who in turn go out and teach in local schools, and to unemployed people and so on. We have now taught about half a million people throughout the country in this way, through our students. So that is really what we are trying to do – **we are trying to create a bush-fire revolution of people getting re-engaged with life again,** starting to have hope, and starting to see that change is possible.

I think billions of people on the planet want a better world and they just want to know how. In fact **everywhere all around you there are innumerable opportunities to make a difference,** in whatever you naturally would be good at. I think that everybody who has that yearning inside should join some cause, should do something, and would find very deep fulfilment in doing it.

And I think, in that sense, all of us are connected. The sufferings of other people are the sufferings of all of us. You can see that economically and politically. Johannesburg is a good example – down in Alexandra township there are a million people living in one square mile, while one mile in the other direction is Sandton City, with the most expensive shops in the whole of Africa, where all the millionaires are living. But the millionaires have to live behind very high walls and they can't enjoy their wealth because they also have to live with the reality of a million people with no running water, no proper electricity, and no meals to eat. They live in fear of hijack and robbery. It is not just acts of violence; it has an effect at every level. It is like a human body – if part of your body is sore, it can even be your little toe, you feel it, and you can't be happy and healthy.

I really do think the whole world has to help each other to become whole and better. Economically it will be better for everybody. It is not in any human being's interest that any other person is poor and suffering. Everybody could be wealthy. In fact everybody could be exponentially more wealthy: emotionally, physically, spiritually, in all ways. All the things that really matter are intangible: love, respect, care, passion, leadership, freedom. All these things are unbounded and infinite. And that is all that really matters. **If you see boundaries, then they are sure as anything there, because you created them in your own mind.**

But this work is wonderful work. What could be more enjoyable than this? Nothing in the whole world. Could I ever have had such a wonderful job?

Don Edkins

Day Zero Productions
www.dayzero.co.za
www.steps.co.za
www.whydemocracy.net

Cape Town, South Africa
Themes: Arts/Media, Health

Don Edkins is a documentary film producer who makes films with a social edge. Over the last few years, with his film production companies, Day Zero and Steps to the Future, he has made a series of films on the themes of HIV/AIDS and democracy. Searching out local film-makers to tell local stories, it is important to him that films get social messages across without being prescriptive. It is about people telling their own stories, in their own ways. For the Steps project, for instance, his team hunted down stories from across Southern Africa which highlight both the dark and light sides of the HIV crisis – from how condoms are used as football fillers in Mozambique, to the life story of Zachie Achmat, founder of Treatment Action Society, one of the leading HIV/AIDS advocacy organisations in South Africa.

To accompany the films Steps also supported an education and distribution campaign around the films, to get them seen and discussed by as many people as possible. Mobile cinemas have been touring the region, broadcasting the films in schools, hospitals, education centres and prisons.

In addition to all of this, Steps has a programme in place for the training of trainers – teaching teams of facilitators how to use the films as educational tools and acting as platforms for further debate and probing into the real life issues.

(Since this interview, one of the films on which Don was the Executive Director, *Taxi to the Dark Side*, went on to win an Oscar in the documentary category in 2007).

You can get so much more from life if you engage with it creatively. There is so much you can do, but it means that you have to go out and do it. It is not just going to fall into your lap or come to you – you have to engage with it.

I started taking photographs when I was quite young – twelve or thirteen. I did a lot of photography while at school. After leaving university I was drafted for the war in Angola. It came at a time when I was becoming more involved in anti-apartheid measures in South Africa. Because I didn't want to join the army, I had two options: either go to jail for six years or leave the country. So I left South Africa. I took the first plane out and it landed in Luxembourg. It took me eighteen years to return.

I moved around a lot during those years. I'd been to the States before, so I decided to live there for a while and then in Guatemala, Canada, Germany and I ended up spending quite a lot of time in Lesotho. This small kingdom, an independent country in the middle of South Africa, was fantastic because

it took me out of apartheid and into an African country where colour was not such an issue. I got involved in small-scale village development projects, mostly focused on poverty alleviation: providing resources so that people could ultimately become more independent. There was a lot of migrant labour in the region that was causing the break-up of families and communities. So I started trying to develop small-scale employment opportunities so that people could remain in Lesotho, living and working together as families and communities. Gradually I became more involved in the media side of the projects. We published a national educational magazine in Sesotho, the local language. I then realised that with documentary film I could get deeper into the stories. As a photographer you can make a feature but it wasn't that easy to get into as much depth as with a documentary film.

My academic training was in development and African languages. I speak Sesotho, which is a beautiful

By being creative, life is a beautiful thing.

language. I have made a lot of films in Lesotho and I have found it is really important to be able to communicate with people in their own language. Living in Lesotho was very important for me as it showed me what life could be like without apartheid. But when it became too difficult to stay in Lesotho [because of South African army activity] I went to Germany where I joined a media group and started to make documentary films. I was about thirty-five at the time.

The group was very involved in social and political documentaries and my time there gave me a chance to understand more fully the process of making films: from the conception of the idea, to the construction of the story and ultimately, the practicalities of making them. I've been involved with media and development for most of my life.

At Day Zero Films we are running two projects at the moment. One is 'Steps for the Future' – a collection of films made by African film-makers about living with HIV/AIDS in Southern Africa. The films aim to provide a different picture of Southern Africa and HIV/AIDS to the world, and more importantly, to engage people in discussions around what HIV/AIDS is. We were seeing that messages being used to educate people about the virus were not working. They were very didactic, formal and not engaging

enough. So we thought that, as film-makers and particularly as documentary film-makers, we could engage people emotionally and intellectually so that the issues would become much more real.

When we started 'Steps', it was not about portraying people dying with HIV/AIDS, it was about people *living* with HIV/AIDS. Making the films was quite a big process, involving a number of international professionals and broadcasters around the world. We approached governments for funding to extend the reach of the films and to develop a training component for young film-makers, especially first-time film-makers. In the end we made 38 documentary and short films, from 6 different countries in Southern Africa, ranging from 4 minutes to 74 minutes. We have been using them for the last number of years to engage people in how to deal with HIV/AIDS in their lives.

We have had a number of mobile cinemas travelling around the region, showing the films in communities and using them to generate discussion. We put a large screen and project the films in public places. And we get so much reaction to them! We take the films into schools, clinics, community centres and more recently into prisons, army camps, police stations ... many different places. To reach people across the region we have versioned a number of them into

129

eighteen local languages. We also started to realise that we needed to teach people how to use the film as an educational tool. So we began a training programme and spent at lot of time developing a methodology of training facilitators to use film to generate discussions – and it has been really effective. We have trained about 300 people, but this is expanding and we hope to reach 800–1,000 trainers in the next couple of years.

The responses we get from the films are really interesting. **Because in the end you are doing this for a purpose and the purpose is to try to change something**: attitude change, behavioural change. Although the impact is hard to measure, people have been saying things like, 'Well I'm not scared now to be in a room with someone who is HIV-positive', or 'I want to do a HIV test, where can I get tested?' That is one way to measure the impact of the films, through feedback.

It is one thing informing people about the issues but I also think the work of the film has to go much further than that. So we build up networks to let people know where they can access the support they need. We have also tried to have some of the characters in the films to be the facilitators of the workshops. They are often HIV-positive, which adds another layer to the discussion. Discussions often revolve around relationships and sexuality. 'How do I manage this relationship?' or 'How do I have a kid if one of the partners is HIV-positive?' The films raise very deep questions. But discussion is not enough. The films are there so that people can see what the issues are, question how

they relate to them and see what they could possibly do about them. And then we try to connect them to resources that they will need when they take action.

Our current project is about democracy. It looks at the political activity which is most important in our society, how we govern ourselves and what we understand by that. So much is done in the name of democracy that might not be democratic, or people have different ideas about what democracy means and how it should be put into practice. So we thought, 'Let's follow up Steps for the Future with a global project'. It's interesting now to have film-makers around the world making films about one topic, but with different points of view and different styles. It is fascinating to see what comes out. We've also been able to learn from the first project and put additional elements into the second project to make it more effective.

I haven't had much time to think about the future! I think we just grab hold of these things and try and make them work. It is fantastic having teams around me and working together. That is one of the things I've learned in my life: that **it is so difficult to work on your own, but when you find people who share your vision and passion, you are able to make things happen.**

Skills

I think it is very important to start understanding stories. You either intuitively know what a story is, or you have to spend a lot of time learning about the structure of story. To find the right stories which resonate with people is very important. So of course, while you need good technical skills, conceptual skills and narrative skills, you need to be able to combine all of those together, because in the end you want to tell stories.

I don't think my work has become any easier now, even twenty years later. But it is about what you are passionate in life about and how you can realise it. I have been learning how to make films that are universally applicable, that tell stories which can be understood by people in many places in the world. It is not about a particular style, but it is about how to approach the story. It is recognising a story and being able to make it into a film that becomes real. It is learning how to make decisions along the way that help finish the film.

Finding the right people is crucial, because making a film is quite difficult emotionally. You need support to be able to take it through right to the end. Being able to do that with someone who is experienced is critical. A good editor is very important for example. It is important be passionately engaged with a story, but you must also be able to cut the things that often take up space.

There is a lot about the ethics of film-making that you also have to know: how far do you go, how far do you allow yourself to get to the people, how far do you exploit them, how far do they know that you are exploiting them or not exploiting them? So it is a journey between yourself and the character where you have to respect very clearly the wishes of the character. You must never lose that goal of respecting people's wishes because they are allowing you into their lives.

I have two boys – what do I tell them? I know how difficult it is, because I see the difficulties they encounter as they keep looking for something that they really want to do, and find a way to do it. **I think it is about opening up your eyes to the possibilities that you have not yet found.** Rely on your own capabilities, your own skills and your own strengths. If there is something that you are looking for, you should go out and try to find it. Take the first step.

I realised that I love the whole process of film-making. Coming up with the idea, developing the project, working with people, making sure it happens and then trying to conclude it in some way. To come back to this thing about creativity: for me particularly it is about working with the people who are film-makers, and working with the characters, or working with the people who are taking the films out there. They are so passionate. It is what their lives are all about. It is a mission for them. That inspires me.

I had to learn so much and I am always thinking how should I do things differently, what do I need to do next, what am I not thinking about, what do I need to be considering? So I always have to push myself to try to move further than where I am. That is when I learn. **But by being creative, life is a beautiful thing!**

Blog extract: Connectors and Connections

My meeting with Don Edkins was a great example of how social networks are so powerful, useful and interesting; and how I can do what I do.

I was introduced to Don by Kim Harte, a manager at Streetwires (see interview with Patrick Schofield), who used to work with him at the production company, Day Zero. I was introduced to Kim by Patrick Schofield, who is the co-founder of Streetwires, and who I stayed with in Cape Town. Patrick also introduced me to Marisa Dean, a young talented woman, who is working with the film-maker Nicky Newman. Marisa put me in touch with Nicky, whom I also interviewed.

It turns out that Nicky also directed one of Don Edkins' films in the Steps project. Turns out also that Don knows the people I stayed with in Dar es Salaam, John and Louise Riber. Don has also put me in touch with a number of film-makers in India, who I can meet up with while there and Nicky in turn has put me in touch with a network of women film-makers around the world (IAWRT).

In a nice reciprocal twist of connections, I also met with a friend of Patrick's, Michaela Howse, who is a talented photographer and interested in getting into documentary-making. So, because I have been fortunate to meet such people along the way, I now can put Michaela in touch with Nicky.

This world is so connected! I love it!

Nicky Newman

See Thru Media
(and International Association
of Women in Radio and Television)

www.iawrt.org

Cape Town, South Africa
Theme: Arts/Media

Nicky Newman: Film-maker. Producer. Editor. Distributor. Storyteller. Juggler!

Founder of a production company called See Thru Media, based in Cape Town, Nicky Newman's eyes and ideas sparkle. Describing her as a 'juggler' seems appropriate given the fact that when I met her she was managing fifteen concurrent film-making projects, talking about each with passion and purpose.

Each of those projects had a social message. One project, for example, was training a group of young film-makers to shoot a series of documentaries about gender-based violence. Another was a documentary about a young American girl, Ellen, setting up an orphanage in one of the townships in Cape Town. Yet another a series of films is about female self-defence. The list went on, enthusiastically.

Interestingly, film-making for Nicky was not some grand plan. When deciding what course to do at university, she ran her finger down a list of entry options and stopped on journalism. It was a reminder that sometimes random choices lead in the right direction.

Africa is dying. It is predicted that by 2010 there will be in the region of 40 million AIDS orphans. I'm from a Jewish family but was not really raised as a practising Jew. However I was raised being constantly reminded of the Holocaust and of the 6 million who died. Now though, there are 6 million people who are HIV-positive in South Africa alone. Six million people in this country, *now*. There is something like 1,000 people dying each day in South Africa from HIV, and there are approximately 1,500 new infections per

day … so if you do the maths, this makes it the Holocaust of today. One can get overwhelmed by the figures, but I have decided to just do what I can do.

I think I'm a bit more sensitive to social justice given the fact that my grandmother and grandfather escaped from persecution during the [Second World] War. If they had not got out, I would not have been born. I understand the repercussions of being killed for who you are or what you are, and of course I never want to see it happen again. But it is happening again, it is happening here, and it needs to change.

My documentaries are about these social issues. One of them, *Simon and I,* is about HIV and homosexuality. I also made a film called *The Architecture of Fear*. I was living in Johannesburg at the time, where crime was rampant.

The rule of law had ceased to work. It is immediately visible how ugly the city is. It's hard to get around and it's particularly dangerous for people who are not in a car. There are huge barriers and walls all around people's homes. I had been living there for about eight years and so decided to make a film about the walls and the spaces that are created, keeping people apart. **The film was a call to people to wake up.** It aimed to show that we are reinforcing fear through the physical spaces we build. During filming I went right into the townships and interviewed gangsters. It's not a very pretty film, and I don't think it had much hope. It did not really offer solutions, and after making it, **I realised that I wanted to make films about what we can do about the problems rather than just expose the issues.**

I have learned that life is circular. The more work you put into something and the more compassionate you are, the more you get back in return.

I chose to study journalism and media studies and then did an honours in psychology at university. I really had no idea what to do. **I ran my finger down the list and it stopped on journalism, and thought to myself 'I can travel with that.'** I did my journalism degree in one of the States of Emergency. It was 1985–86 – the height of apartheid. I registered at Rhodes University, in one of the most politically charged hotspots in the whole country, where I had my eyes rapidly opened to the fact that we were in a war. We were constantly told 'you can't do this, and you can't print that'. As a reaction, I got involved with the whole leftist movement and started working for the student newspaper, which was very left wing. It was one of the only publications in the whole of Grahamstown [where the university is based] that could really say anything. So it had quite a real voice. There I got a crash course in how to shoot a picture from your hip and smuggle the film out. I also got grounded in what you need to do to make a difference, to the point that now, twenty years later, I'm still trying to shrug some of that off.

My journalism course was three years. It was mostly print based and there was a little video section. But in those days you literally held the camera on one shoulder and had the tape in a separate box. It was extremely heavy and, as a woman, I found it virtually impossible to film – the camera really was *so* heavy. So instead of filming, most women would direct or do sound. After the course I spent some time in print media but I realised that the print environment was not really for me. The newsrooms were full of very drunken men. It was bad news, all day, every day, so I said, 'No way!' I stepped back and decided to try to make a little movie. It was called *As Large as Life* and was about how women are portrayed in the media in relation to eating disorders. As I started to work on it, all the people who were to be interviewed refused to be interviewed by a man. I started looking around for a camerawoman in Cape Town but I couldn't find one. There was not one person available, so I realised that there was just this huge gap. I knew I'd better do it, so I trained myself in how to really use the camera. I had done stills photography so it was not a huge leap. I realised I could do this.

Why did I choose eating disorders? Well, a lot of my friends had been hospitalised from eating disorders, and so for my honours thesis in university I decided to look into the issue more. When I graduated I wanted to make a film, and I said 'well I've done the research, so I'll show how women are represented in the media in relation to eating disorders'. I wanted to question if the images of the perpetual skinny woman on the ramp impact on the eating disorders issue or not, and the whole contradiction of wealthy women starving by choice on a continent that has so many people starving from a lack of choice. That little film took me around the world. I wanted the film to get to a broader audience. It got into a film festival and it just started to travel. It was never broadcast on TV, but it was shown in eating disorder clinics and in universities and colleges. Suddenly I became the 'expert' on eating disorders!

Because of the success of the film I realised early on in my career that not all films have to go on TV or in movie theatres. I discovered a whole other market: the educational one. During that film I also hooked up with an organisation called International Association of Women in Radio and Television [IAWRT]. They asked me to travel to the Philippines to show the film and talk about it. I did that and have been working voluntarily with the organisation ever since. I became a member, then a board member, then vice-president and now I just run the website. Through IAWRT, I train women in developing countries how to use digital camera equipment and how to edit on digital equipment. Most of the women are working in development and need to learn how to make their own media to tell their own stories. So I have travelled around the world doing that. I am starting to feel that I want

to do it less now, however. The long-distance flights can knock it out of you! I do love it though.

I'm getting more into fiction recently. For years I could not allow myself to make fiction, because I felt it was frivolous, and I needed to make a 'real' story. I could not get my head around drama. But now I am realising more and more that I have had some of my most profound moments of understanding through fiction films. When I was fourteen, I watched a German film called *H* and I know I'm not a heroin addict today because I saw it. I remember sitting there, watching this horror. I'd never seen such depraved things in my life. I sat there pledging to myself that I would never ever, *ever*, touch hard drugs. I've buried four or five very close friends of mine, all talented and creative, all from very wealthy backgrounds, who all died in one way or another through crack or smack addictions, or who overdosed. So I know that film changed me.

Something odd happened to me at one point in my career though. I was involved in development and social change but I didn't really understand why I was. One day I woke up and said 'this is old hat, this is not where it is at. The struggle is over.' So I started to move away from it, getting more into broadcast television. I directed a series called *Money* on personal finance and some other stuff, which I call 'sausage-factory TV'. But my heart was not in it. Then suddenly my work in social change media just came back. It was like a huge swing. **I needed to move away from it**

to see what I was doing. I also realised that I'd had a faulty belief system that 'cause-based' films' weren't commercial. But I learned how to package the films differently, and it was then that we started *Architecture of Fear*.

The women from IAWRT have inspired and helped me. They share their skills. People think that I'm very developed in my career, but I'm not. I'm learning always. Now and again I feel like I need a little leg-up, or a bit of a helping hand. It can be hard: you put in a lot of hours, projects run for ages, and it is not the most economically viable career. It can be quite traumatic, and at times, filming can be dangerous. I've been hijacked quite violently on a shoot in a township before. So it is not easy.

I have also had to learn the balance of production and direction. **One part of my world requires me to be incredibly creative and the other requires me to be incredibly practical:** cash flows, business development, administration. So I've learned how to juggle and change hats between production and direction. One day I can be teaching in a university, and the next working in production or directing, or doing a camera workshop. Life is never boring – there is never a dull moment. I have the most exciting life. On the whole I would not change it for anything, ever.

I have learned that life is circular. The more work you put into something and the more compassionate you are, the more you get back in return. It can be a whole range of things: emotional, spiritual, financial. When you are empowering people on a real level, it can be the most rewarding thing to see communities grow, evolve and strengthen. It is very dynamic and rewarding. This work opens your eyes. I have learned so much more about myself by working with people who I would not ordinarily be involved with – training with a women's development group in India for example. It is not a group I would ever have had contact with, and suddenly through my work, I do. And I am all the richer for it.

You may laugh when I say 'let's change the world'. But you know I think it happens a day at a time. I used to be very ambitious, saying 'we are going to change the world and it must happen *now*'. But then I would start to doubt and I started to think that probably what I do isn't going to make much of a difference. But I'm glad to say that I've come full circle. I believe that change can happen, but we need to work at it one day at a time.

Sometimes I also say to myself 'let's tell a story for the sake of telling a story, or let's make a picture'. I question whether it needs a social message all the time. But I have realised that yes, in this country it does. I don't know about the rest of the world, but here it does. I also realised that one can make development a lifestyle and a career. I don't make a lot of money doing this. But it is amazing when you start to actually see the changes in the people you are working with as well as the people who are receiving the films. It is just incredible. So if I can make just a small difference, one day at time, that is what I will do. How lucky am I?

Blog extract: The WiseOne Speaketh

I have met many wise men along the way, and I have even met one 'Wiseman'. Yes, that was his name, and sure enough, he lived up to it.

Wiseman is a taxi driver in Cape Town, but he is from Malawi. He came here to earn his fortune. The thing is, the taxi-driver market is a tough world and competition is fierce. There is not much fortune to be had. Wiseman works on a 'kind of' commission basis. Each day he has to pay the owner of the taxi a set amount, about 200 rand (approx. €17). Then he has to pay for petrol, and once that is covered the rest is his. In the winter he tells me that it is difficult to earn the 200 rand a day, but he can make it in the summer when the crowds come.

I hailed his taxi one evening and we got chatting along the way. He told me that there is an Irishman, a businessman, who has said he will pay for him to come to Ireland to work in his catering business for a few months. He told me that this businessman would cover all the travel costs, and arrange for his stay.

When I first heard this I must say the little sceptical part of me kicked into action. 'What made the Irish guy go to those lengths?' And underneath all if I am to be really honest, 'What does Wiseman want out of me?' But my gut told me that Wiseman was a reliable driver. I needed a taxi for next day, and so we exchanged numbers.

I got home. Fifteen minutes later the phone rang. It was Wiseman. I had dropped my wallet in the taxi and he was outside the door, ready to return it. He had driven back from Cape Town to give it back to me. The contents were intact, including some money I had just taken out of an ATM.

The following day, I needed a taxi, and so called Wiseman. As we were driving his story unfolded a little more. 'In Malawi', he told me, 'we are taught not to steal. Honesty is what counts, and hard work. Do you remember I told you about the Irish businessman who has offered to support me to come to Ireland?' I nodded. 'Well, once he left a video camera in the taxi, and I returned it to him. He now wants me to work for him, so that I can earn some extra money, which means I can then return to Malawi to set up my own business.'

Wiseman, it seems, has learned the wisdom of returns. And whenever I now need a taxi in town, he is, of course, the first person I call.

Patrick Schofield

Streetwires

www.streetwires.co.za

Cape Town, South Africa
Themes: Arts/Design, Business

Creative and colourful, the offices of Streetwires, nestled in Cape Town, are no ordinary offices. On the ground floor there is a craft workshop where teams of artists bend, mould and bead wire into the most amazing transformations. On the first floor, a design team, where more experienced and skilled artists get to innovate new wire art designs. Beside that, a shop, where products are displayed and sold, and beside that again, a team of administrators and marketing personnel who keep the business motoring.

In between it all, you will find Patrick Schofield, co-founder of Streetwires, a man with an incredible mind and heart, who has poured his passion and business acumen into making the whole thing happen.

What started out as a team of 3 now is in excess of 150. In that time, Streetwires has helped to rejuvenate the whole wire art industry and put a quality stamp on craftwork.

The business employs local workers from the townships and then provides an environment in which they can earn a steady income and develop a sense of community. It is also a platform to showcase and nurture talent in the townships. In return each artist gets a fair price for each piece that they produce. Those with talent are encouraged to develop it.

Patrick talks enthusiastically about his work, and is always looking for new ideas. The entrepreneurial streak has been in him from early on, starting his first business, a local 'What's On' magazine at the age of twenty-two. Along the way he learned core skills: management, leadership and, essentially, delegation, now letting those with creative talent and marketing flair unleash their potential on the business. All the while he keeps an eye on finances and business ideas coming in. Streetwires is a great example of a social enterprise with both financial and social profit at its core. They happen to make beautiful things too!

In South Africa there is a lot of talk about crime, but if you are going to jabber on about it, either do something about it or shut up! That is a bit harsh, but basically I saw wire art as an area that had huge potential for job creation on a wide scale, not just with Streetwires as a business, but as an industry. You have probably heard, 'Don't give a man a fish, teach him how to fish'. Well, what is the point of that if you don't have a fish market? **We are trying to create the market first, and then we look at how to teach people to fish.**

When I was younger I always enjoyed the creative side of life. I wanted to study art and architecture but I was persuaded by my parents to study business. But the wonderful thing about craft is, it is both. I also wanted to get involved in social development and the preservation of what it means to be an African. When I say 'African' I don't mean in terms of colour, but as a people. I am African. I was born in Zimbabwe to a South African mother, but people often question me: 'you say you are African, but you are white.' Of course I'm African, what else am I supposed to be? So the preservation of what it means to be African, for all its

richness and diversity, is very important to me.

Streetwires started in 2000 when a good friend of mine, Douglas Ochse, and I were looking into ways to preserve African culture through music. We wanted to travel to the rural areas of South Africa to record the music of the tribes and somehow catalyse social development through it. We began to develop a concept called IpiAfrica ('Where in Africa') but due to a lack of experience, we were having difficulty. Around this time one of the wire artists in Cape Town, Issac Dyosi, had become friendly with Douglas and showed him a little wire radio he had made. It was based on a small electronic circuit within a wire-beaded frame, and looked really, really funky. Douglas was so excited about it that one day he came running to me, saying 'you have to see this, it's incredible'. I could see that the radio linked in so well with what we were trying to do in terms of exploring culture through craft and music.

Growing up in Zimbabwe I had seen what an extraordinary effect craft had in the development of Zimbabwean farmers. As tourism developed, craft became a major income generator and

The first step of any project is to understand the need rather than trying to fulfil your need.

a way of bringing traditional heritage into contemporary society. In doing so it also contributed to preserving cultural heritage. So the concept of wire art was very much linked into what we had been looking at doing with IpiAfrica, and I realised that craft could do it as well. Plus it combined three really interesting components: the preservation of culture, job creation/income generation, and poverty alleviation.

We knew from the start that we needed to structure Streetwires as a business and not as a typical NGO. I do think there's a place for NGOs – they can have an important role in providing services in education or heritage systems, for example – but in terms of creating sustainable income for larger groups of people, I don't think they work so well. If you set up an organisation with an NGO culture that creates products to sell, the chances of it surviving are small. Only something like three out of every ten businesses survive the first five years, and that is

when they are wanting to make a profit! So if you say you are going to create an organisation that is not-profit driven but you still want to compete with those which are profit driven, you're making your life very difficult.

So we knew we had to create a sustainable business model to ensure livelihoods for people, while also addressing social issues. Streetwires was set up as craft studios which focus on creating the best environment for the crafters to earn well. We developed an agreement with our crafters about the quality of the work we were expecting from them. It was very much an open agreement and I think it is why we've survived. We then created a structure within the organisation to help address social problems and by segmenting our different agendas within the organisation, we have managed to become sustainable.

So as well as generating income, the studios focus on the social development of the wire artists. Everything from

141

addressing HIV education to financial planning. There are various HIV-positive staff within Streetwires who will support others who are newly diagnosed, bringing them to the clinics to get antiretrovirals and counselling. There are also counsellors who come into Streetwires to give talks on HIV/AIDS. We teach some financial literacy also. Ninety per cent of the people who started working in Streetwires never had a bank account. So representatives from the banks give talks, explaining what an account is or what credit is. On the creative side we also send artists on courses, like drawing and painting, which help them develop their craft. **So we basically look out for each other, which breeds tremendous loyalty.** It is very much like a family.

I studied business at university. I have never actually worked for anyone else in my life, except of course in everything that I do, I am actually working for the people who buy what I create! I started my first little business when I was just out of university – twenty-one or twenty-two at the time. It was a community magazine called *The Billboard*, advertising local tradespeople. It was about supporting people and trade in the local community. I ran it for about three years. The work was tough, having to knock on doors, but I learned lessons. It was an invaluable experience because it taught me how to sell. Once *Billboard* started gathering steam and actually became stable, I brought in people who could run it better than I could. The business is still going and generates a steady income every

month. I still own it, but it is run by other people. After a few years with it, I decided that the advertising industry was not really for me and that I wanted another challenge.

After leaving, I just helped other people to run projects for a while. I was a band manager – that was lots of fun – and I was involved in marketing a bird sanctuary. **Basically I was just in a space looking for where the world was going to take me.** It was around this time that I started working with Douglas.

Once we decided Streetwires was something we would do seriously, I realised we had to get our hands dirty. We had to invest and set up the structures, with quality and consistency of product, which were delivered on time. We realised quickly that through a formal organisation you could ensure a long-term career path for an artist. So, bringing together two more people, Winston Rangwani, one of the best wire artists in South Africa, and Anton Ressel, a friend who had proved his mettle in the hotel industry, we created the team that would build Streetwires.

Ultimately we want to be able to give a fair wage so that people can build a lifestyle we all would be happy living. Sure, we could get people to work for very little money, but do we want to create that sort of society in South Africa? No, absolutely not! We don't want sweatshops. So instead we have to look at how to differentiate ourselves. One way comes through fair trade. We are clear about our principles and ask people to pay more for a product that comes from a place where someone is being paid fairly, and so is able to build a life that you would be happy to live.

We also try to lead in the market through design. We have a very sophisticated design culture within South Africa. By fusing traditional cultural elements with modern design, we can create original, contemporary art. Ten years ago, a lot of the craft bought in South Africa was a sympathy purchase, bought out of pity. But if you are trying to create a sustainable income for someone, don't sell a sympathy product, and don't buy a sympathy product, because it will only be bought once or twice and that is it. However, through design, you can create craft which is bought because it is beautiful. People will invest in it not out of pity, but because they believe it is worth investing in. That, then, is a lot more sustainable.

My role in the day-to-day? Hopefully as little as possible! I'm good at setting up structures and turning ideas into workable solutions, but I am hopeless at doing maintenance: running day-to-day issues. So I recognise that people have different skills and by bringing them together you create something special.

Reliability and consistency are also very important to me. It may be fine in a small organisation if you disappear for a few days, but when there are twenty people and their families relying on your ability to perform, then it is not so funny any more. Working with Streetwires has made me become a lot more responsible. It also allowed me to see the value of building something. **It is in the building and the time that you put into building**

something that can turn a good thing into something extraordinary.

I spent nearly a year travelling from Cape Town through East Africa, and learned so much on the journey. I saw so many failed development projects. I realised that if you are going to invest in people, invest in them, instead of what you think they need. **So the first step of any project is to understand the need rather than trying to fulfil your need.** And it takes time.

I really thought I was very bright when I was younger – I was stupid enough to think so! But I have realised that sometimes entrepreneurs are just not clever enough to get into a corporate. So I really respect those people who can get into corporates and make it. And the other thing is, I wish I had spent the first five years working for other people and learnt my mistakes on their money! That is what most people do, they stuff up in the first few years when they are using some else's cash.

But is incredible when you say 'I want to do something' and get out there and try it. So I would say to others 'if you have an idea, then try it, because if you don't, you will never know what it is like to fail, and if you don't fail once or twice, you will never appreciate success.' That is the beauty of failure. What makes an entrepreneur? It is someone who says 'I have learned from my mistakes and I will use them to grow something better.' **To have the security to know that if you don't make it, you will try again, that sets people apart.**

Blog extract: Farewell to a continent, for now

Africa. It sounds quite whole, really. Whole in sense like 'France', or 'Holland, or 'Australia'. People sometimes say 'I'm going to Africa', or 'I have been to Africa' or even worse, 'I have done Africa'.

But the longer I've been here, the less 'Africa' as a static description, one which conjures notions of stability, uniformity, or completeness, makes any sense to me. The more I have travelled, the more I have seen how varied it is. How stable in parts and fragile in others. How politics affects governance, and how governance affects boundaries. How those boundaries have been shaped through want and warfare, peace and promise. The place, if anything, is complex.

Many of the South Africans I have met do not consider themselves to be part of 'Africa'. The North Africans I have met do not consider themselves to be part of Africa. They are Moroccan, or Egyptian, or Algerian. But that is not Africa, not the real Africa at least, is it? Some Mozambicans tell me they are the real

Africans. But they speak Portuguese and some sip espresso in fancy street cafes. That is not African, is it? Some Tanzanians I have met wear headscarves and pray to Allah five times a day, is that African? The white Zimbabweans I have met have been kicked out of their country for not being African enough. The black Zimbabweans I have met have fled their country and can't get a visa to live in 'Africa'. I have even met some African Americans, who tell me that coming to 'Africa' is like coming home. But where and what they mean, I have no idea.

Very quickly I stopped trying to reach a definition of Africa, because it does not, cannot, and nor do I think should, exist. Definitions limit. They put boundaries on things. 'Africa' is a place that does not need to be contained.

Africa is everything.

It is music that makes your soul come alive. It is life that seeps into every open pore. It is death that hangs over cliff edges, so close, always too close.

It is colour, bright, shocking, glaring colour, which adorns every inch of clothing. It is stench, dark smells that rise from the gutters and hover like omens.

It is sunsets, which give new meaning to orange, to golden, to red, to amber.

It is the woman who carries a baby on her back, laundry in her arms and a bucket on her head. It is a group of grown men playing a giant game of Ludo. It is a child, naked and bare, carrying a younger child in her arms, sharing a piece of chewed maize.

It is houses of mud, which look like they would either crack in the sun or disintegrate in the rain. It is mansions overlooking lakes, with east and west wings full of empty rooms.

It is knowing that every third or fourth person you see probably has AIDS. It is knowing that the life expectancy of some is twenty-seven. It is knowing that there are men in power lining their coffins with gold-leaf. It is knowing that in some places there are no longer enough trees to make coffins.

It is laughter, resounding around street corners.

It is spontaneity, now.

It is hotels with four poster beds and crisp linen. It is hotels with no doors, no beds, no guests.

It is giraffes and elephants and a myriad of multicoloured butterflies. It is nasty ants, termite hills, mosquitoes. It is malaria and the constant fear of malaria. It is mosquito nets being used as fishing nets. It is condoms being used for making footballs.

It is 5,000-year-old baobab trees.

It is early rises, early nights, dreams of better times past, and of better times to come.

It is music blaring out of speeding buses. It is buses with holes in the floor. It is buses meant for fourteen people packing in twenty-four. It is BMWs covered in red dust. It is four-wheel drives with no suspension.

It is when you know you are stinky and dirty, but you really don't care, because there is always someone smellier and someone dirtier.

It is smiles – huge, gaping genuine smiles – which never seem to end. It is children, lots of them, shouting, 'MUZUNGU, how are you?' Then repeating it again, and again, and again, and again.

It is people who care. It is people who don't. It is some who try. It is some who don't know how to try. It is a million angry emotions about to erupt, because they have to go somewhere.

It is hope, despair, frustration, bureaucracy, enchantment, history, death, more death, life teetering on the brink of death, life, more life, and life erupting with potential.

It is all these things, and that is just the beginning.

I have to leave now, but I will return. Not to Africa. But to Uganda, Kenya, Tanzania, Mozambique, South Africa. And who knows, I may even get to some other parts of the continent and discover a few more pieces of the puzzle.

The journey, phase two, is soon to start. Next stop: India. I'll see you there.

Part Three: Asia

Blog extract: Welcome to India

What hits first? The heat.

It comes to slap you in the face like a shout. Very soon, the half-litre bottle of water you were saving is gone, and you can almost wring your clothes out.

Welcome to India.

What next? The colour. Saris, flapping pink, gold, blue, green, everything, in long sleek strands. They are prayer flags. They are bunting. They wave high and bright. The women wrapped in rainbows.

Welcome to India.

What then? More colour. A swarm of black-and-yellow taxi cabs. They are buzzing for fares. There is a herd of them, a hive of them. Pity my driver couldn't find his keys. He looked in the same pocket about twenty times. He was a Sikh. Eventually he found them in his turban.

Welcome to India.

We made our way through the city. It is familiar. It is new. Rickshaws are permitted on the outskirts, rattling at speed (or as fast as their little engines permit) through the taxis. The taxis still going for it. Cyclists braving it. Pedestrians taking a very big chance.

There are lines painted on the motorway to give the option of lanes, but they seem very optional. The 'lanes' morph and blend. Three cars. Five cars. Five cars, a bus and a bicycle. Noise.

I look around. Soaking it in. Thinking ahead. There is no doubt about it: I am here.

Welcome to India!

There is an energy and life in Mumbai, which is distinctive and certainly very different from the Africa I have just travelled through. It is a whirl and frenzy of stimuli that refuse to settle. Every time I step outside, I don't know what to expect. The smells change. The heat changes. The atmosphere changes. I am acutely aware of the fact that I have only just arrived, and it is like standing on the edge of a vast, deep, turbulent lake. I'm only dipping my toe in at the moment, paddling around, testing the waters. But I know, clearly and surely, that there is so much more. Everywhere. The history of this place is ancient; the religion integrated. It plays out on street corners. Like how dried flowers and herbs adorn architraves. How little shrines appear, everywhere, decked in layers of colour and

fresh garlands, candles and offerings.

This morning, a cup of chai – a sweet, milky, spicy concoction which bubbles in steel pots on street corners. I chat with other people who share in the daily practice. It is beginning to become more familiar.

This city is wealth and poverty in a single glance. Today, one moment I am playing a game of firecrackers with a group of street children, and the next, I find myself walking through a fancy courtyard, rimmed with exclusive boutiques and jewellers. I can walk through worlds here. I may stick out like a very sore thumb, but the access is odd. Which world will it be next? Wait, let me have a look around.

This place, this place. The sheer size of it at times overwhelms.

Take these for numbers. Eighteen million inhabitants . . . give or take a few million, no one really knows.

Six million living in the slums . . . give or take a few million, no one really counts.

I have been warned not to travel in rush hour, for I may end up very squashed, and very lost. This is why: 6 million people travel on the trains each day. There are only two main lines into the city. In a nine-carriage train, about 5,000 people push in. Do the maths per carriage – that is a very tight squeeze. Not all make it. There are more deaths from people falling off the trains each year than there have been in all the terrorist attacks in India. But it is not only the trains that are packed. There are a lot of buildings here and on average there are 4.7 inhabitants per room. Then there are the cars, and rickshaws, and taxis, and buses, and carts, and bikes, and trucks . . .

I ask myself, can they really all fit into this place? I am not sure how, but somehow they do. Tightly.

Welcome to India.

Snapshot: Indian Caste System

Despite attempts to ban it, the Indian caste system is a ranking of individuals according to occupation. There are four main classifications:

- Brahmins: priests, holy men
- Kshatriyas: rulers, landowners
- Vaishyas: merchants, businessmen
- Shudras: artisans, agriculturalists

Harijans/'Untouchables'/Dalits are outside the caste system and are restricted to menial labour. There are an estimated 240 million 'untouchables' in India, the majority of which live below the poverty line and often work in unsafe and unhygienic conditions.

While in Mumbai, I stayed in a youth hostel in an area known as Colaba. It is one of the more 'trendy' parts of the city. A bit of a backpacker haven, but where a lot of the accommodation is, and so there I found myself. Every day as I was exiting the building my stomach would turn as I walked past a heap of rubbish on the pavement. The local landfill, which happened to be in someone's backyard. The stench was foul, the sight simply disgusting. Depending on how late I was for a meeting or event, I would sometimes walk the longer and opposite route into town, just to avoid the dump. But one day in Mumbai, I encountered a group of women who spend their whole days on the rubbish heaps of the city. They are rag pickers, eking out their living from what others throw away. It is no way to live but somehow they do. Trying to make things better for them, an organisation called Shree Mukti Sanghatana was established, and to find out more I spent an afternoon on the back of a motorbike, whizzing through the traffic, visiting my favourite places: rubbish dumps.

Blog extract: Shree Mukti Sanghatana

Established by Jyoti Mhapsekar just over thirty years ago, Shree Mukti Sanghatana (Women's Liberation Movement) was one of the first women's organisations in India. They now run a whole series of programmes, targeting the poor, and aiming to improve the conditions of women in Mumbai.

One such programme is Parisar Vikas, a waste management programme which employs women rag pickers, trying to get them a fair price for the waste they collect while both improving their working conditions and combating the huge waste problem in the city. A series of recycling plants, composting plants and biogas production plants have been established, through which a 'zero waste' ideology is espoused. They have the support of the local municipal corporation, which also backs the zero waste movement – calling on all households to separate their wet and dry waste materials. This is not always complied with, and so, when I visited the biogas plant, I found a group of women having to sort through the rubbish.

It is difficult, unpleasant work and admittedly my stomach turned when visiting the dumps. Seeing people rummaging through them barefoot, scrambling for what may make them a few rupees, is not a pretty sight. However, for the women who work in the recycling plants, a steady income is guaranteed, and their health and working conditions are better – with the support of Shree Mukti Sanghatana they can also link into the organisation's other programmes, including a counselling service and microfinance initiatives.

Jyoti emphasised that from the start it has been a huge team effort to keep the organisation running, and growing, and without the dedication of the team, nothing would have happened. Jyoti, who worked for many years as a librarian,

153

is also a playwright and songwriter, and much of the organisation's funding has come through drama productions of her plays, which have toured considerably. The biographical notes for one of her plays, *A Girl is Born*, reads as follows: 'Jyoti Mhapsekar is a librarian by profession and a women's movement activist by choice.'

. . .

My day on the dumps was a trying one for me. My journal extract that evening sums it up.

Here in a day you see it all. The city goes on and on and on. A fringe of smog hovers. The noise is incessant, the heat persistent. But it is in the smaller detail that I have found meaning – the way a little boy who lives on the street beside the hostel I am in beams the most glorious 'hello' every morning, the details of the shrines, the gold-leaf picture frames, the unlimited colour of saris, the way the chai bubbles and boils and how people gather around to partake. And the people, like today when I met Jyoti who, seeing the condition of the lower castes realised that she had to respond. Rather than working on open dumps, the rag pickers are now working in recycling plants, where they get a steady wage for what they do. It is horrible work, but it is income for these women in a way in which their health can be monitored. (I cry as I write this. They are tears for lots of things. Bearing witness to their plight, it is easy for me. I whizz in, look, shake hands, smile, then whizz out again, back to my hostel with shower and clean sheets.)

All this stuff, learning, insights, info, people, connections, futures, understanding, confusion, loneliness, trust, warmth, sadness, deep sadness for what I see, then a realisation that something can be done, has to be done and I have a role to play. Right now it is information overload. Where does it all fit together? How does it all fit together? Will I always just be wandering, forever in search of my contribution? I know that every time I step outside there is so much more to learn.

My tears are because all the time this journey is so intense. They are tears for this city. It is so huge, so crammed. They are tears because I am tired and trying to keep up.

And with that I slept.

Paul Basil

Rural Innovations Network

www.rinovations.org

Chennai, India

Theme: Science/Technology, Business

There is a book on development issues that has been getting a good deal of attention in the last few years. It is called *Fortunes at the Bottom of the Pyramid*. The author, C. K. Prahalad, has claimed that there are markets at the bottom of the poverty pyramid which, if tapped, have huge business and poverty alleviation potential. But as there are fortunes, so too are there innovations – indigenous, local ones – which can provide technological solutions to local needs. It was an idea taken up by Paul Basil and supported through Rural Innovations Network, RIN, which incubates innovations and helps local inventors to design, market and sell their inventions. An insect trap is one example, a manual milking machine is another.

Bringing a product to market is a complex process. An inventor may have a fabulous prototype, but little knowledge of how to scale up production. Or they may have a fantastic marketing and distribution model, but their product design needs tweaking.

RIN tries to identify and coach winning ideas to scale up and to support local entrepreneurs through the highs and lows of the process. Not all products will make it. For the ones that do, they may have the power to transform rural communities. For Paul, that prospect is indeed worth the effort.

I wasn't sure what I was getting into when I founded Rural Innovation Network, RIN, back in 2001. I hadn't done a huge amount of research before I started, but somehow my gut instinct said 'go for it'.

The idea of increasing social impact, but with a commercial focus, really appeals to me. With RIN, I was interested in taking innovative, technology-based ideas from an early stage and helping them develop. I knew from the start that most of the inventions I found wouldn't be successful – that is

155

the nature of innovation. But still, the idea of finding one or two successful ones that have the potential to make a difference to the lives of thousands of people really excited me and still does. So we took on a lot of challenges from the beginning. One of the biggest was the decision to work with grass-roots innovators: these are people who are usually rural based, and who have limited skills, knowledge and networks. RIN is about helping these people and their ideas.

Innovators need support to develop their ideas and create a market for their work. Without a market, it is going to be difficult for any product to have any real social impact, but often the people at the grass roots don't have access to the market or the networks, so RIN tries to create it.

I also realised that that inventors often need some technical support to help them to develop functional prototypes of their ideas – so that is where the RIN process starts. We spend one to one and a half years with a product at that early stage. It usually involves two to three iterations of a prototype. At each stage we take it to a couple of users, get feedback and then further refine the prototype. It may seem like a long time, but when working with rural innovators, in rural settings, it is a slow process. You learn to have patience!

So that is how I started off. After a couple of years I realised that the number of innovations we were successful in getting to the market was pathetic. Most of the innovations at the grass roots were not really scaleable. They were based on local needs and a false assumption that local needs are true and universal across India. I realised that if we were to find the truly innovative technologies, then our selection criteria would have to be more rigorous. So we had to toughen up. We also developed four additional areas of support for the innovators: recognition (an awards programme), funding, mentoring and networks. Our annual innovation awards are quite inspiring. The potential of the two or three winners each year to help people out of poverty is huge.

I'm a mechanical engineer by training. I had no clue about the development sector when I was in college. In my final year, however, I had a couple of friends who strayed from pure engineering into rural management. I was surprised to see their shift, and I

Finding your path is about investigating and exploring what you are good at.

couldn't understand their reasons. So I kept talking to them. Looking back, it was those discussions that nurtured my interest in the development sector.

After engineering I did a course in forestry management. Since forestry is all about rural issues, I started meeting lots of individuals, communities and institutions working in development agriculture. I found the issue fascinating and the challenges huge. After two years of that, and a couple of internships with non-profits, I realised that rural development was where I had to be. I was also pretty certain about my interest in combining commercial discipline with social impact.

The first organisation I joined was the National Dairy Development Board – a kind of an umbrella organisation which helps dairy farmers commercialise milk and by-products. After that I worked with the government of Kerala, in southwest India, on a horticulture project. We were working with small- to medium-sized fruit and vegetable farmers, trying to see how they could generate better returns on their cultivations. I was focused on creating the market for the products, looking at how to sell fruit and vegetables better. That got me into retailing. We set up high-end fruit and vegetable shops in a couple of cities: introducing a little bit of glamour to the fruit market! We had

a shop with an electronic scales, which was new to Kerala at that time. It may sound simple but it shifted the culture of fruit and vegetable buying in Kerala and gave the customer more choice. Prior to this the customers never had an opportunity to pick and choose their fruit, as the seller could tamper with the scales or sneak in a bad fruit into the bag. Instead we gave the customer the freedom to choose. It empowered the customer and raised market standards. I did that for a couple of years, but then moved from Kerala to here, in Chennai, and set about establishing RIN.

One of the most powerful skills I had to learn was networking. We need partners to do the work that we do. We don't exist if we don't have our partners, which means we need to network a lot and manage those networks. I realised that there is a skill in the ability to identify partners with shared vision, and there is skill in the ability to manage those relationships. You need to give your partners respect and most of the credit for the success. In fact, this is true for any team member.

There are also functional skills which were important, like writing business plans, product design, market research, building distribution networks – all of which I had to learn.

I don't think I had 'entrepreneur-ship' in me five years back, and I didn't

take many risks. **But I have had to learn these things.** You have ups and downs. There are days when you start the day asking yourself 'what the hell am I doing?' but by the evening you say 'wow, this is great'. So I think the ability to rise over the ups and downs and believe that it is all going to work out is very important. You almost have to have a blind belief that it is going to happen, but at the same time that belief shouldn't prevent you taking feedback and adapting. With respect to myself, **I think it is blind belief that actually carries me through.**

Another skill I have had to develop is the ability to see a winner, which I suppose is not skill alone, but a combination of gut instinct and skill. Because innovations are new, you don't have the best market research. But you still have to make a decision, which can be very difficult. **Gut instinct is something that gets honed over time.**

Asking the right questions is also a skill you can acquire. If you don't ask the right question, you get the wrong answer. Asking the right questions helps to get a better product. We even have a training programme that helps innovators ask the right questions about their products, which in turn helps them to improve their designs.

We also bring young people into the organisation. They question assumptions. That also helps to keep the whole thing alive.

Looking back, there are a couple of things that I would have like to have done differently, and done better. I would have done much more research and I would

have explored different options. I would have read a bit about everything so that I could gain an overall understanding of the world. I would also have listened more to people to get an understanding of how people act, why they behave in a certain way, what they do, why they do it, why they are successful, why they fail. Meet lots of people, ask questions; there is no better way. Reading and seeing with your own eyes is very important.

I would definitely have done a lot more volunteering too – to broaden my understanding and experience. I would have spent much more time with organisations I'm interested in. I'm interested in the health sector so I would have liked to spend some time working in rural hospitals with the tribal people and volunteering with a professional hospital in the city.

Finding your path is about **investigating and exploring what you are good at.** Because when you are starting out you don't actually know. I recommend that you don't get compartmentalised into a subject or discipline too early. If you do, you will not know the other sides of yourself. I think it is good to get a feel of these things, alternatives, before you narrow down or specialise.

We also all need to **embrace failure . . . you are allowed to fail,** but don't fail continuously! Learn from your mistakes and then take corrective action. Deviations on the journey help you to learn. If I set up this organisation in another place next week, I am sure that it would take half the resources and half the time . . . that is learning!

Blog extract: The queue conundrum

'A good traveller has no fixed plans and is not intent on arriving.' So professed the ancient Chinese wise man, Lao Tse, and I would have been wise to remember the snippet when booking a train ticket yesterday. I certainly got an interesting insight into the operations of the Indian rail system.

I go to purchase a ticket (long queue No. 1). At the front of that queue I am told to move to another counter, with no explanation given (long queue No. 2). At that counter, I ask for the ticket, am given one and pay for it. Not so bad, hey? But soon I realise I was given the wrong ticket. I queue again (long queue No. 3), only to be told that I have to ask at the information counter (No. 4). I get there, to be told that they will not be able to give me the information I need until 3 p.m. (it is now 1 p.m.). I return at 3 p.m. (No. 5), to be told that there are no seats available on the train, but that I should go to another reservation office. I go there and queue for a 'token', so that I can wait in another queue (No. 6). When my token number is called I go to another counter (wow, no queue), but there I am told I have to go to another information desk (No. 7). There I am informed that there is a train the following day and seats are available. So I queue for another token (No. 8), and when my number is called I go to the designated counter. There I am told to go to another counter (No. 9) . . . but at that counter, I get my ticket . . . I am amazed! The thing is I now have two tickets, the one I need, and the one I bought for the wrong train. I ask if there is any way to get a refund. I am told to go back to where I started off . . . (warning, warning) but I queue there (No. 10), and lo and behold, I get my money back.

And it only took three and a half hours!

All that said, it is worth it. Train travel in India is one of the pleasures of the place. Open windows, scenery cantering by, thoughts wandering, chai being served, conversations to be had, reading to be done and, on overnight journeys, falling asleep to the lullaby of the tracks. I would queue for that!

Snapshot: Child Labour

'Child labour is work performed by a child that is likely to interfere with his or her education, or to be harmful to their health, or physical, mental, spiritual, moral or social development.' – Convention on the Rights of the Child, Article 32.1

There are an estimated 218 million child labourers in the world. That is about 1 in every 7 children. Most of these work in agriculture (farming, forestry and fishing), the service industry (retail, hotels, restaurants) and industry (mining, quarrying, manufacturing and construction). It has also been estimated that 22,000 children die in work-related activities each year.

Bonded child labour, which exists throughout India, Nepal and Pakistan, is when individuals are working in servitude to pay off a debt. Where children work as bonded labourers, the debt has been incurred by a parent or relative, or in some cases grandparents or great grandparents. Loans are taken out to pay off costs – from illness-related expenses to dowries. However, interest rates are generally excessive and, with wages being generally low, it can take generations to pay off one debt.

It is estimated that there are 300,000 children working in the carpet industry in India alone, most of these as bonded child labourers.

Kailash Satyarthi

www.kailashsatyarthi.net

www.bba.org.in

www.rugmark.org

Rajasthan, India

Themes: Human Rights, Education, Business

Many people go out on a limb for social change, but Kailash Satyarthi literally risks his. Liberating children from bonded child labour is no easy task. Raiding factories, quarries, and workplaces – where children are often being tortured and abused – Kailash and his team at Bachpan Bachao Andolan (BBA) rescue the children and then rehabilitate them back into the community. There have been death threats and there have been beatings but so far Kailash has liberated over 2,000 children from bonded labour. This is Indiana Jones meets Social Entrepreneurship.

Leaving a promising career as an engineer, Kailash now works to tackle the issue of child labour at both ends of the scale, from the grass roots to international policy and advocacy. He is a leading figure in the 'Education for All' campaign, an international campaign to ensure universal primary education. He also is Chairperson for 'The Global March for Children', a coalition of organisations active in over 140 countries, which demands an end to child labour.

On top of all that, Kailash is also the founder of Rugmark, a labelling system for handmade rugs, which guarantees that they have been manufactured without the use of child labour (see also my interview with Nina Smith in Washington).

The recognition and awards that Kailash has won is testament to his stamina and conviction. He was nominated for a Nobel Prize in 2006 and has received numerous other accolades for his brave and important work.

I was an electrical engineer by training, but my passion and my interest in the fight against child labour and slavery has been deep rooted since my childhood.

I can recall the time I first became aware of the problem of child labour. It was on my first day of school. I saw a boy my age, five or six years old, sitting on the doorstep of my school, polishing shoes with his father. I couldn't understand why he was working instead of attending school. I remember asking my teacher 'why is the child sitting outside not at school?' The teacher replied very simply 'some poor children have to work. It is very common. They are poor and that is why they are working.'

When I came back that afternoon, I found the boy still polishing the shoes. The same thing happened on the next day, and the next and the next. I was feeling bad about it but I didn't know what to do or who to talk to. So I gathered all my courage and went straight to the boy's father and asked him 'why don't you send your son to school?' The father looked at me as if I was asking him the toughest question of his life. After a long pause he said 'because we belong to the lowest caste in Indian society. My father started working at this age. I have been working since my childhood, and so too is my son. Nothing is unusual, we are born to work, we are not born to go to school.' His response raised a much tougher question for me. Even at that age I was trying to understand why some people are exploited and work for others. So that was the first incident in my life where I really became aware of the issues. The boy outside my school

has always been close to my heart, even now. I couldn't do anything directly for him, but it was from that moment when the question was raised within me.

When I was eleven, I realised that many poorer children had to leave school because they didn't have enough money to buy syllabus books. The books and school fees were very expensive so I decided to try to find a solution. On the last day of term, 30 April each year, I remembered that the children graduate from school and that they would no longer need their school books. 'What if I could gather all those books and redistribute them?' I wondered. I convinced one of my friends to help me. We rented a rickshaw and a four-wheel cart. My friend pulled the rickshaw while I stood on it, chanting out loud, 'good morning, mothers, fathers. You should be very happy today because your son or your daughter has graduated.' I was so loud people started coming out of their homes, wondering what all the noise was about. Then I called to the children. 'Listen to me, you have all graduated from school and all your syllabus books are no longer needed. Why don't you give me all your books, I want to distribute them to the children who can't afford new books.' Some of the women started coming and filling the cart with books. It was like wildfire. People were watching us from a distance, running to their rooms and bringing us their books. We were so thrilled. In three or four hours the whole cart was full, and by the evening, it was so full we could hardly pull it. I found a place to store the books and then we did

Kailash Satyarthi (Rugmark)

I believe we are going to see the end of child labour in our lifetime.

a second collection round. We collected something like 2,700 books – much, much more than we had ever expected.

Soon the whole city got to know about what we had done. We went to the headmasters in the area and told them we wanted to give these books to the needy children. I wanted to create a book bank so that children could borrow books for one year, one session, and then return them. One of the headmasters agreed to support us. Over a few months 5,000 books were collected and a few thousand children benefited from it. It was also very funny – I was only eleven years old at the time but eighteen- or nineteen-year-olds were coming and thanking me.

That was a huge turning point for me. It gave me tremendous, tremendous inner power and a strong belief that if you are honest, innovative, committed and determined to do something, even if you go to the people with empty hands but with a strong moral force, then people will come and join you. Even if you are only eleven, people will support. People are looking for some avenue and many want to join in something good. You have to give them that avenue.

That experience was great but it was not until I was at university that I realised the whole depth of child labour and child servitude, and the issue of democracy. I became part of the youth and student movement and was elected as an officer in the student union, which helped to keep my interest alive in this whole thing. However my parents were looking for a bright career for me. Electrical engineering was one of the best careers at that time. I got a scholarship and had go to university, and to keep my parents happy, I kept on doing it. However I became more interested in social issues rather than engineering. I knew that if I built my engineering career it was not going to solve the problems that I was becoming more aware of. But I continued to do engineering because I didn't want to kill my parents' dreams for me.

I realise now that my engineering background has actually helped me. I specialised in transformer design. The basic principle of their design is that there must be minimum input with maximum output, with minimum energy loss – which is a good way to look at how the social sector should work!

I also learned good analytical skills. You can have passion for something, but the backbone of that passion must be a strong mind. You must be able to back up your arguments. This work needs a head-and-heart combination.

My wife, Sumedha, knew before we were even married what I was supposed to do – she has always encouraged me. I think one of the hardest parts of my life was when I left my career and nobody other than her was supporting me. My mother was sad as it was hard for her to

163

understand and also because my father passed away when I was seventeen, my friends were not happy – they were questioning me, almost blaming me, saying 'you crazy, mad person'. I had no money and no resources. But my wife understood me. I told her 'I'm not going to remain an engineer. I don't know what I will do, but one thing is very sure, that I will work for the people and children who are unnoticed, who are unheard.' Surprisingly, she was thrilled!

When I was a student, I loved writing. I used to write in Hindi and sometimes in English in some of the philosophical magazines and journals. So after I left engineering, I, along with some friends and supporters, started a magazine in Hindi, which was called *The Struggle Shall Continue*. This was 1980. I wanted the journal to be devoted to individuals and groups who were totally ignored – people who nobody was writing or talking about. This was before the birth of humanitarian and human rights journalism in my country. My idea was that we should dig out those real-life stories of the people who have enormous survival strength. 'Something is very wrong,' I was saying, 'the people are exploited. What keeps a woman breaking stones when she is eight months, nine months pregnant? What is this all about? We should go and talk to those people and try to understand their lives.'

So I started going and talking to the people. It was very hard. We didn't have money. We had to walk miles. Then someone gave me a bicycle, which really helped. My wife and I, together with our one-year-old son, were subletting a small store room – it was our kitchen and bedroom. My wife belongs to a large family of successful publishers. But her parents were very unhappy with us. Her father had hoped I would take over the business. But my wife and I decided (she was very determined) not to compromise. I did not ask for money either from my wife's or from my family. I know they were thinking that I would, but instead I found some friends who were able to sponsor the magazine.

The magazine was a one-man show – I was the reporter, editor, designer and proofreader. But it was like a spark for me. I was publishing the issues and the stories of the most ignored ones. I also interviewed individuals who were trying to bring about change, because their work was not covered in the mainstream media. They were stories of success, of hope, and it was these that made the magazine work so well.

And then suddenly, one afternoon, a man came to our office. His name was Wasal Khan. He was carrying an old copy of the magazine. When he arrived at the door he didn't have the strength to come into the office – he just sat down on the doorstep and fainted. I rushed to offer some water and tea. When he came around, he told me that he had been running for three days without food to save his daughter and some other people. He explained that he and a number of families had been taken away from Uttar Pradesh to Punjab, to work in brick kilns seventeen years ago. And for seventeen years the families were not allowed to leave the factory, they were never paid anything, and there were one or two watchman with guns always standing to guard.

Wasal Khan had a few children during this time. The eldest one, a daughter, was about fourteen or fififteen years old. She had been born and grew up in the factory, and had never seen the outside world. Wasal Khan told me that his daughter had been taken to the office of the brick kiln owner, and that there were some agents from brothels in Delhi who wanted to buy her. But there was some dispute on the price and they could not make the final deal. The brick kiln owner wanted to sell her for something like 17,000 rupees, but the brothel agents were asking for 10,000, so they did not sell her. She was lucky.

Wasal started crying. He had no idea what to do. So late that night he jumped into a brick-loaded truck and hid in the dark. He knew that every night, at one or two o'clock, the trucks would go to the market. He had jumped into one, not knowing exactly where the truck was going, but knew he needed to get help. The truck had ended up in Chandigarh, the capital of Punjab. When he arrived there he just started wandering on the streets, looking for help. By coincidence he came across a man who subscribed to my magazine and was told to go and find me. The reader of my magazine knew I was calling for action against slavery and child labour – I used to write letters to government departments and make phone calls to raise awareness of the issues.

Wasal Khan came all the way to my office carrying the old copy of the

magazine. It had taken him days to get here. **When I heard his story I spoke to some of my friends and we decided to act, to rescue the girl.** We realised that if we didn't, she could be sold to a brothel. Her name was Sabo. We hired a truck from Chandigarh city. Wasal Khan was very scared, saying that we could be beaten up or even killed. I didn't believe that it could be that dangerous – I was about twenty-six at the time and very idealistic.

When we reached the factory, there was a man holding a gun who asked 'what are you doing here?' I told him that we were journalists and informed him of our plans. Along with three other people I also had a photographer with me. The man with the gun then became scared and drove off on his motorbike. We started to rescue people, shouting to the factory workers, 'Get into the truck, get into the truck. Don't waste time, don't waste time.' People started jumping into the truck but before we were able to leave, the jeep came speeding back, along with the man with the gun, shouting 'who is creating problems here?' When they spotted me they started trashing and manhandling me. They grabbed the camera, smashing it on the wall. They started throwing the people out of the truck and beating them up. Most of us had been beaten up and my driver was also very scared.

We had no option, we had to leave the place empty handed. We drove back to Chandigarh . . . but the story does not end there.

We found a lawyer and were advised to return to Delhi and file a petition against the factory. There is a law in India which stipulates that if somebody is illegally confined against his or her will, then, on their behalf, another individual can file a petition to restore their liberty and freedom. Luckily also, the photographer who was with us had already taken two or three films and hidden them in his pockets before he had his camera smashed. He rushed to his office – one of the leading Indian daily newspapers – and published some of the pictures. So there was a big article and headline, 'Slavery still exists in India', along with pictures of us being beaten. After that many people started calling us, 'what is going on. What is this all about?' Luckily, one of the judges saw the newspapers and ordered the police of Punjab to produce release papers for all the people in the kiln and bring them before the court. **All the people were brought to the court the next evening, the court gave the order. They were all freed!**

That was the first incident of this kind of liberation I was involved in. After that I started getting more information and calls from people, informing me of others who were working in stone quarries or factories being held against their will. I also got some death-threat calls, but I learnt to deal with them.

I would say that the biggest enemy for humankind is fear. One thing very clear is that a day will come when you will die. If you die today or in the future, it is going to happen at some point. So if you die for a good cause it is definitely a multiplication of your message. So you should prepare for that. Sometimes your death is much more powerful than your life. I don't let fear stop me from doing what I know I need to do.

I always say that young people are not the future, they are the present. They should not keep on saying 'we are the future leaders, we are the future entrepreneurs'. No, they are the leaders of today. They have to initiate now. Children means now. Youth means now, not tomorrow.

All young people have potential. They only have to believe in it and use it properly. But the most important thing is the action at a young age. If they don't act now, they may never.

Self-confidence and initiative are so important. Many youth lack them. They feel they have to learn more, or need more resources, or more friends. There is a sense of loneliness sometimes, waiting for external support or guidance. This is something which delays your potential to grow and flourish. Instead of waiting, you can initiate something. You may make mistakes but you shouldn't be worried about making mistakes if they are not done intentionally. You can learn from failure – it is not something

to be frustrated about, it is something to learn from. Something went wrong somewhere that made us fail, but we all have to regain that inner strength and start again. I'm very sure that core strength comes from inside. You have to open up your soul to it. Your potential is enormous.

When we help children, when we change their lives, we go to the root of society and we help to create the future. We are not changing something that went wrong in the past, we are changing something that might go wrong in the future. If policies, laws, verdicts or MDGs [Millennium Development Goals], cannot bring fast change into the lives of children who are trapped into servitude or exploitation, then it is a failure of all those constitutions, MDGs, religions or cultures. For me the child who is trapped into exploitation is the last person in society. Policies and programmes, political decisions and economy, should all be designed to be child-centric. If the fruits of the policies reach a child who is in servitude, it means that they are trickling down to the last person and they will be benefiting a whole range of people in between. So if you touch the last of the last, then whosoever comes in the middle is also benefiting. That is why we say that **if we are abolishing child labour, we are creating a just world.**

I believe we going to see the end of child labour in our lifetime, and it is exciting.

(I joke: 'What will you do then?!')

Letter home

I was on a high after visiting Bal Ashram and meeting Kailash. I couldn't sleep at night. While in Delhi for a few days, I wrote this in a letter home:

In all, the journey is getting richer and deeper every day. I am learning, more and more. The connections are taking place. I can't sleep at night with thoughts of what can be done, and what needs to be done . . . and all the time trying to figure out my role in all of this. Lots of thinking still to do, how to balance the head and heart. It is all rather confusing. World in a bit of a whirl. But isn't it great. Life changes every day, and people have the capacity to change it, if they just step up to act.

Blog extract: Back with DAS

While in Kolkata, I met up with the staff of Development Action Society (DAS), an organisation I got to know through my previous work with Suas. It had been three years since my last visit, and driving out to the area of Ballygunge (close to where they are based), I was amazed to see the change. What once were open fields were now shopping malls. What once was just a petrol station, now new apartments, a café and a boutique. In all, there were many more signs of enterprise and business than I expected. Good, hey? Yes, in some respects. This is becoming the new suburbia, the rising middle class. But for the people with whom DAS works, the ones who do not have the money for coffees and petrol and new fancy clothes, they are being further marginalised. As Sheela Sengupta, the co-founder of DAS, explained to me, for these women, life has not improved much.

After catching up with the wonderful DAS team, I went along to a meeting they had arranged in one of their community centres in another outlying region of the city. They had organised a gathering of local women to address the town councillor, a rare occasion for the women to air some of their concerns and issues. Before the meeting DAS also held one of their outreach dental clinics – to save the women from having to travel in twice to the community centre.

The meeting commenced and the women, one by one, started to speak out. The issues? Alcohol abuse. Domestic violence. Education. Child health.

These women were brave. There was little doubt that what was spoken got back to their husbands, and little doubt too that some of them will have received a beating when they got home. But the women are persistent and want their conditions to change. They have called for another meeting with the town councillor, to which their husbands will be invited where they can raise issues face to face, which DAS will organise.

Whether the councillor actually does anything is ancillary. There is power in these women coming together, the 'power in numbers' paradigm. Colourful power.

My time is India was packed. While this book does not have the space to contain it all, this blog post was an attempt. It captures a lot of what can be done in a short space of time, and with that, it was time to move on.

Farewell to India — for now

I write this on my last night in India.

Seven weeks in India. Seven weeks of what? Of colour, lots of it. Colour as iridescent saris blaze around every street corner. Then the glossy black and yellow of taxis and the glaring orange of festival flowers. The piquant green of tea plantations. The lush green of coconut plantations. The lazy green of cardamom trees. The black of a girl's oiled hair, the black of men's moustaches, the pupils of eyes (you staring at them, them staring at you). The chorus of colour as Diwali swings into life; fireworks painting the sky like a circus. The pink of pickle. The night-blue of night trains. The bright light of bright days.

Seven weeks of bright, busy days. Looking back on my time here I realise I was able to pack more in than I had expected to, things which I would never have imagined when I was back in Ireland. Travelling at speed on the back of motorbikes through the alleyways of Mumbai and Chennai and other, unpronounceable places like Thiruvananthapuram. Wild rickshaw rides. Slow taxi rides. Plenty of traffic jams. Wonderful, long, lulling train journeys. Queues. More queues. Waits. Punctures. Blessings. Grace.

I've been to a school experimenting with science teaching. Another with children's banking. Another with philosophy. I've visited women rag pickers who have joined together to form recycling units. I've been to a biogas plant. I've had a jiving lesson. I've sat in on karate classes. I've been to a surprise party. I've had conversations about venture philanthropy, partnership, business, arranged marriage, female infanticide, terrorism, corruption, altruism, God, schizophrenia, innovations, marketing strategy, Bollywood, home, love. I've lost count of the cups of chai I've drunk.

I've swum in the Arabian Sea. Paddled in the Indian Ocean. I've gone on long walks, got lost, and ended up on longer walks. I've been to a Jatropha

plantation. I've sat with professors, teachers, scientists, social workers, politicians, restaurateurs. I've learned about the long-term commitment needed for rural transformation. I've learned about artificial insemination in cows. I've been to a mushroom farm, a biotechnology lab, a vocational college.

I've been into temples. I've been blessed with blessed water. I've been given flowers, sweets, spontaneous hugs. I've meditated in Auroville's matrimandir. I've seen a solar-powered kitchen and a battery-powered car. I've met people working to combat child sex abuse, child labour, child trafficking. I've met others working to promote rural innovation. I've met a woman who creates beautiful children's literature. I've met another who helps kick-start social ventures. I've met up with old friends from Ireland and met lots of new friends.

I've seen flowers that bloom once every twelve years. I've seen ancient sculpture. I've been to a crocodile farm. I've touched a python. I've seen women stand up for their rights. I've danced with former child labourers and heard the stories of their liberation. I've given puppet shows, with mixed success.

I've given to beggars. Stepped over beggars. Not known how to respond to beggars. I've lost my wallet (again), and had it returned to me, money and cards intact (again). I've been to an adoption centre. I've been to tiny roadside restaurants and five-star hotels. I've been into the homes of people celebrating their sacred festivals.

I've laughed. I've cried. I've been exhausted. I've been exhilarated.

I've been learning. I've been trying to make sense of it all. Seven weeks. I know. I can hardly believe how much can be packed in. A lot has happened, and there is still a lot more to come.

I am thankful. I am lucky. I am learning. And still this journey continues. Onwards. Inwards. Outwards . . .

I went from crazy Kolkata to sanitized Singapore in just a few hours. It was quite a transition. I had also made it all the way through India without even a passing visit from the notorious Delhi Belly. Instead it got renamed: Singapore Belly. Again, all part of the travel package, and so again I had to lie low for a while. From Singapore it was on to Thailand, where I had planned to meet up with Mechai Viravaidya. He, however, was unable to make the meeting in the end. Instead I went along to his innovative restaurant, Condoms and Cabbages.

Blog extract: Cabbages & Condoms.

A condom in Thailand is known colloquially as a 'Mechai'. Mechai Viravaidya, the founder of Population and Community Development Association (PDA) is known in Thailand as 'Mr Condom'. It's no coincidence.

Back in the 1980s, Mechai realised that a potential AIDS epidemic could erupt and knew the time to intervene was critical. So he donned a 'Captain Condom', Superman-esque outfit and started distributing condoms around Bangkok. He'd go into the red light district and host condom-blowing competitions. There was also a Miss Condom beauty competition. He'd travel on buses dressed as Captain Condom and distribute safe sex and health information. He said at the time 'if Thais remain unaware of the dangers of AIDS, it will soon be too late to prevent the deadly disease from spreading. We have to try to keep the disease under control.'

Mechai's antics were laughed at, but he got noticed. More importantly, so did his message, not only by the public, but also by the government.

The government saw the need to intervene on a wider scale. The army was mobilised and 326 army-controlled radio stations and the army-run TV station launched a three-year educational campaign to help prevent the further spread of HIV. The business community was also targeted, with Mechai proclaiming 'dead staff don't produce and dead customers don't buy'. Businesses listened. About 100 corporations enrolled in PDA's 'Corporate Education Programme', training staff about AIDS.

Over the next few years PDA was at the forefront of health education in Thailand, working across all sections of society: with sex workers, in factories, in prisons, in villages, in schools, and at border crossings. It continued to mobilise government interest and also set the tone among the NGO world, reducing the stigma around condom use.

The statistics around STD prevalence rates this time are a testament to the intervention work. In 1989 the Ministry of Public Health reported 410,406 STD cases, representing 7.69 cases per 1,000 of the population. By 1997 this had fallen to 22,765 cases, or 0.38 per 1,000, and since that time has continued to fall. Condom use has also increased, dramatically. The use of condoms by commercial sex workers in 1989 was reported to be 25 per cent, by 1993 it was up to 92 per cent. In all, sexual behaviour was radically altered, saving lives.

PDA has grown and diversified over the years. Family planning. Refugee education. Rural development. Microfinance. Post-tsunami rehabilitation. Each strand taking innovative measures to create change. There is a book in this alone!

Interestingly too, PDA runs commercial businesses including two resorts and a restaurant called *Cabbages & Condoms*.

I had set up an interview with Mechai, but unfortunately it fell through at the last moment as something else cropped up for him. But I did get to sample a meal in the *Cabbages & Condoms* restaurant in Bangkok and spent a weekend camping at one of the resorts in the hills north of Bangkok. Quirky, fun, beautiful settings and, importantly, profits get driven back into PDA. I'll drink to that, and eat to that, and swim to that, and camp to that. . . .

(Mechai was named by Time Asia Magazine as one the heroes of the last sixty years. He is one of two Thai people named; the other is the King.)

From Thailand it was on to Cambodia.

Blog extract: Arrival in Cambodia

The line for visas is like a factory conveyor belt. I fill in a form. Hand over a passport photo. Hand over my passport. It gets passed along a line of ten very official-looking officials. At the end of the counter I hand over $20 and am handed back my passport, visa inserted. Stamp, stamp. Easy enough, I'm in.

The lovely Bec Cook, who I'll stay with while here (a friend of a friend), has arranged for a tuk tuk driver to meet me. I see a bright-eyed, smiling man holding up a sign: 'Ms Clare Mulvany'. When I meet him it turns out that he was expecting two people, Clare and Mulvany. 'Two just became one,' I inform him, showing him the name on my passport to prove that I am actually Clare and Mulvany all rolled into one. He smiles. Laughs. Runs to get his tuk tuk.

His tuk tuk is spanking new. Black and red glossy leatherette, with silver poles swirling to a black and red canopy. I am reminded of a carousel, and step up into it, imaging plastic horses bobbing up and down with me going around in circles. I ask the driver his name. 'Mr Gogo.' Appropriate enough for a tuk tuk driver, don't you think? We go.

The 5-km drive immediately reminds me that I am not in a so-called 'developed country', and as we pass by the life on the streets, past the thriving little restaurants, the sounds of children's play, the barber shop on the footpath, I'm thinking 'so if Ireland is meant to be "developed", does that make this "undeveloped"?' I think not.

There is so much energy on the streets, and so many forms of transport. Scooters and mopeds, all going in different directions. I'm sitting, thinking 'I love the chaos, somehow it feels so much more natural than the highways and concrete of Bangkok'.

Over the next couple of days I start to notice more and more what is carried on the scooters. Two people is probably average. But then you see families, kids hanging on. Father, mother, granny, baby, chicken. You see people carrying all sorts of things. A fridge. A computer. A ladder. Cabbages. Packs of noodles. Fifty or so chickens strapped around the handlebars and saddle. Eggs, all stacked in trays on the back. Then you see the things that are fixed to the side of the mopeds, like a mobile restaurant: park and set up a business. This is a city on the move. Two-wheel moves. Phnom Penh. Phenomenal.

Sébastien Marot

Friends International
www.friends-international.org

Phnom Penh, Cambodia
Themes: Education, Business, Human Rights

On his way to live in Japan, Sébastien Marot decided to stop off in Cambodia. Twelve years later he was still there. He never made it to Japan. Instead he went about establishing Friends International, a dynamic organisation based in Phnom Penh which works to protect marginalised and vulnerable children across East Asia.

Friends specifically looks at ways of supporting street children and breaking the cycle that leads children to the streets in the first place.

The list of projects is comprehensive, so comprehensive in fact that an hour into a conversation with Sébastien we were still on the overview! Their first and most established, however, is Mith Samlanh (or 'Friends') in Phnom Penh, a residential centre with vocational training, education, health and hygiene programmes, cultural activities, and emotional support for street children and their families. Alongside it is a restaurant where young adults are trained in the service and catering industries, and which has proven to be popular with tourists and locals alike. Alongside it again is a commercial outlet, where clothes, jewellery and bags made by the parents of the children are sold. The list goes on.

Sébastien spoke with clarity about understanding the system which results in having children on the streets. Prevention, he explained, starts with the family, so that is where their programmes start. It also involves working with all sectors of society – the police, hotel owners, taxi drivers, government, etc. – to help combat child trafficking and abuse. Complex problems demand comprehensive solutions. It is a model that is being replicated internationally, a move which Sébastien and his team are eager to drive.

And Japan? Well, 'maybe one day'. It seems that there is work to do first.

176

When I was younger I didn't have a clue what to do. I had dreams of archaeology, oceanography – lots of different things. **There was a lot of family pressure to get a good job. Blah Blah! But I really didn't have a clue about my life, myself, who I was or what I wanted to do.** I suppose it is a complaint of many young people.

I studied at the Political Science Institute in Paris, which basically allows students to become anything they want. I got a general education, which allowed me to become quite multidisciplinary. I still left not knowing a thing about what I wanted to do. Most people go from there into journalism, which ultimately did not appeal to me. Others go into politics (boring), or administration (hell). So I still had no clue. But I was very lucky. France at the time still had the military service but instead of joining the military I was lucky enough to be sent to Japan to work in the French

Embassy. It was there I got the Asian 'bug', and it was absolutely fantastic. I spent a year and a half working in the French embassy, and afterwards worked with a radio and TV station in Japan – just so I could stay a little longer in the country. It was an interesting job, and a good opportunity, but after a while I decided my time was up. I found Japan increasingly difficult. I loved the language and the culture but sometimes it just got to me.

I decided to take my backpack, starting out in China and ending up in Australia, on a one-year-long trip, spending the money I had made in Japan – and then the money I didn't. But again, it was a fantastic experience. It helped me to open up and explore different things. **I highly recommend the backpack to everyone.** But when I returned to France with all this fantastic experience, I still had no clue what to do.

Eventually, after looking around, I was hired by a cosmetics company. I didn't know much about marketing but I did one year in sales (which everyone has to do), and a little more than one year in marketing. I hated every single minute of it. *Hated it.* I really didn't enjoy the work or living in Paris, which was way too expensive. After a couple of years I said 'enough is enough, I'm going back to Japan, the only place I was really happy'. So even though I knew that Japan could be a difficult place, I decided to return. I had some money saved and decided to stop somewhere en route for a holiday. 'Eenie, meenie, minie, mo – Cambodia.' The country had just opened up. It was 1994, and UNTAC [United Nations Transitional Authority in Cambodia] had just left. I was going to spend a few months in the region then head off to Japan.

I arrived in Cambodia. It was hell on earth: no electricity, no running water, no streets, and gunshots all the time. It was awful. But it was meeting some of the kids on the streets that really changed things for me. One evening, when I was leaving a restaurant at around ten o'clock (which was late by Cambodian standards at the time, really late) I saw about twenty kids sleeping on cardboard and then saw a big Mercedes driving by with tinted windows. Somehow the image moved me. I had seen street kids in Asia before. I had seen things in China you would not believe – kids wounding themselves to make money – but somehow this incident and the situation here in Cambodia made me even more upset. I knew there was a lot of money being pumped into the country and that there was no reason for these kids to be on

You have to keep the bigger picture in mind all the time.

the street. 'The West' had come for years and put so much money in, but what was there to show for it? Nothing. If you say you are interested in reconstructing the country, then surely you start by looking after the children. I know my reaction was a little innocent, because I see now that everything is linked, but this one incident really made me react. Many people still ask me why do I do this. **Honestly, only for one reason: social justice.** I've always been very sensitive to it, so seeing very rich people alongside the very poor was just horrible.

I started working with the kids. I was in Cambodia with my then girlfriend, Barbara, and a friend called Mark. The three of us began providing bread to the children but we realised fast that providing bread was very stupid and dangerous because it was actually keeping the kids on the street. It's just like giving money: it is not a solution. So we talked with the kids, gradually breaking down the barriers and asking them what they wanted. It was then that the basic idea of Friends emerged, a residential centre with outreach.

Honestly, I thought that within three months the Khmers would be running it. I was a little innocent then. But if you are not at all naive and innocent you don't start. Barbara and Mark were working at the time, so they said to me 'you do it'. When I think about it now – the thought of a white man starting

a programme for street kids – Alarm, Alarm, Alarm, Alarm, Alarm! But that is exactly what happened. People would look at me, 'who is this weirdo, what is he doing?' I was stupid, but if you are not, you would not start anything.

I made all the mistakes you have to make, including not listening to the kids. It is always the biggest mistake: not listening to the people you are trying to help. But I learned from the mistakes. The best example happened when I was setting up the first centre. Instead of beds the kids asked for mats on the floor. But I insisted. 'The children are not animals, they should have mattresses.' Mattresses – what a stupid idea! It is humid and hot here. The tiles of the floor are cooler than mattresses and everyone sleeps on floor mats. So my mattresses were a total waste of money. Eventually I learned to listen. Then slowly I was able to build up the organisation.

It was only myself working full-time at first. I was twenty-eight or twenty-nine at this stage. Then some people came in and helped out. I developed a map, or vision, of what I wanted to do: outreach, residential centre, reintegration, and vocational training – which still is the core of what we do now. I didn't have it all, but I had a few chunks of it. But I had no more money. For two years I used all my savings and begged all the money I could from everyone else. I worked at night translating a newspaper from French into English, and I worked as a consultant for the UN to get money. I fed all the money into the centre.

After two years of constant struggling I said 'enough is enough. I'm tired. I can't do this any longer'. Really, I was exhausted. But just as I was about to quit, a guy from Save the Children contacted me. He had seen the vision for the centre and said 'this guy knows where he wants to go'. We wrote a proposal for funding together and submitted it to AusAID, Australia's overseas aid programme. This was 1996. So on a Friday night I had told everyone 'this is finished, I have no more money. I'm exhausted', but on the Monday morning I got a call saying 'you've got the money'. The rest is history. **You only need one donor to start trusting you and then the rest follows**. I was so close to giving up, but now am still here, over fourteen years later and expanding the services across the region.

When Barbara and Mark told me at the start, 'you are in charge', I didn't sleep for two nights. I was trying to take into account the life change it would bring. It would mean not going back to Japan for a while – I didn't realise that would be for fourteen years. For two nights I weighed up the pros and cons and I finally decided to go for it. I knew it would be hard, but I did not know just how difficult it would be. It was especially so at the beginning. It is somewhat easier now because we are more established and have more experience. **But really, it is not a job for me, it is a way of life.** It is also the best

'job' you can dream of. It is amazing. I am very lucky!

You have to be careful not to get burned out in this work, and in order for that to happen you have to do things that are difficult – like not getting emotionally involved with the kids. It is hard to do and initially I made a few mistakes. The kids clung to me. They called me 'papa'. Now it is very different. I give them what they need, including affection when they need it (and I will not be scarce with it, because they really need it) but at the same time I know it is part of what I have to do for them, it is not something I have to do for myself. **And that is what the difference is: it is not about you, it is about them. It is not about fulfilling your needs, it is theirs.**

I hear so many people who come to me saying 'I have been through a difficult divorce, and I would like to help'. Basically I tell them to go through therapy. We are not here to give them therapy. If people come, they are here to work. This kind of work does attract a few disturbed people and so there are a few things you have to be very careful about. If you have needs, go elsewhere to treat them. At the end of the day, it is not about yourself and you need to be clear about why you are doing it. You are here to work with the Khmers who will in turn work with the children. So you have to be very modest and humble. You need to keep yourself in check, all the time. It is important to question yourself and to be critical. Why do you do this? Are you good enough for this? Are you careful enough? You really have to be so careful.

In terms of my day-to-day job, unfortunately I have put myself in a position where I do the boring stuff so that others can do the good stuff. My job is to help others function properly: writing proposals, writing reports, making sure the accounting systems work. At the same time I know I'm not a specialist, so we have to have accountants who do this with me. As a native French speaker, I have had to work on improving my English and I also learned how to speak Khmer. I wish I had more time to work with the teams – it is what I really like doing. It takes a lot of discipline to focus on what I need to do. But, as I said, it is not about you, it is about the greater picture. **You have to keep the bigger picture in mind all the time.**

Having good people working with me has been critical. And then having a great partner in life also helps. I met my wife, Dana, two weeks before she was due to leave Cambodia for the US. She actually did leave, but I invited her to Paris – the ultimate weapon for a Frenchman – and it worked! She decided to return to Cambodia to be with me. It was pretty courageous and pretty crazy, but sometimes you have to trust your instinct. We now have a son, and another on the way. Being a father has had an impact on the way I work. I have less time now and so I've had to learn to delegate. I also hire single people with no kids. That is a trick for a manager – to hire young people with lots of energy. However, the problem is they too fall in love! Private life is much more unstable with young people. But they are young and dynamic and I would rather work with those people anyway. Friends is never boring.

Don't be afraid to have an adventure, and once you have found what you want … go for it. This is going to sound corny, but it really is about seeing the chances when they appear and grabbing them. If you are happy with them, just work your ass off and you will make it. And **if it doesn't work, try something else – it is not the end of the world.**

I have learned that it is OK not to know where to go. Just take the chances when they arrive, because they are always knocking. You just have to see them. Then go for the ride.

Youk Chhang
Documentation Centre of Cambodia
www.dccam.org

Phnom Penh, Cambodia
Themes: Human Rights, Law

To understand contemporary Cambodia it is vital to step back over thirty years to the start of the Cambodian Genocide. It is a shocking, violent, traumatic history in which, in the space of just over three and a half years, over 1.7 million people lost their lives under Pol Pot's Khmer Rouge. To ignore it is to step over a huge scar in the country, one which is still healing and shaping the growth of the country.

Ignoring it, however, is something Youk Chhang is certainly not about. Youk is just one of the many who suffered huge loss as a result of the genocide. He survived, but his father, siblings, aunts, uncles and cousins did not. Youk started the Documentation Centre of Cambodia as a means of recording the history of the genocide, showing the world what happened. 'It's about family', he told me first off. He lost his. He craves for it. But knowing what happened and sharing those stories is a way for him to show the world the depravity to which it can stoop, so that we can hold a hand up high and say 'never again'.

Youk and his team have interviewed over 6,000 individuals involved in the genocide, both persecutors and victims. It amounts to over 600,000 pages of documents, maps and transcripts. They then set up a genocide museum in one of the former Khmer prisons, Tuol Sleng, also known as S21, where between 1975 and 1979 an estimated 11,000 prisoners were tortured and killed. Walking around Tuol Sleng, encountering hundreds of black-and -white portraits of prisoners and images of their abuse, is hauntingly bleak. It is seeing the worst of humanity, enlarged. But despite the horrors and the pain, Chhang and his team have been determined not to bury the past. The documentation centre is now acting as a resource for the Khmer Rouge Tribunal, providing access to witness accounts and prison records, so that perpetrators maybe held accountable.

Youk spent his teenage years at a refugee camp in Thailand separated from his family. But what he admits started out as a quest for revenge, is now one of justice: for himself, for his mother, for humanity.

(Chhang was named in 2007 as one of the Top 100 most influential people in the world by *Time* Magazine).

I lost my family in the genocide. My mother survived but my father, sister, uncles, aunts, and some cousins, didn't. I used to feel such hatred because of it and when I started this job, I wanted revenge. It's the love the Khmer Rouge took away; it's the most cruel thing anyone could have done. I thought that

revenge was justice, but after I began my work I realised that revenge was not the answer.

People, including the Cambodian people, see the genocide issue in Cambodia as being too sensitive, too political, too dangerous. But it has to do with living today and we had to face our past. The victims wanted to share their stories and wanted people to hear them. Sharing the stories somehow offered hope. **I knew I could not bring back the people who died, or fix the houses, or make people happy but by listening at least I could given them some hope for the future.** Not a single person has refused to speak to me about their stories in the last ten years.

A lot of people in Cambodia are very poor. You can see how poor they are when you sit in their homes. But among all the victims we spoke with, no one asked for money. Instead, they want to know what happened, to share their stories, and to fight for their own justice.

I went to visit one lady in Kandal Province whose son was a Khmer Rouge soldier who had been missing for twenty-five years. She wanted to know what happened to him. We later found out that he had died. When I returned to tell her, she cried for hours. She then turned to me and said 'thank you for letting me know my son is dead. I no longer have to wait for him.'

During our research, we also found a cassette tape of some prisoners. Many of the families recognised the voices of their missing children or cousins or uncles. We made copies of the tape and gave them to the relatives. It became a symbol of hope and love for their family. They are proud that their children sacrificed their lives for their country. For them it is no longer a horrible story but something they can show their children and be proud of. They can talk about the good things: how handsome the uncle was, or how kind. **You can't bring back their relatives but it is important for them to remember and to know what really happened.** It is important for them to be a part of the history and to know that people still care, even after twenty-five years.

The tribunal isn't that important for a lot of the people. Some do need to have

Our work here creates lessons about where we've come from. I believe they can help shape our future. It's not a good history but it is our history. There is no way we can escape that shadow, but perhaps we can help prevent it happening elsewhere.

that final judgement. It's an important process that some survivors are looking for: a resolution or a sign of social obligation from the state to the whole country. But for me, whether tribunal or not, the victims are the ultimate judge.

While I did have academic training to do this job, it is not what I really use. You don't have to be a lawyer to understand that killing is a crime. Human instinct responds to it. I am a victim as well. I lost so many of my family members in this. When I go to the mass grave site I can feel the bones. I can feel flesh. I can feel it come alive. I am one of them and I have survived. I'm proud of being a survivor and being able to tell my story. So I thank God for being a victim and surviving and having the opportunity to do this. This is for me, my mother and the other victims.

There is a saying 'the truth will set you free'. At first I found it difficult to cope because everyone had such horrible stories. I could see blood when I read the documents. I could feel international pressure because this it isn't just about Cambodia, it's about humanity. But I had to confront this with a loud voice, rather than being silent. Looking for this truth sets me free each day. Understanding what happened is healing: for me, for the people of Cambodia and for the rest of the world.

It's helpful to see this work in the global context. **We need a global response to genocide: it is the only way to prevent it.** It is important for the world that we tell the story of what happened here in Cambodia. Our history has shown that narrow-mindedness leads to extreme, violent behaviour. Our work here creates lessons about where we've come from. I believe they can help shape our future. It's not a good history but it is our history. There is no way we can escape that shadow, but perhaps we can help prevent it happening elsewhere. There is nothing to be proud about in the Cambodian genocide, but to be free from it, to be in charge of our own history and to share it with the world is something I am very proud of.

I tell the children of the Killing Fields to talk to their parents, to listen to their stories. For others, I tell them to take one day to think about what happened in Cambodia and to listen to this story. It's about humanity. It can happen anywhere in the world. **Each of us has an obligation to understand but listening will have an impact on the world.** Put pressure on politicians, policy-makers and lawmakers to think about this before they go to war, before they support a country that has genocide. Being able to share our stories is one of the best medicines for healing. It is a gift from heaven.

Letter home from Cambodia

Friends,

As I type this, I have been sitting in pause trying to figure out what I want to say to you all. Since August so much has happened – new insights, new friends, new places. Since the last time I wrote, I have been to: Mumbai, Panjim, Palolem, Cochin, Munnar, Thiruvananthapuram, Vellenad, Pondicherry, Mallalapuram, Auroville, Chennai, Coimbatore, Delhi, Rajasthan, Kolkata, Singapore, Bangkok, Sap Tai, Chiang Mai, Ubon Ratchathani, Phnom Penh, Siem Reap, Battambang . . . and a few smaller places in between which I can hardly remember the names of.

There have been a lot of buses, trains, taxis, rickshaws, walks, motorbikes, back of pick-ups, planes, boats and bicycles. It's been a lot of figuring out routes, buying tickets, haggling, queues, waits and long, lingering journeys. When travelling such distances, distance itself takes on new dimensions. I think nothing now of a fourteen-hour train journey, an eight-hour bus ride, or a one-hour motorbike ride. When a town is four hours away, it really does come to feel like it is just down the road. 'Just down the road' seems to get longer and longer the more time I am on the road. And I'm not even halfway around the world yet . . . but getting there!

That has been the physical journey, the more tangible one, but there has been a mental and emotional journey too. It is the latter I find sometimes a little more challenging, a little less clear as to when the journey will end. This is a good thing.

When I set out on this journey, part of me was seeking clarity, seeking solutions and trying to figure out what particularly little contribution I could make to this world. I suppose I was looking for the 'right' answers, a way to differentiate the black from the white, clear the path, move on. When I started out, I thought that six months into the journey my head would be a lot clearer, and my own understanding of my contribution more certain. But I'll be really honest, six months in, and about eighty interviews later, I am even more confused! Why? Because I am realising more and more that there is no right answer. What there are is right intentions, and solutions are driven by those intentions, but everything has its pros and cons. Not one project that I have visited is perfect. Not one person that I have interviewed is without demon or vice. Not one place is free from damage, or pain, or suffering. And now, funnily, when I meet someone who claims they have the right answer, then I start to become suspicious. What is right in one place is not necessarily right in another. What is good for one set of people, may not suit another. Where there have been benefits there have most likely been blunders. Right is becoming more and more relative.

But don't get me wrong. The confusion in many respects is comforting because I am realising that the pros and cons are part of the package. It's the way the world works. Where projects and people have been successful it is where they are aware of the positive and negative, and strive to set the balance towards the positive.

Let me give an example: Last night I went out to a hip hop dance practice in Phnom Penh. There was a group of about twenty kids and a young guy, KK, who was their trainer, all gathered in an upstairs room of KK's home to work on their moves. I watched the practice for about an hour – the kids were incredible, twisting and contorting in magical ways, working hard to improve. KK had set up the group as a way to give the kids a focus, keep them off the streets. From the outside looking in, it was cool, funky, all positive, the kids looking like a bunch of innocent kids. But chatting to KK later, about his own background and about some of the challenges of working with the kids, it was not all so clear-cut. The kids themselves are from mixed backgrounds. Many come from broken homes. Some are orphans. Some are HIV+. Some come from abusive settings. They are learning to dance out their frustrations on the dance floor, but they don't necessarily leave them behind. There have been fights, arguments, stealing equipment, not turning up for practices, letting the group down. The older kids get paid to teach other communities how to dance. But they don't always show up, or they are not always motivated.

KK himself has a chequered background. At twenty-nine he looks hardened and streetwise. We didn't go into too much detail, but when he was six months old his family moved to California, and he grew up there, learning hip hop, and getting heavily tattooed along the way (he has an

incredible tattoo of Angkor Wat on his back). But something happened (not sure what) and he was deported from the States three years ago – sent 'back' to Cambodia. This, apparently, is some 'silly' US law, which is a 'strike once and you are out' policy. Also apparently there are many deportees in Cambodia now, people who veered off the so-called straight path in the States, were not given a chance and were kicked out of the country. Many have landed in Cambodia with no jobs, no family, drug habits and no support.

KK landed in Phnom Penh alone and jobless. But rather than sitting around and falling further, he made a choice: to create his own life again here, to build networks, contacts, and to start dancing again. He started volunteering with a local NGO, worked for eight months without pay, then eventually got a paid position as a drugs and HIV outreach worker. When he comes home from work at six, he starts dance practice with the kids. He has built relationships with the kids, becoming a role model for them. He has even taken five of them on as his own – kids who are orphans, or where home is too unsafe. They stay with him and he helps them with school fees.

So this is someone that was kicked out of the States because he wasn't making a positive contribution to society? KK is no puritan cookie, nor are the kids. But they try. They are making choices day by day to improve their lot. It's people at risk working to help each other out. KK doesn't claim to have the answers for these kids, he doesn't claim that dance will be their redemption or their solution, but he does know that they are talented, they

love to dance, and at least for the hours they are in the room, they are safe. It's not everything but it is something better than nothing. He knows he may not be the ideal role model, but he willing to give it a try and take on the responsibility. This is something I really admire. It's all about choice.

Choice is something I am learning more about. But choice in a mental setting. When travelling, I can choose the route, the means, the way. But I am learning that creating a positive experience is also very much about the lens and mind-frame in which I view that experience. If I expect a situation to be bad or difficult, it usually is. If I start thinking that a fourteen-hour bus journey is going to be uncomfortable, it probably will be because that is what I have geared myself up for – but when I am making the choice to put on the open lens, the one which lets me explore and be open to experiences, then things start to shift into positive swing.

So it is about making a choice, and I've learned with so many of the people I have interviewed along the way, it has come down to those day-to-day choices to shift things to increase the pros. They didn't start out with grand plans. They just made choices to do something positive, those choices grew and grew.

So while I remain confused, I am also comforted. Part of me is still looking for clarity, but I think I have shifted from looking for the answer, to looking for direction. I'm not sure whether this journey will lead me in the 'right' direction, but one thing for sure is that it is leading me to a better understanding of myself and of others. With four months to go, I still have some time to figure out the directions. It's not about finding the road map, it's about creating one.

Now where did I put my markers?

KK
Tiny Toonz

Phnom Penh, Cambodia
Themes: Arts, Youth

I used to breakdance in the States, in Long Beach, California. I started when I was eight. By twelve I knew all the moves.

But I got mixing with the wrong crowd. I had no role models. I got into drugs and crime and I was deported from the States.

When I first got here I had already lost everything. I had nobody here. But I had to motivate myself. Find a job. Do something.

I volunteered for an NGO working with HIV and drugs users. I volunteered for eight months: no pay.

We were going around, looking for drug users. As we went around, I was meeting all these street kids. They were dancing and people were telling them what I work at. They were saying 'you want to dance, go to KK. He is very talented'. So they came and asked. I said 'no, I don't want to do that'. They asked me three times. Third time I said, 'all right, I will give it a try'.

After that try, they got me. I never stopped. Still more kids come.

Part Four: Australasia Pacific

From Cambodia, things took on a different shape and form. Following a few days in Vietnam, I then travelled on to Australia and New Zealand, where I met up with . . . my mother! This was her first long trip away, and so I cut back the interview schedule and we both enjoyed each other's company. I was buzzing from my travels in India and Southeast Asia, and it took a while to slow down and travel at a different pace. But when I did, I started to notice . . .

One Very Literate Bird

Kea are beautiful, naughty, playful birds: the clowns of the New Zealand crop. Their underfeathers are a myriad of red and blue and their backs a jade green which flickers in the light.

They are entertainers too, this one typically so, which I found picking the notice off the post.

Do not feed the Kea

Gareth Morgan

Morgan Charitable Trust and World by Bike

www.morgancharity.org

www.worldbybike.com

Wellington, New Zealand

Themes: Philanthropy, Business

So what do you do when a good investment turns into a NZ$47-million bonus? If you are Gareth Morgan, you give it all away.

I first came across Gareth not through his philanthropic streak, but his adventurous one. Gareth, his wife Joanna, and a team of others take long-distance motorbike trips around the world. So far: an Indian journey across the Himalayas; another across Korea; an epic retracing of the journey of Marco Polo from Venice to Beijing across the Silk Road; another through Africa, and, no doubt, more on the way. Photos and astute commentary are captured on their blog (www.worldbybike.com), which I read before setting out on my own journey.

For Gareth and Jo, travels are both a reminder of the cultural and geographical diversity of the globe, and also of the 'haves' and 'have nots' which punctuate it with disparity. So when Gareth's investment came through, he decided to set up the Morgan Charitable Trust, and seek ways of redistributing his gains.

The money came as a result of the sale of Trade Me (New Zealand's equivalent of eBay), which Gareth's son, Sam, had set up. At the time when Sam's business was getting going, Gareth saw the investment potential and placed his bets. The horse came in a winner.

Seeing investment potential is something out of which Gareth himself has made a business. Trained as an economist, Gareth set up Gareth Morgan Investments, which now has a portfolio of 'about NZ$1 billion'. He is also a director of Infometrics, an economic forecasting company based in Wellington. Between all that, his bike trips, and being a father to four, and grandfather to a growing number, he still has had time to write several books on financial investment including the recent New Zealand bestseller, *Pension Panic*, which he wrote while on his US bike trip (he packs a PDA, a fold-up keyboard and a satellite phone on all his trips). On top of that Gareth is a regular contributor to New Zealand's *Dominion Post* and *Christchurch Press*, where his economic ramblings are expounded with wit and charisma. He is also a regular voice on radio with dispatches while on his bike trips (including one from Iran when he and fellow travellers were under house arrest!)

Gareth speaks with a slight lisp, a remnant from an early cleft palate, which he said made him a prime bullying target. School was troublesome; grades were weak. It was not until university that his academic focus was found. But by the time he had his PhD in economics from Massey University in Wellington, with a wife and two kids, he wanted a break, a break that has turned into a very long adventure.

Gareth was named *North by South* magazine's New Zealander of the Year in 2007.

The choices I made to bring me to this point? Well, I think you need an individualistic streak. I describe myself as 'unemployable'. But where does that come from? I've always had a real resentment of authority for the sake of authority, stemming from when I was back in school. I was bullied because of my lisp. But I had the 'smarts' and I could organise the tough guys to come to my defence. From there, I've always had an eye out for the underdog. I was also a bit of a troublemaker – suspended three times, but I did sit my A Levels. I was very single-minded and focused. I went on to do an undergraduate degree, then to do honours, then my PhD. I was exhausted by that stage, and we (my wife, Joanne, and I) had two kiddies by then, so we decided to go and live on a bus.

I had to keep working to fill up the tank of the bus – it only did two or three miles to the gallon, so there were lots of odd jobs to keep us on the road. But after a while I realised I had to decide what to do. I knew what I didn't want and that was to work for a large corporate. So I decided to set up my own business. I set up a horse-racing system measuring gallopers' performance and racing times. There were really high costs involved at the time and I blew a million dollars in the end. None of it was my money, fortunately. So that business went splat. It all sounds crazy now but Joanne was driving a bus trying to keep us alive!

After that I set up this company Infometrics. It was 1981 or 1982 by this time. I managed to fast-talk my way around the corporate boys and the company grew and grew. By the end of the 1980s it was pretty profitable and I had to think about what I would do with the money. Some guys need superyachts but all that wasn't for me. So I started investing the money and my business partner said 'you'd better make a business out of investing money or we're going to have to sack you because you're spending your time doing that!' I said 'that's a great idea'. So I began the investment business, which grew to be much bigger than Infometrics. This business is pretty successful now too.

Then of course my son, Sam, set up his own business, TradeMe, which really took off. The family used to go around to car parks putting stuff on people's windscreens or in their letterboxes to help get it off the ground. We even got arrested once for putting flyers on people's cars. I was one of the initial investors in it, which is why when he sold it, I got a piece of the pie.

The bike trips came later in life. We've been doing them since 2001. It's cool. It's a whole new education. People everywhere are just wonderful. And I think the problem is if you spend as many years as I have in a corporate environment in one country, you get a very myopic view of the world. I'm good with economics literature, number crunching and stuff like that, but I'm not very familiar with people, really, because it's not that kind of business. But you go on trips like these and all of the sudden the lights come on.

I'd advise others to **get a technical skill of some sort under your belt but don't get sucked into the system. Don't say 'well I'm now an engineer** **and engineers work for engineering companies'. Stop right there and open up your horizons.** A lot of people in New Zealand spend some time overseas right after university and then come back. I never did that – I went straight through the system, education all the way. So it's weird to be doing my overseas experience now. I get a lot of feedback from people my age saying 'I wish I could do what you're doing'. They've gotten themselves stuck in a rut. One of the hazards for people is that they can get trapped by their frame of mind, and you can also get trapped by thinking you need this or that. And it sounds pathetic but it's real. Joanne and I were perfectly happy when we were on the bus with nothing . . . Joanne says 'just stop buying stuff'. She wears the kids' hand-me-downs.

Now I run the investment strategy for the company, so I don't manage the day-to-day any more. I only need the laptop, which means I have the flexibility to travel.

My mother still asks me 'when are you gonna get a proper job?'

Diary extract: Back in Tonga

Spin the globe around many times and randomly select a place. Do this over and over again. Chances are you won't land on Tonga. The reason being, there isn't very much to land on. Just before starting university, I travelled to the South Pacific for a year, volunteering with some community projects and a school. Ten years on, this trip afforded an opportunity to return, reunite and compare.

To be official, the Kingdom of Tonga is an archipelago in the South Pacific: 176 islands; 36 (last count) inhabited. Population 98,000 (last count). Some islands so small you can walk around them in five minutes. I ran around one and it took me ten. Think palm trees. Think white sandy beaches. Think pineapples. Think coral reef. And importantly, think ocean, lots and lots of it.

That is Tonga. That's the bit the few visitors that make it here get to see. But given the size of the place, there is so much more.

There are a few basic rules to survival in Tonga. Follow them, and you'll be a step ahead in finding out what that 'more' is.

1. *Don't be in a rush. Things don't happen quickly here, so what is there to rush to? You'll be amazed at what you notice when you slow down.*

2. *Like your vowels. Because at least every second letter is going to be one.*

3. *Don't be on an Atkins diet. Carbs are in here. Taro, yam, tapioca, breadfruit, potatoes . . . often all on the one plate at the same time.*

4. *Stop and chat. It is the way this place works. If you can't think of anything to talk about, talk about carbohydrates. They are really popular.*

5. *If you don't swim, learn to. And get a snorkel – there is a magical world of reef and colour just below the surface, waiting to be explored. Dive in.*

6. *Swim with most of your clothes on. Bikinis are NOT in. Togs are very 2050. Try shorts and a T-shirt instead. You'll fit in better.*

7. *Go to church. You don't have to believe in it, but at least appreciate the singing. It will give you a glimpse into the Tongan soul.*

8. *Share. Share whatever: smiles, sweets, greetings. People give here. They give a lot. Give a little in return.*

9. *Get off the main island. The capitol of Nuku'alofa may seem like a one-street wonder, but it is a metropolis compared to the rest of the islands. Hop on a ferry. Hop on a plane. Explore.*

10. *I'll say it again: slow down.*

Ten years on but it felt like someone had just pressed rewind. Returning to my old haunt of Vava'u, one of the northern groups of islands, it felt so familiar. The sights and sounds: crickets at dusk, a gecko's chirp, cockerels crowing at ungodly hours, church bells ringing out for attention, palm trees everywhere, green, green land, and still more ocean. The pigs still tormented the dogs, the dogs still tormented each other. The Vava'u high school uniform: deep wine pinafores, white shirts and bright yellow ribbons. The students still waving gestures of welcome. Women in mourning, dressed in black, with traditional woven mats tied around their waists. The colourful shops selling not much at all or overpriced imported goods.

Returning, I had expected many changes, but what I saw is not as dramatic as I anticipated. Change, I realised, can take a lot of time. I did, however, see too many cars, too many plastic bags and more yachts in the harbour. There were some more shops, more restaurants – but not that many more. The market had moved closer to the wharf. There were a few Internet cafes. The post office was looking a bit more bedraggled while it still took two months for a letter to arrive from Europe, and that's by airmail! There was now an ATM machine, making life a lot easier. The roads had been resurfaced. What once was like negotiating a deep

ravine was now a smooth cruise (EU-funding made it here). The graveyards were even more colourful, with knitted quilts adorning loved ones' gravesides. The mosquitoes still were biting. The coral around my regular swimming spot had grown. I've saw new fish that I had never seen before – all a myriad of colour, stripes and shapes bringing new meaning to magnificent. The water was still a warm bath and the snorkelling a meditation on diversity.

Returning, however, I did see many a change at the school I used to work with as my blog entry recounts . . .

Tongan Ocean of Light

When you live on a small island, far from even other small islands, life takes on unusual dimensions, and challenges.

One of those challenges is getting a quality education. There are schools of course – a primary school in each village, and a secondary or high school in the large towns, but the standard is low, class sizes large and resources limited. This makes for some frustrated brains.

However, ten years ago, the founders of the Ocean of Light Primary School decided to take on the challenge and in doing so are raising the educational bar in Tonga.

Back when I was last in Tonga, I worked for some time at the then infant Ocean of Light Primary School. It had just twenty-seven pupils and was still trying to find its feet. Ten years later, with new school buildings and a pupil

intake of about 340, its feet have clearly been found. There is now a kindergarten and a secondary school, and plans for more buildings. The school has just recently opted for the Cambridge International School certificate, and now students can take A Levels and compete for university places in whatever part of the globe they wish. The exams are tough, the standard high – and given the relative shortage of local teachers who are available to teach at A-level standard, it's hard to get staff. But still the school continues, believing that just because you may live in an isolated place, it doesn't mean opportunities have to be isolated too.

Interestingly too, the school takes moral education and pastoral care as a very high priority. Although inspired by the principles of the Baha'i Faith, the school uses 'The Virtues Guide' which is a methodology for teaching social and moral behaviour across the religious and cultural spectrum. The principal of the secondary school, Nick Flegg, told me that about one-third of the current pupils are Baha'i while the remainder are from the many other denominations which make up the Tongan population – Methodist, Baptist, Seventh-day Adventist, Mormon – all seeing advantage in the methodology.

Ten years on, it was fantastic to see the growth of the school. The challenges are still there (funding, staff, resources), but the school is committed to tackling them, and keeping the bar high. I hear, too, that other schools on the islands are sitting up and taking note, which is a great sign for educational opportunity in the region.

. . .

After Tonga, there were a few days in Samoa, and then on to the United States, to let the games continue . . .

Part Five: United States

Jim Fruchterman

Benetech

www.benetech.org

Palo Alto, California, USA

Themes: Science/Technology, Human Rights, Business

Outside Jim Fruchterman's office there is a picture of a rocket ship exploding. It is one he helped to build. The picture, he said, reminds him that sometimes it is just as well things explode. Had it not, it is unlikely that he would be where he is now, the founder of Benetech, a non-profit tech company based in Silicon Valley.

Benetech design and implement technology solutions that benefit humanity. Starting off with a reading machine for the blind, the company have gone on to produce and market a variety of software and literacy products including project management software for human rights activists and Bookshare, an online library for people with disabilities. It is a great example of the merging of technology with social entrepreneurship.

By Jim's own admission he is a 'nerd'. But he is also proof of what brains can do when applied to solving the world's problems. Jim and Benetech have been the recipient of many a prize, including the MacArthur 'Genius' Fellowship for his endeavours. The 'nerd' has done well.

I was a nerd, 'an anorak'. I went to one of the top technical universities in the US, Caltech. Back then my major worry was that I wouldn't come up with an original idea. Everyone else was coming up with original ideas but I was thinking to myself 'I'm pond scum.' I would walk around wondering **'how am I ever going to come up with an idea?'**

But it did happen. Back in the 1970s I was in an advanced class studying optical systems, learning how smart missiles can recognise patterns. This was when the examples of technology were drawn from the military – technology and the military were very closely aligned. After class I went back to my dorm room thinking 'rather than blowing things up, I wonder if there is a socially beneficial application to this pattern recognition technology?' Then I **had the one idea that I had in college:** 'you can make a reading machine for the blind with it.' I got very excited. I went to talk to my professor who told me it was probably impractical. Still, I remained really charged up about the idea, but because of timing I knew I had to put it on hold for a little while. Instead, I went to Stanford to get a PhD in one of my other interest areas – I was interested in rockets and being an astronaut.

While at Stanford someone came in to give a talk about a private rocket company they were running, and offered me a job. So I left the PhD programme and joined the rocket company. Joining a rocket company was an atypical career move. People ask me 'did you ever end up getting your PhD?' and I say 'heck no, I got to blow up a rocket! I got to fly aeroplanes. I got to start up a company.' You see, when we actually tried to launch the rocket it blew up on the launch pad. But afterwards I knew I didn't want to go back to university. I was thinking to myself 'if they can start a company to build a rocket, **anything is possible**'.

After the first attempt I decided to try to start my own rocket company and needed to raise $300 million to do it. No one gave me the $300 million, which naturally was problematic. I needed to rethink my plans. After a year my business partner introduced me to a friend of his, Eric, a chip designer. Eric wanted to start a company that would specifically do something new, something that could not have been done before his chip technology. He was thinking about a chip that could read texts, so then I said 'you could make a reading machine for the blind with that!'

During the 1980s we raised $25 million in venture capital and built a scanning machine that could read anything. That was our big technical breakthrough. When we started, reading machines could only read certain fonts but our scanner changed all that. It cost $40,000, and we then used it to build a prototype reading machine for the blind. I ended up being the Vice-President of Finance for the company, and then Marketing. We showed the reading machine to our investors who said 'Jim this is cool. You are the VP for marketing, what is the market size for reading machines for the blind?' 'About $1 million per year.' Then there was silence. One of our investors eventually said, 'So what is the relationship to the $25 million we have invested in your firm?'

And that really is the core problem Benetech is trying to solve. Back then, if there wasn't a $100-million market for a product, venture capitalists wouldn't get interested – the returns were not enough money to justify taking the risk. And so, even though the reading machine was cool, even though it had good PR and the employees loved the idea of the technology being used to help blind people, our board said 'look, we've got to make a lot of money and you promised us this $100 million market'. The reading machine had to be put on the shelf, and so a couple of years went by.

After a few years the venture capitalists replaced our CEO and I decided to quit. The new CEO was freaked out because he thought I'd compete with my own company and pry away all the engineers. So I said 'why don't we sign a severance deal – you give me six months' salary, I promise not to compete'. I also asked for the right to develop the reading machine into a non-profit company. That was 1989 and it is how I actually got started in the social enterprise arena.

We started a charity that operated like a business. At the time, a non-profit high-tech company was an oxymoron. Our job now is to develop information technology applications in the social sector that don't make a lot of money (so nobody in Silicon Valley is going to develop them on their financially motivated steam) but that have a big social impact. **We don't give charity, we give access to a tool**. We make the tools affordable. People then use them to get an education, get a job, and keep a job. That is the essence of the social entrepreneurship movement.

Our next big breakthrough came. Rather than making a custom reading machine, we made one based on the personal computer. For under $5,000 we could turn a PC into a reading machine. It read about a dozen different languages and was in sixty countries. Also, because it was PC-based it got cheaper every year. During the 1990s we sold $5 million worth annually – almost 40,000 units. We were profitable but every time we made profits we would plough them back into the business and subsidise some machines so people in need could afford them. For the next ten years we essentially did that, branching out somewhat to develop a reading system for dyslexic people.

After ten years we came up with a plan for expanding. Rather than doing one new project every ten years, we decided to do one or two projects a year. In order to do this we sold the reading machine for the blind business to a for-profit in 2000 and raised $5 million. Then we started Bookshare and Martus (our grass-roots human rights software).

I had been working in this way for ten years before I realised I was a social entrepreneur and that there were other people like me. Up until that moment **I was the one nut-job in Silicon Valley not trying to make millions of dollars.** In late 1999 everyone was saying 'Jim, all you have to do is look at an idea to start a company and you will make millions.' But I said 'no, I'm happy doing what I do'. My dream is that technology gets 1 per cent of the social budget and makes the social budget 20 per cent more effective. I know that a little bit of money goes a long way.

I was one of the more technically oriented kids in high school. My dad wanted me to be a doctor, and I wanted to be a professor of science, or an astronaut. I did applied physics and electrical engineering. Applied physics was the optics, lasers, the stuff that is the boundary between engineering and physics, but is practical. I always knew that I was going to become a techie.

In high school I had some teachers who really got me interested in technology. I went to a Catholic boys high school and got close to the head of the maths department, the physics professor, and the computer science guy

– and they all made me more interested in the subjects. We also had a paper-tape-based computer. That was a key thing for me: encountering a computer as a sophomore in high school, and having the opportunity to write programmes. 'Oh, this is cool, I can do this.' It was a turning point.

So that was the career track I was on. The only thing that derailed me was when somebody in Silicon Valley said 'hey, you can try to start up a rocket company'. 'Oh wow, do I want to spend the next five years getting my PhD thesis or do I want to go off and launch a rocket?'

I learned a few key things about myself while working on the rocket project. I learned that I was really good at getting things done – better than doing research – so I switched from becoming a PhD to becoming an entrepreneur. Like many people I was casting around for what I should be doing in life; looking for something I would find pleasure or satisfaction from working on. Getting rich was not on the agenda. It wasn't there in high school or in college. It probably wasn't until I went to graduate school that I started to realise that getting rich could be part of the deal. I did make some money, but then I decided that I had enough, and so said 'let's go off and do the fun stuff'.

When I started the non-profit, I also started a for-profit company. I was the head of both for six years. It was another pattern recognition company, routing the mail for the postal service in the US. It is still out there, but I stepped down as CEO after six years because I had to pick one or the other and I picked the non-profit. It has been an easier choice for me to make because I had reasonably good financial success early on, so I could buy a house in Silicon Valley – which is usually the big thing, and I have probably made more on my house than on my first company!

In the last five or six years I have worked hard on learning how to communicate better: public speaking and writing. It became clear that if I wanted to do a lot more and raise money, I had to be more articulate about what I was doing. So I took a couple of public-speaking courses and got some lessons from an expert speech coach. I say 'you know' when I am speaking less often now. My staff once counted seventy-five 'you knows' in an eight-minute talk. But you can learn to get rid of some of those!

I also learned about **the importance of network**. You don't realise that your peers in college, especially if you are going to a pretty good college, are going to end up being the business leaders, engineers, government leaders, and politicians of tomorrow. And if you are interested in starting companies or non-profits, **you have to build these networks to make it possible to get access to the people and the help you will need to make it successful**. This is just as true in the for-profit world as it is in the non-profit world.

You can turn network building into several kinds of practices. For example, if someone you respect tells you to go and meet with someone – even if you can't for the life of you figure out why you would want to meet with them – go. Odds are that you will figure out some sort of connection. It is part of **honouring that network**. If someone thought it was important enough to actually introduce you, show up. That is how we got our high-tech companies off the ground. Our venture capitalists would interview us and then send us off to other entrepreneurs. They in turn would tell us what it was like having venture capitalists invest. Then they would pass on feedback: 'yes, these guys are able to do it.' It is how networks function and the same thing goes on in the non-profit sector.

I also put it in terms of the 'karma bank'. I get requests to do more things to help people than I can possibly do, but I still try to set aside 5–10 per cent of my time to do stuff where the pay-off for Benetech or me is not clear. The one thing that I am certain of is this: if you put in a lot of deposits into the karma bank, occasionally you will get some withdrawals. And do you always know where it is going to lead? No, you don't, but you just keep doing things. Wouldn't you rather be regarded as someone who is helpful and supportive, than not?

Another thing is that the gap between you and changing the world, you and starting a successful company, or you and coming up with some new technology, new insight, is a lot smaller than you have been led to believe. But if you are not willing to work at it or if you are not willing to be stupid for a while, it won't happen. I think just about any smart engineer can become a participant at the leading edge of any technical field

within a year – or let's say 90 per cent of them. **The gap really is not that big.** So if you find something that you are really interested in, learn about it and you will find that **the field is much smaller than you think**. Learn about the players in the field. Maybe you know of some clever people doing some great work, so figure out what they are doing and learn from them.

The story of my career is that fortune favours the prepared mind. You may end up doing something you didn't expect to do, but if you learn a lot and build a wide network, then opportunities will present themselves. You also have to be enough of a risk-taker to take advantage of them. It is so important to **take risks**. People say 'wow, you have been so successful'. But I tell them 'well, actually I started seven high-tech companies, but you just see the ones that were successful'. Part of it is taking risks. If they don't pay off, just set them aside and move on. Most communities don't encourage risk-taking – this is hugely apparent in the social sector where the incentives are to be risk averse. **But the world's problems are big enough that we need to take more risks. We need a culture which encourages risk-taking and some tolerance for failure.** This is particularly true for the coming decades because the problems are such that incremental changes in what we are doing aren't going to be enough.

So I will say it again, take risks!

Victor d'Allant

Social Edge

www.socialedge.org

California, USA

Themes: Media, Technology

Victor d'Allant's fascination with social change started with eggs. Yes, eggs! In his late teens, as a volunteer community worker in Burkina Faso, alarmed at the levels of malnutrition, he donated a hen house to the community. Eggs = protein = fuller, healthier bellies. Or so he thought, until a couple of years later a friend of his returned from the village with news that there was no sign of the chickens, or the eggs.

Therein was a lesson for Victor. He realised that had he set up a local entrepreneur in business with the hen house, the probability of it still being there was much higher. Plus someone would have a business. It was a lesson he took with him throughout his career.

Following stints as a photojournalist, a magazine editor and involvement in a media consultancy, he is now Executive Director of Social Edge, an online media site promoting the work of social entrepreneurs internationally. The site is about inspiring others with stories, sharing resources and building a global network for social change. It is amazing what can be done from a handheld mobile device these days.

I simply love my work. It's wonderful to help change the world by connecting people online, virtually. I've had people all over the world tell me that they find Social Edge useful. From San Francisco to Kolkata, people are able to connect and share their experiences. **At the end of the day we are trying to tell stories to motivate people, to inspire them, and show them that we can all contribute to making this world a better place.**

Being around the social entrepreneurs I work with drives me. I'm totally inspired by them. Talking with them I have realised that they have no choice but to do what they do. They are smart and clever; they could have chosen another way. They could be working in investment banks, making a lot of money and leading very comfortable lives. But they're not. They have decided to try to change the world.

Listening to their stories is humbling.

I was born in Paris but quickly realised there was lot more beyond just France. I started travelling when I was quite young. At eighteen I went to Burkina Faso to work as a volunteer in a hospital. When I returned to France I raised some money with my friends – washing cars, painting apartments – and went back to Burkina Faso to build a community hen house in a village, thinking that the eggs would be a good source of protein for the villagers. But I made a mistake: I decided to give the hen house to the village for free. In retrospect I should have sold the hen house to one of the villagers – I found out a few years later that the roof was stolen and all the chickens were gone. Had I sold the hen house, the villager would have been able to profit from the sale of the eggs and there would have been more of an incentive to look after it properly. But you learn from your mistakes. When you travel you realise that your own principles of generosity

may not always be the best way. **I learned that there is the difference between charity and helping a community to get out of a mess.** There is definitely room for giving, but one should give with a strategy. When the community is closely involved, the project becomes theirs and they care more about the outcomes.

After my experiences in Burkina Faso, I decided to become a photo-journalist, believing the image to be a very powerful tool to explore and understand the world. I was self-taught, learning while I was still at university (at the time I was doing a master's in anthropology at the Sorbonne in Paris). After my studies I went to India for a year, working as a reporter with the World Health Organisation, mostly in psychiatric hospitals. After that I continued to travel a lot: Turkey, Syria, Brazil, Bangladesh. I would return to Paris every so often and camp out with friends, but then I'd head off again with my camera.

After a few years of travel and reporting I thought it would be more powerful to switch from the editorial side of magazine publishing to the business side. I decided to get an MBA and came to the US – to Berkeley. I followed the MBA with a stint in publishing for a few years, then discovered digital media – the Internet. I became the CEO of Ascribe, an Internet-based newswire for non-profit organisations. Then I saw the job at Social Edge and jumped at the chance. Social Edge feels like all the pieces of the puzzle coming together for me. It is Internet-based, draws on my language, media and business skills,

I have learned that there is no shame in starting small. Most successful social ventures started with only one person, but one with a vision.

plus has a social dimension. Finding the job was like a dream come true. It is so rare to do something in your life where everything fits. I breathe Social Edge. I'm always online. It is a big passion for me. I also love gadgets – I carry a handheld device so I can have access to the site everywhere.

Success stories seem obvious when they are almost over, but along the way they can be painful. My journey to get here has been difficult. I never really followed a straight path, and following a straight path is much easier. Deciding to become a photojournalist, for example, is always a difficult choice. You don't just knock on the door of CNN, a newspaper or a photo agency and say 'hey, I want to become a photojournalist'. You have to go out and do it first. You have to raise enough money to buy the equipment, find a topic, take pictures and then you knock on the doors and say 'hey, here are some pictures, are you interested?' Usually the answer is no and you have to try again, and again, and again. It can take years and a lot of effort. 'Blood, sweat, and tears' is really what it takes to succeed. As a photojournalist you often go to places where people don't want you to report. It is risky. I spent some time in jail, in places where being in jail is not always nice. It can be very scary stuff.

So of course there were obstacles along the way, but if there are none it means that we are not really trying hard enough. Friction is challenging, but it is interesting. I have no idea what the next step will be, but I am sure there will be more friction along the way.

I keeping asking myself 'what can I do and how can I do it better?' I have learned that there is no shame in starting small. Most successful social ventures started with only one person, but one with a vision. Try one step at a time, and it if works, try again and again. Don't take it for granted that what has been done in the past should be done again in the future. Start small and grow as much as you can, always with the vision to think big. Stopping because you think others are doing it better and bigger is not an excuse. There is so much to do – we need more people at every level. **Whatever one can contribute is significant.** Even doing a little bit is more than most people will be doing. If you can only give an hour a week, it is more than most. Start in your local community, in your town, with your friends. It may be small at first, but it could easily grow into something bigger. We need more people to get involved. But if we don't start, nothing will grow.

Snapshot: Microfinance & Microcredit

Around the world 1.2 billion people live on less than $1 a day; 2.8 billion people (nearly half the world's population) live on less than $2 a day.

Living in poverty or in isolated locations, over 80 per cent of the world's population do not have access to traditional financial services or banks. Microfinance – the provision of financial services to the poor – is, however, helping to lift them out of poverty. Microfinance includes access to loans (microcredit), savings, insurances, collateral and money transfers.

To date, over 10,000 microfinance institutions (MFIs) have assisted over 100 million people globally. MFIs can be any organisation, including NGOs, credit unions, self-help groups and co-operatives which offer financial services to poor people. Their services are aimed at both the rural and urban poor and are accessed mainly by microentrepreneurs and farmers. The majority of borrowers are also women.

Most MFIs are based on a business model using interest on the loans as a means to cover their running costs. Microcredit loans are typically small (less than $20) and are both short and flexible. Unlike traditional banks, no collateral is required to be eligible for a loan or other service.

Muhammad Yunus, social entrepreneur and 2006 Nobel Prize winner, is a pioneer in microfinance. His work has helped to lift over 6 million people out of poverty in Bangladesh. Yunus became a role model for Matt and Jessica Flannery, founders of Kiva. Together they are helping to extend financial services to people who previously had difficulty accessing loans

Matt Flannery

Kiva

www.kiva.org

California, USA

Themes: Microfinance, Business

Matt Flannery keeps a blog on socialedge.org (see interview with Victor d'Allant), of which I'm an avid follower. It is an insider's guide to setting up a social venture. He should know – he had been doing it for the two years prior to my meeting him. The result of his work is Kiva, an online peer-to-peer microfinance lending platform, where lenders meet borrows online; a kind of dating agency for new business ventures.

Here's an example. Take, let's say, Wilson, a 25-year-old man in Kampala, Uganda, who is setting up a bike repair business. Wilson, with a wife and family, has the usual bills to pay. He also wants to support his younger brother's education, but he can't do that until he can get his bike business off the ground. So he decides to take out a small loan, goes to a microfinance institution (small loan bank) to borrow the money. Pause there and meet Joan.

Joan, a thirty-year old school teacher, lives in Dublin. She has never visited Uganda, but is interested in getting more involved with development issues. She is in a bit of a quandary about how. She has given money to larger charities before but would like to know more about exactly where her donation goes.

Basically, Kiva help to make some introductions. Wilson meet Joan, Joan meet Wilson.

Joan reads about Wilson's business online and decides to invest money with him directly. The loan is made via the Kiva website to Wilson's local microfinance institution and then on to Wilson. As Wilson pays back the loan, Joan can track it online and get regular update reports.

Wilson and Joan introduced. Wilson's business off the ground. Joan is eventually paid back, and can either have the money returned, or pass it on to another would-be entrepreneur.

That's Kiva in a nutshell.

It was Matt and his 'amazing wife', Jessica, (his words – ahh) who rallied the support for Kiva and continue to build the website, along with a growing team in San Francisco. Other unrelated but fortunate events have helped to speed Kiva's growth, including Muhammad Yunus winning the Nobel Prize for building the microfinance field with the Grameen Bank.

Kiva has seen rapid growth and popularity since its launch. Getting going and keeping it going has been a lot of hard work, a lot of commitment, and a lot of introductions. Oh, and broadband is a bonus.

Kiva? I'll give you my elevator pitch! Kiva is an online lending platform for microfinance. Through Kiva you can lend to a low-income entrepreneur in the developing world, someone who is a goat herder, a fish seller, a farmer, a taxi driver, but has very little access to formal financial systems. With the Internet we are able to connect lenders to borrowers through the intermediaries of microfinance institutions (MFIs) so that socially conscious lenders can make an impact in starting a business, and partner with someone in an equal and equitable relationship . . .
(Me: Bing, forth floor)

That wasn't so good! I can do that one faster, and more precisely!

Kiva all started out with stories. **Very early on I saw the loan as a medium for connecting with other people far away.** It is a lot different from just donating money. After you make a loan to a person you think about them. You wonder if you are going to get repaid, or not repaid, and you want updates on their progress.

Kiva was our own personal website for a while, there was no organisation behind it initially. Our story really starts out when my wife and I were working with microfinance in East Africa. We had a really amazing experience and when we came back to the US we stayed in touch with people we had met there. We decided to build a website around it. The Kiva website today is just an extension of that personal experience, to allow others to participate in that same type of exchange.

In 2003 I married an amazing woman, Jessica. Before we got married we saw Muhammad Yunus – a famous microfinance pioneer from Bangladesh – give a talk. After hearing him speak, Jessica said 'I want to commit my career to being involved with microfinance in Africa'. I don't know why she said Africa, but she did. I had always said, however, that I wanted to start up a business in the Bay Area and be a Silicon Valley entrepreneur. So we had this potential rupture simmering and we didn't know how to solve it. Jessica got a consulting job to do some microfinance work in East Africa and I went out to visit in the middle of that time and saw what she was doing. It was my first time in

At the very beginning it was hard to get supporters . . . We tried to knock on a lot of doors and it didn't work. So we stopped knocking and started doing work.

Africa. So in one sense the whole Kiva story started out as that long-distance relationship.

Around the time we started Kiva, I was in San Francisco and was on the phone with Jess, who was in Uganda. As I was talking to her, the phrase 'Sponsor a Business' raged through my head. **Once I had that phrase, I had the whole business. All I needed was those three words: 'Sponsor a Business'. They set the chain in motion and the idea evolved.**

I had grown up sponsoring children in the developing world, but as an adult I didn't want to sponsor adults like children. Instead I wanted to partner with them in business. I really get a kick out of working in teams, so I thought 'maybe I will make a loan and we can work on a business plan together, and then they can pay me back. Maybe I will even make a small return on the money.'

At the time I was working as a computer programmer for a company in the Bay Area, developing pause and rewind TV. I did a lot of that in college. I have a pretty eclectic background. I did my undergraduate degree in something called symbolic systems, which is like cognitive science with a combination of computer science, linguistics, psychology, logic and artificial intelligence. I also got a master's degree in philosophy. Then I

went to work as an engineer! I am the type of person who changes a lot, and when I get into something, I go all out.

In the Bay Area there is a culture that holds up the entrepreneur and it is a great culture. Everyone here wants to be the next Google founder. So it has just been beautiful to be based here. It is like a renaissance – there are so many creative people around. You have extraordinarily talented people who care about what they do and who want to apply their skills for socially responsible action. So you have all these resources at your disposal. A guy who might make six figures somewhere else is coming to Kiva and working for nothing in his spare time. It is amazing to be able to draft up that talent. In the few years that I've been doing this, I've been overwhelmed with amazing people who have remarkable generosity. It has been mind-boggling. It inspires me.

I quit my job to do this, but before quitting my job while I was trying to do it in my spare time, I had a harder time getting people to contribute. It was because I wasn't fully committing to what I was doing either. But after I made the leap of faith, going off the deep end, demonstrating commitment, and saying 'I am serious about this', a chain of wonderful events started to happen. Every week someone would get behind the idea or an amazing thing would happen. Going out on a limb and building trust was something others could rally behind.

One thing that has enabled me to get anywhere, or enabled Kiva to get anywhere, is getting things done every day. It was hard to start but we figured out a way to boil the Kiva model down to one place, one example – one 'use' case. Because we were able to start with that example and we could prove it, we were able to get some traction. So if you have a big idea, can you boil it down to one example, one 'use' case? Figure out how to do it in one place. Get it started little by little by little. Let it be contagious. That was my lifeline and once we were able to prove it in one place, we were able to grow.

At the very beginning it was hard to get supporters. You have an idea but it does not carry a lot of weight. Some people might think that it is great idea, but after meeting, nothing happens. You don't get a lot of momentum so you have to bootstrap your way. We tried to knock on a lot of doors and it didn't work. So we stopped knocking and started doing work. How can we do work today, not how can we get support today? How can we build a website today? How can we start connecting with a microfinance institution today? How can we make a loan today? How can we start a business today? How can we get blogs on our website today? **So we started doing all the work ourselves.** We did our own legal work, called the regulators, and whenever there was a barrier, we just asked 'how can we do

it?', without waiting around and getting a lot of people to help.

Jessica also went back to business school during this whole thing. Working together with my wife has been both the best and the worst thing. When it is good, it is the best, but when it is bad, it can be really difficult – it is not as if you can go home to escape it. We definitely reached a point where we were saturated and work took over our relationship too much. So we had to learn to balance and we are still learning how to do it. We cut ourselves off from working together for a while and now we are finding it again. You have to keep your priorities straight. Even though what we are doing is great, if really hurts our relationship, I would rather not do it.

At the very beginning of Kiva we also started an MFI in Africa. We actually hired staff in East Africa and were lending money through them. But that became pretty unwieldy. To run an MFI or an international development organisation is a very complex task. I learned – the hard way – how difficult it really is. However to build a website is a pretty solvable task, so we shifted our focus. We now work through a network of local microfinance institutions, which are small village banks, medium-sized banks sometimes that lend in their communities. Since Yunus started the Grameen Bank about thirty years ago, thousands of microfinance institutions have sprouted up. What we are simply doing is connecting our website to those MFIs.

On the Kiva website we have tried to create a market-site feel, eBay-type model, where new businesses are posted up every hour, every minute sometimes. It constantly changes. People can lend as little as $25. Lenders pay with credit card and PayPal, and we send the money to the MFI via wire transfer. Developing this model where we partner with MFIs in the developing world has unlocked an order of magnitude of growth for us, because we don't have to do the job of the MFIs. They do their job, we do ours.

We needed a lot of support to get this idea off the ground. We needed funding, respect from people, networks. There was a lot of politics, a lot of networking, a lot of making deals. I have sought mentors to help me along the way. I'm a pretty inexperienced businessman, so especially early on I needed someone to watch my back. Luckily I have people older than me with a lot of experience offering support; people who could really carry weight in a meeting in that first year. Right now we have something to speak of: we started something, we have a staff and several million dollars in loans and Kiva now has popularity. But when we started out we had nothing like that. So how do you get that leverage? It is hard – you need some political leverage by being associated with people who really believe in you. That is almost the difficult bit.

There have also been a lot of fortuitous events where Kiva has been in the right place at the right time. Muhammad Yunus winning the Nobel Prize for instance. Who would have known that the same year we started this business that microfinance would

become world-renowned? So man, were we lucky! I didn't plan on that.

My highest priority now is to stabilise the company so that it is smooth to work there and that everything is covered. We were so understaffed for so long that there were big holes and some balls got dropped. So I want to build a stable, well-run company getting us over this period of hypergrowth. We are doing pretty well. Every month it gets smoother and smoother.

I'm really comfortable doing this job now and I feel that it fulfils my needs more than any other job I have done. At the same time I'm not sure if I really get to decide how long I can do it. We have a board of directors and governors and they will make the decision. I just feel I am doing my best at what I am doing today.

Tony Deifell

Seeing Beyond Sight
WDYDWYD?
www.seeingbeyondsight.org
www.wdydwyd.com

San Francisco, California, USA
Themes: Arts, Media

Following your calling sometimes means going against the flow.

Tony Deifell is a talent bundle. He has an unusual blend of analysis and creativity, which have lead him in fascinating ways. From photography to social activism, from non-profit strategy development to social entrepreneurship, it's a diverse mix of skills, which Tony calls 'living in the slashes'. For him, innovation happens where disciplines meet.

Tony is author of *Seeing Beyond Sight*, a photography book which collates images from his days of teaching photography to visually impaired students. He is also curator of WDYDWYD?, a mass photography project which captures people's response to the question 'Why do you do what you do?'.

With an MBA from Harvard Business School, he has been able to bring the arts and business together. He was previously founding director of KaBOOM!, an organisaiton which builds playgrounds in neighbourhoods across the US, and was Executive Director of the Institute of Public Media Arts, which promoted diversity across colleges in the US.

Passing through the San Francisco, I made a point of meeting up with Tony, whose photography exhibition, Seeing Beyond Sight,was just opening in a gallery in the city. Tony also happens to be married to the wonderful Mardie Oaks, fellow social entrepreneur (see next profile). I'm telling you, that's one heck of a household!

218

I feel our communities are what make us our best selves. Everybody has selfishness and greed, they are human qualities, but if we are around communities that support better qualities, the more altruistic side of ourselves, then we will be that way also. It is the communities we choose to be in that bring out our best, which is why I believe it is so important to help build them.

There is a folk tale about the creator of the world who was holding a lamp, bringing light into the world. But the creator dropped the lamp and it broke into a million pieces. Today each one of us is in possession of a piece of that lamp and our work in the world is about bringing the pieces back together. It is about mending the world so that the lamp can bring light again. That is our collective work. The problem is that each of us has one piece of the lamp but we think we have the whole lamp. And sometimes people think that their piece is the whole lamp – the solution. It happens when religions clash and it happens with people working for social change too. They focus on just a single issue or problem when the reality is

much more complex than that. You should not think that one thing alone will solve everything. **There is no single magic glue.** We have to try out different things. That is our challenge.

My work is trying to build communities and help others put the pieces of the lamp together. However, I find I always have to pause when I describe exactly what I do, because I never know what sort of bucket to put it in. I am in a hybrid space between for-profits and non-profits.

I was on the founding board of KaBOOM! and have been involved in helping the organisation grow and expand. During that time I was also running a non-profit called the Institute for Public Media Arts, based around community media work. We had a radio production studio for teenagers, helping colleges to use video in classrooms to address 'isms', particularly racism. The programme ended up being in colleges and universities all across the country. We had seventeen staff at one point and funding from Ford and Kellogg. But interestingly, we didn't set out to build a large organisation. **We set out**

to take the next step we needed to take, and it grew from there.

As KaBOOM! was growing they needed someone who understood business frameworks and practices to help it expand. So after a few years I went back to business school and did an MBA at Harvard (which is where I also met my wife, Mardie). Currently I'm on the board of the Social Enterprise Alliance, which is the sort of trade association for social enterprise in the US. I love this kind of field-building work and developing the whole area of social enterprise and social entrepreneurship.

As an undergraduate I studied sociocultural anthropology, doing a lot of photography on the side. I shot for newspapers and took a lot of journalism classes. But I decided I wanted a broader humanitarian education and that I didn't want to make my living out of photography. It's hard to make a living that way and when you do, you end up doing the kind of photography you don't like doing, which for me is wedding photography. I love photography but I don't want to have to chase money to do it. I would rather just do my own projects, which is partly why I went to business school to learn how to use what I know about running non-profits and make a living from that. I can then do other arts projects, which would never happen if I had to depend on money. The Seeing Beyond Sight project and 'Why do you do what you do?' (WDYDWYD.com) are two examples. I've never made a dime on them!

When you start non-profits or projects, you often have to go on fumes. A lot of people in organisations don't get paid the first year and they work off their credit cards. It is just like making a film: social entrepreneurs are like film-makers too – they make a film, get it to Sundance, put it on their credit card! **It is about having a passion and believing in it.**

When I used to shoot photography in a journalistic way, I loved meeting people directly and being invited to their homes. I would have access to things as a photographer that were really moving to me. I could tell stories that could reach a broad audience. But after a while it felt too micro – like I was in the grass roots of things. I wanted to get a bigger picture and think systemically, which is how I got interested in systems change and public policy. I see **systems as large levers** and a place where you can tell stories on a different scale.

It was probably my parents who got me started in this kind of work. My father is a minister. Our dinner-time conversation would involve my Dad pushing religious conversations, which I hated at the time, but they made me think. It made me ask questions like 'how do I want to live my life?' or 'what is my purpose?' So even though I wanted to watch MTV instead, the questions still sunk into me.

While my parents certainly influenced me, **I also really believe in people finding their path by walking.** Part of the path of where you are now is because of the step you took right before now and right before that. When

I think about my own path I know there were people every step of the way who helped me to get to where I am now. One person, for example, was Joel Fleishman. He was a mentor to me, deliberately taking me under his wing. He worked in philanthropy and taught me a lot about the area. Interestingly he never married and I remember asking him 'do you have regrets? Did something prevent you from doing it?' He said no, explaining his belief that it was not his calling in the world to have a family. He is Jewish and has a strong sense of God. He told me he believed God called him to have a different impact in the world and explained that he could not have done the work he does if he had a family. So all of a sudden he validated that there is another way of being in the world, even career-wise. He showed me that **following your calling sometimes means going against the flow.**

Sometimes I wonder what could have led me down an entirely different path, politically and otherwise. I don't know how far off I was from it. I certainly don't think my work is innate within me. Opportunities just opened up and it is still a puzzle to me how I got here. Except that **the next step just kept on leading me to it**. And is great now because, as the field of social entrepreneurship grows, people are becoming more comfortable with taking alternative career and life paths. A while ago it was just anathema to not have a job at a brilliant company. Now people accept it more.

I learned a lot from the people who I worked with on the Seeing Beyond Sight project – Luwanda, for instance, who was visually impaired. She was one of the students in the photography class at the school for the blind. One day she took a picture of sidewalks and I thought they were a mistake, that she had intended to point the camera somewhere else. But she corrected me – and I learned something that has really shaped my thinking. 'I wanted to take a picture of the cracks in the sidewalk because they are a problem for me. I want to send the photos to the superintendent and ask for the sidewalks to be fixed.' So we sat down at the typewriter and she wrote a letter to the superintendent saying, 'Since you have the privilege of sight, you probably walk on these cracks every day and don't notice them. Here are pictures: proof of the damage. They are a problem for me because my cane gets stuck. Can you please fix them?'

This may seem like a very simple event but the experience represents

a larger metaphor to me: **that cracks exist throughout the world which need healing**. Often people have blind spots and don't see cracks along the fault lines of race or poverty or gender, or indeed any of the cracks which make our world unjust and in need of healing. It takes work to notice the cracks, to pay attention to them, and then to mend them. But the problem is we don't always see them because we are privileged. It may be that we live in the US, or we are white, or middle class, or have college education – all of these things can blind us. And so for me, media seems like one of the best vehicles through which people can **see the cracks**, or have a voice to tell other people about the cracks they notice. I want to use media to give people opportunities to be self-reflective, by seeing or reading something, or being moved by it. If they can engage with it and participate with it, all the better. WDYDWYD? and the Seeing Beyond Sight Challenge are some of these projects.

I almost have two different résumés. I just applied for a grant and didn't put Harvard Business School on it. If anything, it will make people in the arts world misperceive me. But when I apply for jobs that use more strategy or are with for-profit businesses, then I don't put my art residencies on it. I sometimes feel I have done twice the work for half the résumé! I realise, however, it is about figuring out your audience and deciding how to slice it.

It is easy to say 'follow what you believe in', and I do believe that, but you also have to understand the key component that will make it successful. You need **persistence**. The *Seeing Beyond Sight* book is a good example – it took fifteen years to get it published. If I wasn't so bull-headed and passionate about it, there is just no way it would have happened. You just have to knock on doors and **keep knocking on doors**. People just don't get it. They don't see the possibilities like you can. I had to realise that people have limited time and they were not as invested in it as I was. But I had to be persistent. I would **try every angle**. I tried to find agents. I couldn't find any so I went directly to a bunch of publishers. I knocked on at least fifty different doors and tried numerous different paths. Finally, Chronicle Books published the book and it got tons of great press, including the *New York Times* Book Review. I think organisations are the same. You have to believe totally in your project. However being persistent doesn't mean being stubborn. You have to **be willing to modify your approach based on feedback** . . . and then not give up.

And also you have to **learn how to deal with ambiguity**. I feel that most of the innovative things in the world are between the cracks, between known things. **It is when people live in the hybrid, or the hyphen between worlds, that innovation happens.** But that space is also the least defined. It is the most ambiguous. It is the most lonely. But it is also the place of new ideas, new solutions, new possibilities. It is an exciting place to be, and I feel so lucky to be here.

Mardie Oaks

Hallmark Community Solutions

www.hallmarksolutions.org

San Francisco, California, USA

Themes: Design, Environment

Mardie Oaks was trained as an architect. But not only does she design buildings, she designs communities. Through innovative design she helps to integrate people with disabilities into local communities by buying and renovating existing homes to suit their particular needs.

Believing that life can be enriched through creative design, she has combined her background in architecture, finance and development to create a business model with high-quality, affordable housing at its core. Houses in the San Francisco area are remodelled with sustainable and safe materials. Non-slip tiles, bamboo flooring, wheelchair ramps, lower countertops, and easy-to-clean surfaces are features which combine to provide safe, comfortable and beautiful spaces.

With over 350,000 homeless people in San Francisco alone, her work is an example of how people on the margins of society can be integrated into the local community when their needs are incorporated from an early stage into the design process.

In 2006, Mardie was awarded an Echoing Green Fellowship for her innovative efforts.

I have always followed what I find interesting, which has been pretty consistent throughout my life: design and buildings. **By meandering and following my intuition, it always surprises me that I can draw a pretty linear path to where I am right now.** It was not particularly calculated or deliberate and I have never done a big job search. One thing comes up, which I think might be interesting, I follow it, and it happens. I have never been a big planner. But somehow I got here.

I am currently the Executive Director of a non-profit called Hallmark Community Solutions. It has nothing to do with the card company – the name is a constant source of pain for me! I stepped into an existing registered charity that was dormant, which is why the name stuck. The organisation is the master developer of a housing project in California to develop community-integrated homes for people with developmental disabilities. We develop housing for people with Autism, Down Syndrome, or for people with disabilities from brain injury.

We have been working on a project to rehouse individuals who have been living in a residential institution. It was built in the 1880s as California's first insane asylum: the Great Asylum for the Insane. At its height it had 4,500 people in residence and now has about 250. The State plans to close it and intends to shift people into other institutions or traditional group housing models. However this type of housing is not particularly appealing and doesn't attract the highest level of care. So instead we are developing a new model. We are buying existing houses throughout the San Francisco Bay Area, renovating them and making them accessible for people with disabilities. We adapt the housing to suit the individual's needs. The goal is that each house feels like a home and not a little institution. We work from scratch: from getting the finance together, buying the properties, to working with the construction managers. It is fantastic to be able to bring all those elements together with the client's needs in mind. I feel like I matter when I am able to solve the problems that come up.

I studied architecture as an undergraduate – I always loved buildings. When I was a child I remember going on field trips and, rather than describing where I had been, I would describe the rooms I had been in. I've always enjoyed just going on house tours and looking at buildings, which is why I decided study architecture.

I had a blast at university but when I tried to work full-time as an architect it was not such a blast. When you are studying architecture you have no budget and no clients; you are just dreaming and it is very disconnected from the practice in the field. I did a five-year degree and between fourth and fifth year I worked in an architectural firm. It was during that year I realised I didn't want to be an architect, but I didn't know what else to do so I decided to go back and finish the last year. In my final year I took a class on housing and urban development. I was one of only five people who had signed up for it and because the numbers were so small, they were going to cancel. But I begged them not to. They decided to run the class and because of that **the trajectory of my life totally changed.**

It led me to learn about community development and its history in the US. It was a pretty new movement in Houston, where I was studying. I met a bunch of organisations that were dabbling in it and ended up interning in my last semester for a group who were involved in community redevelopment, working in Houston's lowest-income neighbourhood. I did that for about five years, becoming a project manager and helping to develop innovative single-family homes. The organisation I was working with did great work bringing new housing and energy to the neighbourhood and **I learned that if you have the intention and the creativity** you can build something much better for the same price. I also learned that you have to understand the systems of how things happen and that **you have to know how to scale something to really make any kind of a dent.** There was no point building one or two homes, we needed to transform the way things are built. And that is what led me to business school.

It was funny how I got to there. I had gone on vacation, feeling frustrated about work, and ran into a friend who I had done my undergrad with. He had just finished at Harvard Business School. We went out to dinner and I started talking about the things I was interested in. I still remember meeting him so vividly: he just looked at me and said 'you have to go to Harvard Business School'. It was so funny because it had never occurred to me to go to business school – at that point I was filling out applications for social work degrees. He just talked to me about the database of alumni and contacts he had made, and the people who can help make things happen. So that very day I was convinced that business school was for me. I applied to do an MBA at Harvard and got in. Good job, because I hadn't applied anywhere else!

There are moments however when I miss the pre-MBA Mardie. It was easier when I was a little naive about how things really are. Now I'm much more aware of how much effort is required to make real change, to make systemic change. **Systems are big, heavy and hard to move but if you don't tackle problems at a high level,**

then I think that you are just applying the 'band-aid solution'. Sometimes working at this level does frighten me, but it depends on the day you ask me. Mostly I feel optimistic and know that there are ways to make a difference. It just takes time, effort and big-picture thinking.

I have realised the value of being able to follow the funding money: where it comes from and where it goes. It is empowering to have an influence on where funding goes and connecting the money to outcomes that are good for the world. It is what I love about this work right now – the source of the money is completely connected to the outcome and it is funnelling through my organisation. We are connecting the pieces in the whole chain of events to build the best houses for people who need them. So that is fun!

I sometimes find it hard being a leader of an organisation where people want me to make decisions all the time but when I have very little information to make the decision. They have no idea how much pain I am in when they ask me to make a decision when I know they understand the context better than I do. I have probably got better at making decisions over time, and I also have enough experience to know that even though I may not have made the best ones all the time, nothing ever blew up, nothing fell apart, nothing really bad happened. There might have been a better outcome had I had more information or more time, but generally there are not many times when you totally screw up – thankfully!

The skills I have had to learn along the way? Being able to communicate clearly. I try to use **correspondence as an opportunity to connect and educate**. My emails tend to be long, but I hope it helps people know where I am coming from and why I'm asking for something.

I have also developed my analytical skills – that is what business school does for you. I love spreadsheets now. I spend a lot of time on them, and I actually really enjoy understanding how numbers tell a story. I didn't have that skill five years ago.

My management style is '**kill them with kindness**'. I try to make people want to do their best job because they want to, and be pleased that they got the job done. I suppose I have a soft, personal style. I also just try to be myself in the office and I even have a habit of doing little dances! I kick off my shoes and run around if I need to. I did have some insecurity around that early on, thinking that it was not so professional – but it has yet to bite me in the ass!

I like my work the most when I feel like the journey I have taken, which has pulled together a lot of different disciplines, helps to solve particular problems. I particularly enjoy my work when I think not many other people could do the particular piece of the job I have been working on. It is great to feel that the choices you have taken can make a difference for others – it is just so rewarding!

Kyle Zimmer

First Book

www.firstbook.org

Washington DC, USA

Themes: Education, Business

First Book is a clever organisation – very clever. Their aim is to give children from low-income homes the magic of their first books.

What's clever (aside from the concept) is the way they have managed to team up with corporations to form mutually beneficial deals. Take First Book's marketplace as an example: an online book site that sells to local reading groups at discount rates. The publishers often have excess books that they can't sell, but to store them costs money. The local reading groups may have some money to buy books, but not much. This is where First Book comes in, acting as a mass purchaser and distributor of low-cost, quality books. The publishing companies are happy, because they get to sell their stock copies, and so too the reading groups, who now have a chance to buy up-to-date books at a very low price. As a result books are getting into homes that they ordinarily wouldn't.

Kyle Zimmer, one of the founders of First Book, started out over fifteen years ago. Back then she thought it would be a job for only a year or two . . . little did she know. Leaving a successful career in law, her legal colleagues found it hard to believe what she was doing. But Kyle persisted and ended up using her lawyer boardroom experience to negotiate deals for First Book. Over 60 million books later, she and the team are still going strong, and getting stronger.

I went to law school and practised law for years. When I was in training I was very interested in the environmental movement, so I practised in the field of energy law. But because I had to make money to pay back my educational loans, most of my work was in corporate law. It was great training and experience, but **it was never really where my heart was.**

When I was in practice, I started tutoring a little boy in a well-known soup kitchen in Washington. I went in once

or twice a week and learned a couple of things really fast. Firstly, that I'm not a teacher. I have profound respect for people with that gift, but it is not me. I tutored for six years and learned more than anyone I taught. But once I started, I also noticed that the centre had no books. I remember thinking 'gosh, if this programme, which is highly touted in the Washington community, doesn't have books, what is going on with the others?' So I started looking around. I reached out to a couple of friends of mine, Washington lawyers, and we started piecing First Book together. I had done a lot of political work and understood how to put a local operation together, and **we just kind of began**.

In our first year we gave out 12,000 books. None of us had quit our jobs at that point. There was a young man who came in and helped us run the organisation for a while, but soon it became clear that if we really were to crank it up, then one of us would have to work full-time. I said I'd do it for a couple of years, and here I still am! **This is the most fun I've ever had.** Every day I come to work with people who are infinitely smarter than I am, who are incredibly gifted and incredibly dedicated. I work with a growing network of people who are absolutely inspiring.

I think that I've always been someone with a very strong public-sector, **mission-focused heart**, but I also have a very **private-sector head**. Working in the private sector never really fulfilled my personal mission. Sometimes I was lucky enough to work

You have to learn to love the game.

with clients who I thoroughly believed in. I represented the Navajo nation for a number of years, for example, and that was incredibly transformative work. It taught me important lessons about humility and the gifts each of us has been given.

On the corporate side, working in the private sector gave me a strong understanding of business principles and an appreciation of the pressures involved. I've been in boardrooms on the other side of the table. Now I'm in there for different reasons, but because of my corporate experience I don't find it daunting or mysterious, and that gives me a lot of confidence. There are, of course, some businesses that have behaved wrongly – there are some who have profoundly worsened the social sector movement, and without a doubt there are people with bad intentions – but it is not everybody. The corporate sector is the biggest jet engine out there and if you can figure out a way to harness the power of that economic engine – now we are talking.

The culture of First Book is strongly private sector. The design of our business from day one was in recognition of the fact that we wanted publishers to get to the table. Publishing has narrow margins and isn't a big cash cow. Like the movie industry, some books don't make much money or make no money, so they are dependent upon the superstar Harry Potters to significantly move the needle of their business. We knew

that if we went to publishers asking for money and books, then it was going to be a pretty short conversation. We knew it would have to be sustainable for them. When the market takes a turn for the worse they have to protect their company. From the start we had to build a system fundamentally based on purchased books, at thin margins, so that no matter what happened, the industry would stay engaged. **You can't have the kind of cultural impact in the US, or anywhere else, if you are dependent on the crumbs that fall off the table.** We needed the best authors, we needed the most engaging illustrators, we needed to engage these kids with the most powerful tools we could bring to them. They deserve it.

About seven years into our work, in 1988 or 1989, we began to realise how many millions of books were being destroyed every year. We sat with the publishers and asked 'what goes on?' We knew these weren't people with horns who love throwing their books out! So we inquired. 'What are the economic pressures that bring you to that decision?' We understood from their responses that they do what they can, but they are getting thousands of phone calls from people in preschools and after-school programmes asking them to send small boxes of books. It is not the cost of the books that is the problem, it is all the exchange: talking to the person who calls, getting the address right, calling the warehouse, packing a

small box . . . Multiply that by a few thousand and YIKES, it is a lot of work! The publishers did what they could, but there is a limit.

That is where we stepped in. We designed a system called the First Book National Book Bank. We recruited donated warehouse space all over the country. Some of it is private sector from businesses that may have spare warehouse space for a few months. So we step in, use it and have staff to manage it. Then we created a software system, funded by a phone company, which allows the people running preschools and after-school programmes to register with us. They give us their bona fides to prove that they are working with kids who need the books. We also became the signature charity of the US Coast Guard. It may seem like an odd choice but, because they move equipment, they taught us gigantic lessons in logistics. In the end, we created a wildly efficient system to place books. Now we are

placing 7 million books annually, and it is all based on industry excess – excess warehouse capacity, excess inventories – and a software system to place it all. It is fabulously powerful! (Can you tell I love my job? I can barely sit still after all these years. It's not just the coffee!)

Even in the States everybody assumes the streets are paved with gold. Some of them are, but not the streets we work on. So profound is the difference that in one recent study it was reported that in a middle-income neighbourhood there are thirteen books per child. However, in the lowest-income neighbourhood there is only one book for every 300 kids. One for every 300 – that is inconceivable! Even if the researcher was having a wildly bad day, and even if she was off by a hundredfold, it is still one book for every three kids. It is still a train wreck. So we have a lot of work to do and we have been watching those statistics, saying to ourselves 'we need something else, this is not adequate, what more can we do?' That is the symptom of a social entrepreneur – it is never enough.

So next we created the First Book Marketplace – the first ever retail site for books for people serving or working with low-income children. Word is getting out. In twenty months we went from 4,000 to 17,000 groups signed up with First Book to receive new books. Interestingly, the people who are building the registry for us, this online community, are 24- and 25-year-olds. They are incredibly smart and dedicated. They will tease me sometimes, saying 'does anyone know that the people putting this database together is being run by 24-year-olds?'. **They are young people who are highly motivated and who want to change the world.** It doesn't matter if they are 17 or 23 or 135 like me, they are doing it and the results are tangible. It is very, very cool stuff.

Good analytical thinking is critical to this work. Over the years you learn not to fall in love with the deal or the specific thing you are thinking about, whether that be launching First Book in colleges or trying to forge a deal with a company you think makes perfect sense to you. Instead, you have to force yourself to pull back. I loved the concept of the First Book Marketplace but we forced ourselves to back off and write a business plan. We had to ask 'is this going to work? What is our motivation? Will this be sustainable if the economy drops?'

And you have to learn to love the game. You can't get discouraged. I had to learn to love it when I came to First Book in a way I never had before. **If this were easy work, somebody else would already have done it and we could be off sipping cocktails. This is hard, it is so hard.** Some days you come in and an idea you loved is failing or something crashes that you didn't expect to crash, or a million other things – a million obstacles. You have to teach your brain not to go down the chute of despair. You have to pull up and say 'this is new, bring it on'. It is like playing a game of tennis. When there is someone on the other side who has an ace of a serve, you can't get in the headspace of 'I'm going to get creased'. You have to say 'I hope it is ninety miles per hour, bring it on! **Bring it on because we will figure this out.'**

A while ago I attended a book distribution in Ohio, not far from where I grew up. A little boy, about eight, came running up to me and said, in his deepest southern Ohio accent, 'Do you have any Spanish books?' I asked him, 'Honey, are you taking Spanish?' He responded, 'No, but I know it is out there and this is my big chance.' That really is the power of this work, and this little kid knew it. He wanted the opportunity. Kids are so hungry for learning. They know the big world is out there but they know they are only getting one view of it. This is our big chance to really change them and open them up to the world. So at 2 a.m., when I'm up trying to finish something or have a deadline, that is what keeps me racing. Bring it on, I say!

Coming Full Circle

Extract from last letter home: almost home.

Friends, greetings.

It is time to revert to a cliché. Time flies. Or I could just put a bit of a spin on the formulaic and say, time glides. Either way, there is truth in it. Wasn't it just the other week I was packing my bags in Dublin and watching the dawn sweep from under me as I flew out on this trip? Didn't that just happen? Obviously not, for my calendar tells me that I have about two weeks left before that plane takes me back to a Dublin dawn. The last leg of the trip is sprinting to the finish line, and I am somewhere behind it trying to catch up (I was never that good at sprinting!).

These few weeks in the States (from San Francisco and now DC) have been packed and rightly so – meeting more good folk en route, making connections with some of the organisations I met along the way, and in the late hours of the night reflecting on what has happened while thinking about what is ahead. It seems like there is a lot to think about.

Which brings me to this. Those of you who know me well, know that I have a slight fetish for motivational quotes. I seem to hoard them as others would shoes, or fluff, or whatever takes your fancy. Thanks to some cheesy travel photography book I was looking at the other day, and thanks to the poetry of Rumi, I just added another to my collection. Let me share: 'Journeys bring power and love back to you' – Rumi.

OK, so this one is fairly high on the cheese-alert factor – even I admit it, but despite the stilton, brie or even Wensleydale-with-cranberries whiff to it, it did resonate, a lot. You see, when I set out on this journey, the world seemed like a big place. Well now, eleven months on, it seems even bigger. Setting out, the world seemed like a beautifully complex place. Well now it seems even more beautiful and even more complex. The more places I travel to, the more I want to return to. The more I learn, the more I know I have yet to learn. The more I push myself to explore my own 'power' or potential, the more I realise that there is to explore. And the more I question what love there is in this world, the more I am reminded with each turn and glance that it is there in abundance. It is just a matter of seeing it.

Phew, that was some paragraph – but I mean it. When I look back on this trip, I know without a sliver of doubt that it was the right thing to do. It was not all clear at the start, plans bordered on the nebulous most of the time, but being open to suggestions led me to places I never thought I would get to go, externally and internally.

Of course, it hasn't all been fun fun frolics. There have been tough, challenging moments: the bumpy roads, the missed connections, the travel hiccups, but mostly the scale of poverty that human dignity should not have to bear witness to, the dichotomies that go unjustified, the sheer abundance of wasted talent that circumstances of birth dictate.

But nestled in the tough times are the good times. Learning is a hotchpotch of highs and lows, and if it was all plain sailing I would return wondering if I really had set sail at all. So in all, good and bad, highs and lows, rough and tumble, the circle is soon to be turned, and I am on my way home.

I was sitting with a friend in a coffee shop in San Francisco last week and she basically summarised where I am heading to: 'So you have no job, no house, don't really know where you want to live, what you want to do and you have no money.' 'Yep', was my reply and we both laughed. Taking the facts for what they are I seem a rather sorry case. But my friend gets this too: it is also rather hopeful. You see, this time a year ago, I think I would have panicked not knowing. But now, thankfully, things are different. I have lots of ideas about what I want to do, lots of things I still want to explore, I have a book to write, and experience to condense. My odd lack of fear now comes down to trust. Somehow, deep down, I know it is going to be fine. If anything, this trip has taught me about trust. Trust that I'll meet the right people. Trust that I'll be given the right phone number. Trusting my gut. Trusting my instinct. Trusting that I'm doing something worthwhile, which will lead to something worthwhile. Trusting that the bus which has already broken down three times will actually, eventually, get me there. My trip so far has been more than fine, so why should the future suddenly stop being so?

A little word of warning – when I come home I may appear to have my head in the sand, but no, it will be in the clouds, searching for the stars. I'll also have a sign on my door, whichever one I may be at, which will read: Open for Business.

Until then, wishing you love and power, C.

Nina Smith

Rugmark

www.rugmark.org

Washington DC, USA

Themes: Business, Education, Human Rights

My visit to Washington linked me back to my visit to Bal Ashram, the rehabilitation centre for former child labourers in Rajasthan, India, established by Kailash Satyarthi. One of the many interesting dimensions to his work is his effort to eliminate child labour, industry by industry – the carpet industry being one of them. To help, he set up Rugmark, a certification label that guarantees a rug to be child-labour free.

To find out more about Rugmark's operations in a 'developed country', I met up with Nina Smith, who is the Executive Director of the Rugmark Foundation USA. Nina came to Rugmark from twelve years of work in the fair trade movement and an involvement with the 'The Craft Centre', a non-profit which promoted the fair trading of handicrafts from artisans, mainly from South America.

Talking to Nina was a certainly an insight into the level of work which is required to make system-wide change. It's as much about rescuing the children from the factories (as Kailash does), as about how products are labelled on shelves back in the US. Making the link between the two is one of the reasons why Rugmark has been successful.

Rugmark is tackling the problem through market demand, allowing consumers of conscience to purchase products, knowing that the rugs they buy are not made by children. Since the introduction of the label the numbers of child labourers in the industry has fallen from approximately 1 million to 300,000. The numbers are still huge, but they are going in the right direction.

Rugmark is a great example of collaborative social entrepreneurship, thinking about how problems can be approached through incentivising positive consumer choice, rather than just laying blame.

234

There are so many problems you can't solve all of them — no one person can do that. But focus and be satisfied with making a difference in your chosen area. If we all do that we can make a collective difference.

My first job after university was with an international newspaper. It exposed me to all kinds of global issues and people. I did it for four years and it was a great way to engage in what was going on in the world. But I knew that I was not exactly in the right place for me at the time – I wanted to explore the world. So in 1993 I took a trip to Central and South America and it was a life-changing experience. One day I was at a market in Guatemala and was about to buy a weaving from a woman, but I couldn't pay the amount of money she wanted and walked away. She chased me down the street, willing to sell the textile at any price. I realised that she was so desperate that she would lose money on it. I started feeling responsible that people like me could go to a place like Guatemala and squeeze the producers to sell us beautiful hand-weavings for a dollar – when even the materials alone cost more than that. The people are so poor that they just need to sell their products to get a meal on the table. The experience got me thinking about global markets and how they are creating situations like this.

After the trip I started to ask 'how **can I bridge this gap between those who have money and those who don't?'**

I wanted to connect the consumers with the producers, educating them in the process about the reality of the countries where the goods are made. I didn't know what fair trade was at the time but I had an idea to start a company that would sell handmade products while educating people about the artisans and the conditions in which they live. I saw it as a way of getting more money and improving the conditions for the producers. As I started to work on it, I realised that there was already a whole network of organisations under the auspices of fair trade. So I got involved. I volunteered with a fair trade conference initially and met a lot of people in the area. The next thing I knew I was offered a job to go to India with a fair trade company. I went to the mountains, to Dharamsala (which is where the Dalai Lama is) to work with a Tibetan refugee employment project. I was there for a year and have stayed involved over the years. My time there helped me to gain hands-on experience of working with small producers.

When I came back to the US I got involved with another non-profit called the Craft Centre, where I worked for five years. It was based on the idea of linking the artists, or producers, into networks and markets, connecting them to potential buyers, or to loans or funds for their businesses. I was working with the Craft Centre when I heard that Rugmark was getting started in the US. I was drawn to Rugmark, because it offered an opportunity to test my theory that when consumers are educated about working conditions they will make humanitarian choices. So when I heard about the launch of Rugmark, I jumped at the chance to bring it to life in the US.

Rugmark International is a network of non-profits working against child slavery in the carpet industry. We certify rugs as child-labour-free and ask businesses and consumers to select them over rugs that could be made by exploited labour. Companies that sign up to Rugmark agree to randomised inspections at their production sites – to ensure that children are not being employed. A portion of the licence fee for the certification then goes back into the rehabilitation and schooling of former child labourers. If we can convince consumers in Europe and the US to refuse to buy goods made by children then a message is sent down the supply chain and manufacturers will stop using child labour. So that is the simple theory, but it is backed up by a complicated operation.

The Rugmark story starts with Kailash Satyarthi, back in India. Kailash had been working in raid and rescue, bringing children from factories into ashrams, or rehabilitation centres. But he realised that if you keep rescuing children, others will take their place

– there needed to be a way to create a disincentive for people to employ children in the first place. He decided to start with the carpet industry, where there was a huge problem of child labour. Rugmark began in 1994, starting in India and Germany and then branching out to different countries.

A group of people also wanted to bring Rugmark to the US. They started campaigning against child labour but they had a strong anti-industry, or anti-business position, and ultimately weren't making any friends. I realised this would need to change. In 1999 I met one of these campaigners who asked if I wanted to work with Rugmark and launch the office here. So I decided to investigate.

The idea of Rugmark appealed to me because of my involvement with fair trade labelling and I really believed in certification. I liked the focus of this initiative on child labour in the carpet industry – I knew it was a finite market in which you could reach consumers and businesses. But it has been a lot harder to change the system than I originally anticipated. Rugmark works with businesses and at the same time pushes them to improve their practices.

At the beginning there was a lot of door-knocking, but I think that is where my natural orientation is: building networks and relationships. When I started, I was just trying to find someone interested in talking to me! I found one person in the carpet industry interested in getting Rugmark off the ground here in the US and getting that support was critical.

I am a very stubborn person; I don't want to stop until I've won. I also have wonderful colleagues, both here and overseas – people like Kailash – which make my job easier and a lot of fun. I love working with these people and I really believe in what I am doing. I think a lot of what sustains me is the people I come in contact with and, of course, the children in our rehabilitation schools. We have over 3,000 children in schools, vocational training and day-care, and we are changing individual lives all the time. So sometimes when I get discouraged I think about that and feel fortunate to be able to do this work.

I've found a niche working in fair trade. I'll probably always work in this area in one way or another because it's where I can make a difference. I can't say that I'm expert, but I have learned some skills along the way. The big one for me was learning how to straddle the private sector and the activist worlds. **Being able to put on a business suit and talk to businesses as a partner is so important.** It hasn't always been easy, but I have got better at it over time. I like to bring people together around initiatives or campaigns, getting people behind a strategy and making it work . . . and winning!

Young people don't necessarily need experience to get involved with meaningful work. My advice is: just go out and do it. Don't let lack of experience be a hindrance.

Sometimes people think they have to take a traditional path to get to where they want to be, but I don't believe that. Volunteering is a great way to get involved initially and learn about issues or causes.

Approach everything with confidence. If you don't have the confidence that you can do it, you won't do it. Growing Rugmark has been really difficult. There has been a lot of opposition along the way: there hasn't been the funding, there hasn't been the support we needed at times and it has been discouraging. But keeping focused on the long-term success has helped, so have the confidence. There will be lots of ups and downs and maybe at times you may get discouraged, but you have got to stick with it.

No one person can change the whole world, but you can make a difference in your small part, and I think that is enough. There are so many problems you can't solve all of them – no one person can do that. But focus and be satisfied with making a difference in your chosen area. If we all do that we can make a collective difference. Oh, and if you are going to buy a rug, make it Rugmark!

Sarah Symons and John Berger

The Emancipation Network

www.emancipationnetwork.org

www.madebysurvivors.com

Cape Cod, Massachusetts, USA

Themes: Business, Design

Watching a film changed Sarah Symons' life . . . and her husband's, and her childrens', and her neighbours', and the lives of groups of women from Cambodia to India.

The film was *The Day My God Died*; the topic: child sex trafficking; her response: 'what can I do about it'?' That question led her and her husband, John, to set up The Emancipation Network (TEN), which buys and imports handmade products from survivors of trafficking and people who are at a high risk of being trafficked. It is done in a belief that when alternative income streams for families and communities are sourced, the risk of trafficking is radically reduced.

TEN now imports goods and products from many different organisations across East Asia and continues to expand its reach. John and Sarah's home in Cape Cod became their office and storage depot and it operates in a flurry of activity. Arriving to their home I was quickly taken on the grand tour, introduced to large boxes of goods – from hand-embroidered bags to handmade paper – and told about the story of the people behind the products.

Once the goods are purchased they are then distributed and sold though a series of 'Awareness Parties': a Tupperware model of sales, organised though a network of volunteers. The parties are a chance not only to sell the goods (thus providing an income to the artisans) but also to increase awareness about sex trafficking.

You do it because you believe in it.

Sarah: Believe it or not, seeing a movie changed my life. I'm a songwriter and a few years ago I was at the New York Film Festival because I had a song in one of the films. One afternoon during the festival I went to see *The Day My God Died*, a film about human trafficking between Nepal and India. The film profiles two NGOs, Maiti Nepal and Sanlaap, who are working to combat human trafficking. It shows how the organisations have created an underground network of prevention of trafficking by working at borders, conducting rescues with the International Justice Mission and raising awareness about trafficking in the villages. It shows how girls who have been rescued are going back into the brothels to rescue others. It is really amazing and after watching it, I thought **'if they can do it after what they have been through, then I in Cape Cod – a** very affluent area – can help. There must be something I can do'.**

The funny thing is I didn't want to see the film that day and had actually said to myself 'I won't be going to that'. I had a lot of misconceptions about human trafficking. My initial reaction to the film was fear and that, as a parent, it would be too painful to watch. My children were very young at the time and I just felt 'why would I go to see something that I can't do anything about'. But I was wrong because I know now that something can be done.

A couple of hours after watching the film, I met John for lunch. I remember telling him 'I just saw a film that's going to change my entire life'. He was very supportive and wanted to hear more . . . he didn't realise that it was going to change his life too!

I decided to contact the two NGOs

profiled in the film. Maiti Nepal immediately responded and put me in touch with a group in Boston who were already representing them. This group graciously invited me to volunteer with them, which I did for a year. All the time I was studying and reading a lot about the issues online.

About a year later the Boston group asked if I wanted to join them on a visit to Maiti Nepal – of course I did! When I visited I met Anuradha Koirala, their inspirational founder, who was interviewed in the film, and I asked what she needed most. She told me she needed help with the economic self-sufficiency and income-generation programmes for the women. So we spent some time brainstorming and thinking about what that could mean: chef training, working in hotels, accountancy – we had all sorts of different ideas. However, the next day while walking around the shelter I came across a room full of 'sparkly stuff'. It was full of amazing handicrafts: bags, scarves, and jewellery. So I just put the two ideas together. I realised that they already had nearly everything they needed – talent, people power, facilities and great products – but they didn't have a sufficient market for them. So I just followed their signposts and decided to sell the crafts in the US.

John came up with the idea of doing home parties. It was a way we could link the sales with raising awareness about issues. We spent nine months preparing and getting our non-profit status. We initially knew nothing about importing or retailing so we basically had to figure it out as we went along. We enlisted some volunteers and got a little money together between ourselves and some friends to buy the first inventory of goods. We figured out how to import the products and in 2005 we got the first shipment from our first four partners in Nepal, India, Thailand and Cambodia. One of our first partners was Maiti Nepal, and a few years later we have also been able to partner with the other organisation in the film, Sanlaap. That first year we had some really committed friends who helped us take the business to the next level. There was also a TV screening of *The Day My God Died*, and I was able to link up with the station. From the screening we got about thirty volunteers who also started helping us. We started growing very quickly.

In the beginning we had no office or real base – we were basically just an email address. Our basement was the storeroom and main depot. John was still working full-time in finance, while I was working unpaid. Around Christmas in our first year we started doing pretty well. We had partnered with another TV station, Lifetime TV and were able to get some more hosts for parties from that.

John: My decision to quit my job came around this time. When Sarah came back from Nepal she was very clear about what she wanted to do – sell the products – but she needed the right model to do it. I had been an investment banker for almost twenty years and in that job you get to see every kind of investment model in the world. You learn to analyse business models very

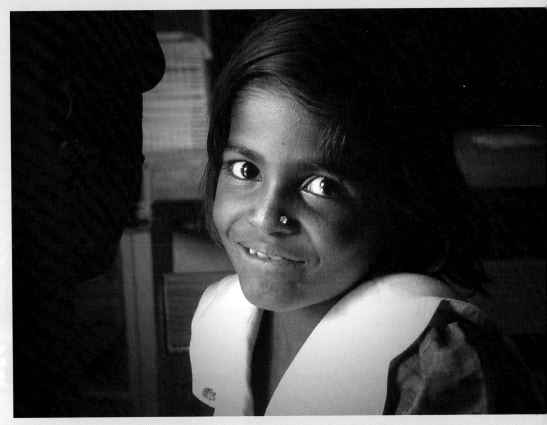

quickly. So when Sarah started telling me she wanted to sell the products, I knew the home-party model would work well. It has great awareness-raising potential plus the model doesn't require a lot of mark up – so you can get a good price for the producers. We didn't have a huge amount of money to invest in the business either, so we needed a model which we could fund with a relatively small amount of capital and which could then grow virally. Home parties are great for this: you invite ten people over and two of them may then have their own party. So the model is relatively easy to set up and run.

I was still working in banking for the first year while Sarah was in test mode. Our first year was really just 'proof of concept', showing that the

model worked and figuring out the products. I still had the day job. I would come home, spend time with the kids and then go to work on the website or whatever was needed. Towards the end of the Christmas season of 2005 we had a couple of volunteers and sold $40,000 in a month. It convinced me of the potential in what we were doing.

The next bit of our story demonstrates how totally different Sarah and I think – almost the opposite in fact. At this stage Sarah was shouting 'YEAH!' – she was so excited about the sales. But I said 'you are in trouble'. The model clearly worked but we had no infrastructure in place. The accounting wasn't automatic, we didn't know where all the inventory was, and the website was not up to scratch. I was afraid of

241

the 'Oprah' effect – if we ever got in *O*, the Oprah magazine, or achieved high levels of PR, we wouldn't have been in a position to deal with it. So **we had to prepare for success.**

That was when I decided to quit my banking job. It was perfect timing really. I had been thinking of getting out of what I was doing anyway. The market was changing in a way I didn't really enjoy and I was getting bored with it. I also had a horrible commute. I was leaving home at 5 a.m. and getting in at 7 p.m. at best. I wanted to spend more time with my kids. I had already come up with a couple of business ideas of my own but had never gone through with any of them. They were all in finance, doing what I already knew I could do. So I think I was in the right place for this job. I wanted something new. I also really like developing infrastructure and systems, so getting the accounting and IT system in place was perfect for me.

Sarah: This is a head-and-heart business. John is more pragmatic than I am – so it works well! We have an interesting combination of skills and we are very different. People often wonder how we ever got together! Our kids are also very supportive of what we do and we couldn't do it if we had high-maintenance children – they are fantastic. They have also developed an interest in the issue and love seeing the products coming to the house. It gives them a foundation and perspective on life, which I hope will help them form their own futures.

John: We are also lucky because we had a house and we have been able to use some of the equity in it to set up the business. It is like anything else – it is a risk. You have to get the business to a certain size before it is self-sufficient. We could pay ourselves a salary right now, but then we would not have the money to grow or to find new partners. We are gambling . . . it is interim. We committed to doing this for a couple of years to get it to the point where it would be able to sustain itself. But we do want to start paying ourselves a salary at some point soon!

Sarah: This is often the choice of people who start any entrepreneurial businesses, whether it is charitable or not. **You do it because you believe in it.** A lot of people go into this kind of work but don't really start doing anything until they get a grant. We didn't want to do that. These survivors can't wait for us and getting a grant could take years. We knew that once we built our credibility, the grants would come. So we decided that we had to come up with our own income stream. Between us we already had skills, and we knew we could create the market. John had the business side. I had a background in social work, so we said 'let's just do it'. And it seems to be working. We just keep growing and growing. Now we have many organisations overseas approaching us to take and market their products. We know there is huge need out there and our dream is to help them all!

Diary extract: on board the flight home

Boston. The very last leg.

I'm sitting on the plane, waiting to take off. Closing the circle, it feels like it is about to begin. 'Did that really happen?' I ask myself. 'Was that just a dream?' Dream or not, the images I am left with are plentiful, the friendships multiple, the learning intense, the solutions real.

I celebrate this by returning to friendships, all the stronger for absence. I celebrate it with a renewed sense of this crazy, beautiful world. Mostly, as the engines now fire up and the plane takes to the open skies, I applaud the people I have met along the way who have the vision and audacity to think big.

They are indeed living their one wild and precious lives.

Conclusion

One year on . . .

In many ways, the conclusion to this book has yet to be written. What started when I set off through the departure gates in Dublin Airport will, I think, take years to unravel. What started was a new way to see and frame the world – a world replete with possibility and potential. Witnessing at first hand what can be done when goodwill, courage, vision and passion are aligned filled me with the belief that things can be different. Once new parameters are drawn, it is hard to go back; that was the whole point of the journey.

But, there is a but: returning and settling back into Ireland was, by far, the hardest part of this adventure. Returning to friends and family was wonderful, but I also returned to a deep sense of unease within myself, rattled with the questions of 'What do I do now? What do I do next? Oh my gosh, what on earth just happened?' Frankly, it was frightening. There were months when I felt that my whole world had been shaken and, as I started to think about all the amazing people I met along the way and the choices they were making to make this world a better place, there were moments when I just froze, unable to make my own choices – it was all just a bit overwhelming. I did not anticipate that reaction, even towards the end of my travels, and that in turn was quite a shock. But now I see that bearing witness is a passage to responsibility and back in Ireland, here was I faced with my own responsibility to act.

It takes time for dust to settle, but settle it does. So in figuring out my next moves, I spent time trying to distil the many lessons from the journey into bite-size chunks. Here are my top ten, in no particular order:

Trust

Trust, I learned, gets you places. Trusting gut instinct. Trusting the good in people. Trusting that there is a better solution. The people I met on my travels trusted in their own vision and ability to make things happen, and then put their trust into hundreds of others to help make that vision a reality.

Acquiring skills to serve humanity

The people I met could see clearly that the world needs to change but they also spent time acquiring the skills to help make it happen. The world, they understand, needs many more 'doers' who come from all walks of life and fields. It needs more accountants, carpenters, medics, teachers and communicators who are advocates and agents of change.

When it comes to serving humanity, having practical, transferable skills is a huge bonus. Whatever it is, with a skill you have something tangible to offer, and the more skills you have, the more you have to offer. And the great thing is that you can pick new skills up along the way.

The power of vision

'If you have an idea, picture it in your head', Caroline Casey reminded me. All the people I met had a strong vision of what they wanted to create. From Mary Davis' team seeing the Special Olympic Games coming to Ireland, to Matt Flannery's conceptualisation of Kiva, each drew a picture in their head of what success would look like. With that clarity and vision they powered their dreams. Vision is direction, vision is a path to action.

The power of connections and networks to make things happen

Jim Fruchterman said, 'Honour your networks'. He is right. Without contacts and connections this journey could never have happened. For each of the people I met, it was their networks and contacts that built bridges of support. Networks are also reciprocal: if you put something in, you will get something back – that is their magic. They can come in many guises: college alumni, old school friends, social networking websites, hobby groups, and each can have something unique to offer.

The phrase 'networking' has got some bad stick in recent times. Think of it instead as bridge building. And just like any network, the stronger the connections, the stronger the structure. So, in a social context, the stronger network, the stronger the community.

There are no right answers/living with ambiguity

Nothing is perfect, ideas are flawed, things will inevitably go wrong at some point, times change. What is right in one place, may not be right in another. What works for someone, may not for another. Friction and ambiguity create space for learning and if we wait for the perfect moment to act, we will be waiting a long time. None of the people I met waited until they knew all the answers or had all the resources. That is partly what differentiates them.

Seizing Opportunities

As Taddy Blecher reminded me, everywhere around us there are innumerable opportunities to make a difference – we just have to open ourselves up to them. However, seizing opportunities can also mean taking risks. We may have to push ourselves beyond our comfort zone but it is at our margins where rich and lasting learning resides.

However, there is a caveat with this one. Deep in the mantle of what makes us tick should also be a commitment to sustaining our own personal energy and health. Burnout, stress and exhaustion are common in this work, and it takes time and attention to keep our own reserves in positive swing. We are no good to anyone else if our own physical, mental and spiritual health is depleted. Top-up comes by way of taking time out, spending time with nature or family, reading a good book, exercising, or whatever it is that replenishes and uplifts. Without a release valve, pressure mounts and implosion is pretty much guaranteed. So, discovering your own release valve and then using it, is vital to an effective and sustainable life of commitment.

In it for the long haul

Lasting and meaningful change takes time. Commitment must be combined with patience if real change is to occur. This is a long-haul race, which needs long distance runners.

Passion is there to be followed

Passion fuels and fires ambition. Passion is contagious and can rally others to want to have a slice of it. By tapping into their own passions, each of the people I met enriched both their own lives and the lives of others. Passion also helped to sustain them through tough times.

Leadership is about choice

Leadership, I believe, is not innate. It is a set of lenses through which we choose to view the world, and with them, we have a choice to influence others.

The power of choice is a remarkable thing. I met people who were choosing to make the best of their skills and talents to have a social impact, irrespective of geography, economics or social conditions. They are choosing to act, learn, follow their passions, seize opportunities, take risks and trust others to help make their visions reality.

Whether born into the slums of Mumbai or the wealth of Manhattan, the option to exercise that choice is universal. When it is exercised in the service of others that is true leadership.

Enjoy the ride!

Have fun while getting the job done – it makes life all the more beautiful!

. . .

Looking into the future now, I know there is reason to be optimistic. I only met a handful of people on my travels but I could have met handfuls and handfuls more. There is a quiet revolution taking place in the world that is not making headline news: it is the revolution of people starting to take action, to stand up for their rights, to demand change, to take ownership of the planet on behalf of its peoples. True, the challenges that the world faces are huge, but the willingness to take action on a global scale is also growing pace rapidly.

These lessons are my own personal take-aways. They are lessons I will carry with me for life and will take a lifetime to live up to. So as Goethe started, so too will he finish:

'Whatever you can do, or dream you can, begin it. Boldness has genius power and magic in it.'

And so, now, I begin.

Resources

Planning your own trip? Some travel tips from how I planned mine.

Committing to the idea of the trip was one of the hardest parts. When I say committing, I mean *really* committing. Despite the fact that I did not have all the money to do it, there was a moment when I had to say 'I will do it no matter what'. Once I did that, lots of things started happening to help me along the way. For instance: I was chatting to a man one evening at an event in Dublin. I was telling him what I was planning to do, explaining why and my intended route. At the end of a long conversation he asked for my address. Two days later there was a cheque in the post with enough money to cover my main airfares. Nice man! I was on my way.

A friend of mine posted a note about me on a social networking website called Omidyar.net (now closed). Within hours, I had offers of places to stay all around the world. Sofas and floors were becoming available from Nairobi to San Francisco. The response was overwhelming.

Friends and family gave me some sponsorship. It all amounted to enough to get me going. I had a small amount of savings, which I used, and now that I had places to stay around the world, I would be able to keep costs down.

Planning the trip seemed like a huge task to begin with. Who would I meet, where would I go? To start with I pulled the world map off my bedroom wall and decided on a rough route. I purposely choose some countries to which I had been before or at least had a connection with. That way, I thought that finding people to interview would be easier. I had already spent time in Kenya, South Africa, India, Tonga, Samoa and the United States, they were points of relative familiarity en route. The rest was all new to me. Once I had the route, it was easier to decide who to interview.

There was a bit of give and take when I went into the travel agent to book the trip due to flight availability and flight routes. Initially I also wanted to travel to South America, but financially, I realised that things were stretched as they were, and that South America would have to wait for another trip.

Word of mouth got out about what I wanted to do. Soon people whom I had never met or never heard of before, were emailing me with recommendations of people I could interview along the route. The list was growing bigger and bigger.

I made contact with a few key organisations which would also be able to put me in touch with interviewees. Social Entrepreneurs Ireland initially put me in touch with people in their Irish network. Ashoka, an organisation which identifies and supports social entrepreneurs around the world, liked my idea and put me in touch with staff in their offices around the world. These contacts were invaluable as I travelled.

I looked through the websites for the Skoll Foundation, Echoing Green and the Schwab Foundation, three additional organisations which support social entrepreneurs. My potential interviewee list was growing and growing.

Along the way, I would always buy a local newspaper and see who was making the news. Perhaps there were people mentioned there whom I could interview? I tracked down Youk Chhang in Cambodia and Gareth Morgan in New Zealand this way.

Google also became my friend. We spent a lot of time together researching and planning. We remain good pals.

Word of mouth is also a powerful connector. I asked each person I met for recommendations – not only for people to interview, but places to stay, foods to eat, local things to see and do.

I set up a blog site and became active on Flickr. People contacted me through both of them, recommending interviewees or sharing ideas. They were a fantastic way to communicate and share ideas. The blog became a crucial piece in my planning. I would send the link on to people I was going to interview or stay with. That way they had a much better sense of what I was doing before I met them. It also meant that we could get straight into the interview and I would not have to explain so much about the 'why' behind my travels when I met them. If they were limited for time, it meant we could make best use of the interview.

Computing

I bought a little Mac iBook G4 before I travelled. It was a reliable friend. I also had two 80 GB external hard drives for music, backup and photo storage.

Photographic

I had a loan of a Fuji Finepix S620 Zoom digital camera before I went. This refused to work about halfway through the trip and I decided to purchase a Canon EOS 350D and 18–55 mm lens. I also had couple of disposable cameras (in case something happened the digital) and a basic point-and-shoot digital, which, in fact, I never used.

Audio

I had an Olympus digital voice recorder on which I recorded all the interviews in MP3 format, and then backed up on to my laptop. I backed up interviews (and photos) in three places and carried them in different bags, with one in a sealed trouser pocket when en route. I had an iPod, which gracefully provided the soundtrack to my travels and backup for my files.

Telephones

I carried two mobile phones – one with an Irish SIM card and one with local SIM cards. I only ever used my Irish phone for text messages, as otherwise it would have been too expensive. In nearly every country I bought a local SIM card, which meant I had a local mobile number. This was a huge help when it came to arranging interviews and particularly when needing to clarify directions. I also felt safer with it.

Clothing and luggage

I never carried what looked like explicitly like a camera bag or laptop bag. I stuck out enough in many places as it was, so wanted to remain as inconspicuous as possible. My clothes were decent enough to go to interviews in, but nothing too fancy or flash. Mostly long, loose trousers (with side pockets), a few below-the-knee skirts, loose shirts, and a pair of jeans. My clothes were light and included layers, which I could wear in number if I was chilly. I had a warm fleece that functioned as a pillow when I didn't need to wear it. I had a light sleeping bag and a mosquito net and also carried a sarong – the all-essential travel idea, which at various times was a skirt, towel, pillow, sheet, door, bag, and tablecloth. My shoes were two good pairs of Birkenstocks, boots and sandals (not a high heel in sight for a year – bliss!) Before setting off, I bought a good 'female' backpack and had it fitted to my back. Prior to departure I walked up and down the stairs with the full weight and, realising it was too heavy, left some things behind. Along the way it still got too heavy and I would constantly have try to reduce the weight, not always successfully as some of my hosts will confirm!

I carried a writing journal and would pick up other reading material en route, often doing book exchanges in youth hostels or the people I stayed with. I always seemed to be short of a pen when I needed one. I tended to pick up a lot of literature about the organisations I would visit – this would get very heavy, so I posted a few batches back to Ireland.

I carried a basic first aid kit, a sterile syringe kit, a penknife, and just basic toiletries and essentials. Clean, but not glamorous was the plan.

I had photocopies of my passport in a few places and memorised my passport number. I also scanned essential documents and emailed them back to myself. I hid a small amount of money in a few locations, in case of emergency. I took out a good insurance policy in case all else failed.

Money-wise, I travelled with as little cash as possible. I had one credit card, which I put into credit before setting off. That way, when I withdrew money from an ATM machine I wasn't charged a hefty withdrawal fee. I kept a small amount in traveller's cheques in case of emergency.

I had a battery charger, rechargeable batteries and a universal travel adaptor (essential).

What I should have brought

There are a few bits of equipment that I did not have, and now regret not bringing. The main one is a video camera. Photos and words are great, but they are only part of the picture. I regret not videotaping the interviews. Next time! This, however, would have meant a very different trip. For video interviews, light, sound and location become more important. It would have meant a lot more time setting up the interviews; which probably would have meant meeting fewer people. A toss-up. I also would have invested in a proper digital SLR camera from the beginning, with a proper portrait lens. But it was only really when I was well into the journey that I realised what a difference it would make to the photos. Investing in better equipment up front (and learning how to use it) would have increased the quality of the interviews. Again, next time!

Accommodation and travel

I stayed in many different types of places en route – hostels, campsites, bus stations, overnight trains, motels, but the best was when I stayed with other people in their homes. This was a great way to gain some local insight, plus I gained some lifelong friends.

The rest?
A bit of luck and a lot of trust.

Web Resources

International Support Organisations for Social Entrepreneurs

Ashoka: global organisation identifying and investing in social entrepreneurs. www.ashoka.org

Community Action Network: supporting social enterprise. UK-based.   www.can-online.org.uk

Echoing Green: US support organisation for social entrepreneurs. www.echoinggreen.org

New Profit: US-based. Helps social entrepreneurs grow their organisations.   www.newprofit.org

The School for Social Entrepreneurs: UK-based training for social benefit. www.sse.org.uk

The Schwab Foundation for Social Entrepreneurs: investing in global social entrepreneurs. www.schwabfound.org

Skoll Foundation: Supporting the growth of social entrepreneurship internationally. www.skollfoundation.org

Social Entrepreneurs Ireland: support and network organisation for social entrepreneurs in Ireland www.socialentrepreneurs.ie

Social Enterprise Alliance: US-based membership organisation for social enterprise. www.se-alliance.org

Social Enterprise Coalition: UK's national body for social enterprise.   www.socialenterprise.org.uk

Unltd*: UK-based support organisation for social entrepreneurs. www.unltd.org.uk

Wavelength: study tours, conferences and events supporting social enterprise. UK-based. www.thesamewavelength.com

YouthVenture: youth branch of Ashoka. Building a generation of young changemakers. www.genv.net

Youth Social Enterprise Initiative: supporting youth social entrepreneurs in Southeast Asia www.ysei.org

Irish-Based Resources and Organisations for Social Change

Dóchas: Irish Association for Non-Governmental Organisations. www.dochas.ie

Irish Aid: Irish Government's Official Overseas Development Assistance.   www.irishaid.ie

National Foundation for Teaching Entrepreneurship (Ireland): Teaching young people business skills. www.nfte.ie

Social Entrepreneurs Ireland: support and network organisation for social entrepreneurs in Ireland. www.socialentrepreneurs.ie

Philanthropy Ireland: promoting giving. www.philanthropy.ie

The Wheel: support, advocacy and leadership for community and voluntary activity. www.wheel.ie

Young Social Innovators: supporting young people to create change. www.youngsocialinnovators.ie

Volunteering (Irish-Based Resources)

Irish Aid Volunteering and Information Centre: O'Connell Street, Dublin Centre to explore volunteering and development issues. www.irishaid.gov.ie/centre/

Volunteering Centres of Ireland: National network of regional volunteering centres. www.volunteer.ie

Volunteering Ireland: Online resources and information about local volunteering. www.volunteeringireland.com

Volunteering Options: Resource and information about global volunteering. www.volunteeringoptions.ie

Books

The Billionaire Who Wasn't. Conor O'Clery. The story of Atlantic Philanthropies founder, Chuck Feeney.

Creating a World Without Poverty. Muhammad Yunus. Nobel Prize winner tells his story of setting up the Grameen Foundation. www.muhammadyunus.org